Desert Landscaping for Beginners

Desert Landscaping for Beginners

Tips and Techniques for Success in an Arid Climate

Arizona Master Gardeners

Lucy K. Bradley, George Chott, Marylou Coffman, Sharon Dewey,
Donna DiFrancesco, Shanyn Hosier, Frank Martin, Kirti Mathura,
Rod McKusick, Terry Mikel, Michelle Rauscher, and Catherine Rymer

Edited by Cathy Cromell
Illustrations and Cover Design by Carole Palmer
Cover Photo by Nancy Christensen

Arizona Master Gardener Press
in cooperation with The University of Arizona
Maricopa County Cooperative Extension

Printed in the United States of America

05 04 03 02   4 3 2 1

**Publisher's Cataloging in Publication
(Provided by Quality Books, Inc.)**

Desert landscaping for beginners : tips and techniques for
   success in an arid climate / Lucy K. Bradley ... [et
al.] ; edited by Cathy Cromell. — 1st ed.
   p. cm.
   Includes bibliographical references and index.
   LCCN: 00-109172
   ISBN: 0-9651987-3-1

   1. Desert gardening—Southwest, New. 2. Landscape
gardening—Southwest, New. 3. Landscape plants—
Southwest, New.   I. Bradley, Lucy K. II. Cromell,
Cathy.

SB427.5.D47 2000   635.9'525'0979
                           QBI00-829

Issued in furtherance of Cooperative Extension work, acts of May 8 and June 30, 1914, in cooperation with the U.S.
Department of Agriculture, James A. Christenson, Director, Cooperative Extension, College of Agriculture and Life Sciences, The University of Arizona.

Arizona Master Gardener Press
Phoenix, AZ 85040

Table of Contents

Table of Contents

Foreword

Most garden books are written for other parts of the country by authors who have no experience growing anything in the low desert. The books, although fun to peruse, have little relevance for the challenges we face. *Desert Landscaping for Beginners* fills that gap on the bookshelves: it was written by low desert gardeners specifically for our conditions.

How did we decide what to cover in this book? The Master Gardener Hotline at Maricopa County Cooperative Extension in Phoenix receives about 25,000 calls each year. Many are from new residents, unsure how to grow plants in the low desert. The chapters in this book correspond to the types of questions that we typically receive.

I am always impressed by the generosity and enthusiasm of gardeners. It has been my experience that people who love plants and digging in the soil also love to share that knowledge with others. I am particularly impressed with the gardeners who took time from their overloaded schedules to write for this book. As you read their bios at the end of each chapter, you will see that they are all experts in their fields. They have years of hands-on experience and many of them are educators, sharing their knowledge with the public in a variety of venues. They are well-known among "plant people" in the Phoenix area, and if questions arise, these are the gardeners with the answers. I thank each of them for their willingness to tackle a chapter and their patience through the publication process.

Frank Martin starts the book with an overview of adaptations that desert plants have made over eons to survive in challenging conditions. In Chapter 2, Shanyn Hosier details how to select a healthy plant and prepare the transplanting hole to give the plant the best possible start. Most problems that plants suffer are due to improper watering, and Donna DiFranceso explains how to water for healthy plants and water conservation in Chapter 3.

Lucy Bradley describes pruning techniques in Chapter 4, a skill that some desert dwellers lack if the sad condition of many area trees and shrubs can be used as an indicator. Lucy and Shanyn cover plant problems in Chapter 5, including nutrient deficiencies. There is also a discussion on integrated pest management, which focuses on prevention and the least toxic methods of insect control. Appendix A contains a handy method to follow for diagnosing problems. Terry Mikel continues the discussion in Chapter 6 with entertaining descriptions of insects and diseases that appear seasonally in the low desert. Yes, we do get hit with frost here, and Lucy shows how to protect plants from freezing temperatures in Chapter 7.

The wondrous variety of cacti and succulents seduces most gardeners. Kirti Mathura explains how to care for these unusual plants and lists some of the best ones to grow in Chapter 8. We've all seen the photos of wildflowers creating carpets of color across the desert. In Chapter 9, Michelle Rauscher shows how easy it is to sow your own wildflower patch. Catherine Rymer provides detailed information on inviting butterflies and hummingbirds to your backyard wildlife habitat in Chapter 10. She includes an extensive plant list for attracting native wildlife.

Citrus in December is an Arizona bragging right, and George Chott tells which varieties do best and how best to grow them in Chapter 11. Did you know that over 40 percent of the rose bushes sold throughout the U.S. are grown in Maricopa County? In Chapter 12, Marylou Coffman and Rod McKusick provide detailed instructions on planting and caring for these popular flowers. Appendix B contains their recommendations for specific varieties. Finally, a turf area can be part of a well-designed Xeriscape, and Sharon Dewey details the steps to create a healthy lawn with appropriate watering, fertilizing, and mowing in Chapter 13.

Gardening concepts have been skillfully illustrated by Carole Palmer, another expert both on the computer and in the garden, with herbs her passion and specialty. I am grateful for her good humor and perseverance.

The authors have covered just about everything you need to know to understand most desert landscaping topics. They have written detailed, yet easy-to-understand information to help you create your own attractive, low-maintenance, and environmentally friendly landscape. Their combined experience is now yours simply for the reading. I hope you learn as much as I did!

Cathy Cromell
Urban Horticulture Department
Maricopa County Cooperative Extension
The University of Arizona

Acknowledgements

The printing of this book was made possible by a Community Challenge Grant sponsored by the Arizona State Land Department and the Arizona Community Tree Council, Inc. We would like to gratefully acknowledge Ron Romatzke and Louise Wakem, with the State Land Department and the ACTC, respectively, for their coordination of this grant.

We also gratefully acknowledge assistance from Western Sod in the production of this book.

Many people were involved in the book's content development, review, and production. *Desert Landscaping for Beginners* would not exist without their input. We would like to thank the following people for their generous gift of time, support, and expertise.

Rita Jo Anthony, Owner, Wild Seed, Inc.

Cathy Babcock, Assistant Director of Horticulture, Old World Succulent Horticulturist, Desert Botanical Garden

Diane Barker, Agave and Yucca Horticulturist, Desert Botanical Garden

Hall Bradshaw, Consulting Rosarian

Leroy Brady, Consulting Rosarian

Carolyn Chard, Maricopa County Cooperative Extension

Nancy Christensen, Gardening Editor, *Phoenix Home & Garden* magazine

Jim Christenson, Associate Dean & Director, College of Agriculture & Life Sciences, University of Arizona Cooperative Extension

Korene Charnofsky Cohen, Freelance Writer

Maeve Dion, University of Arizona Cooperative Extension Master Gardener

Robin Dunn, University of Arizona Cooperative Extension Master Gardener

Floyd Evans, Consulting Rosarian and University of Arizona Cooperative Extension Master Gardener

Stan Farlin, County Director, Maricopa County Cooperative Extension

Roberta Gibson, Entomologist, University of Arizona Cooperative Extension Master Gardener

Russell A. Haughey, Habitat Program Manager, Arizona Game And Fish Department

Connie Heaton, University of Arizona Cooperative Extension Master Gardener

Mike Hills, Research Agronomist, Seed Research of Oregon and University of Arizona Master Gardener

Michael Jepson, Consulting Rosarian

David Kopec, Extension Specialist, Turf & Pasture Grasses, University of Arizona Cooperative Extension

Charlotte Kraft, University of Arizona Cooperative Extension Master Gardener

Joanne Littlefield, Maricopa County Cooperative Extension

César Mazier, Superintendent of Horticulture, Desert Botanical Garden

Mesa-East Valley (Arizona) Rose Society members

Judy Mielke, Author and Landscape Architect, Logan, Simpson and Dye

Cathy Munger, Maricopa County Cooperative Extension

Kent Newland, Water Resources Specialist, City of Phoenix Water Services

Carol Noyes, Maricopa County Cooperative Extension

Jim Oravetz, Summer Winds Nursery

Leslie Pauli, University of Arizona Cooperative Extension Master Gardener

Kathleen Peterson, Maricopa County Cooperative Extension

Steve Priebe, Horticulturist, City of Phoenix Street Transportation

Patrick Quirk, Cactus Horticulturist, Desert Botanical Garden

Diana Rogers, University of Arizona Cooperative Extension Master Gardener

Marjorie Sykes, University of Arizona Cooperative Extension Master Gardener

Andy Terrey, Program Manager, Recycled Water, City of Phoenix Water Services

The late Jimmy Tipton, Ph.D, University of Arizona Cooperative Extension

James Truman, Citrus Farm Manager, University of Arizona

CC Willis, General Manager, Western Sod

Production

Editor

Cathy Cromell learned to garden from her parents while growing up in northern Minnesota. It was her duty to deadhead the pansies and harvest all of the garden peas. She performed these chores with perhaps too much gusto, secretly consuming most of the peas before heading back to the kitchen. Cathy is an Instructional Specialist in urban horticulture with the University of Arizona Maricopa County Cooperative Extension. Her role is to publish books and materials specific to gardening in the Sonoran Desert. Cathy also writes a monthly column for *Phoenix Home & Garden* magazine and a bi-weekly column as southwest regional editor for the National Gardening Association. She still enjoys deadheading pansies and prefers eating peas straight from the plant.

Illustrator

Carole Palmer has been intimately involved with plants since she ate leaves as "crackers" while still a toddler. A University of Arizona Cooperative Extension Master Gardener, graduate of the Desert Botanical Garden's Desert Landscaper School, and a member of the Arizona Herb Association, Carole has been in the publishing field since 1986 as a writer, editor, and graphic designer. She appreciates the balance her landscape provides to her ever-computerized lifestyle and is particularly amused when the dill decides to volunteer next to the cacti. A Michigan transplant who moved to the Valley of the Sun in 1987, Carole would also like to thank the many plants which have given their lives so that she might become better educated about gardening in the low desert.

Photographer

Nancy Christensen's love of gardening didn't take root until a move to Arizona prompted a shift in careers. After receiving her degree in mass communications from the University of Wisconsin-Milwaukee, she spent the next five years working as a photographer's assistant. Her love of writing and photography came together when she was hired at *Phoenix Home & Garden* magazine, where she currently is managing editor and garden editor. Her knowledge of Southwest horticultural practices continues to grow, as does her garden.

Chapter 1

The Magic of Desert Plants

By Frank Martin

The Sonoran Desert's indigenous peoples, including the Akimel and Tohono O'odham, held desert plants in high esteem. They depended on plants for food, shelter, and medicine and were keen observers of nature. There was very little about the budding of a leaf or the opening of a flower that they did not notice. They were so in tune with native plants that they used them as a calendar to signal when to plant their cultivated crops. When the mesquite trees leafed out, usually in late February or early March, it was nature's signal to plant corn, beans, and squash. The same crops, as well as amaranth, gourds, and sorghum, were planted when the saguaro fruit ripened around the latter part of June to early July, which coincided with the onset of summer rains.

Native peoples viewed the desert not as a parched wasteland, but rather as a place that gave them life and sustenance. They gleaned the desert for food with respect and wonderment. Their cultivated crops were often at the mercy of favorable rains, but the native plants were a stable mainstay.

Survival Ability

Although we no longer depend on desert plants for food and shelter, modern-day desert dwellers appreciate the incredible ability of these plants to survive, which seems almost magical. Consider how these plants grow in their native surroundings: no one needs to drag a garden hose out to water a creosote bush or buy fertilizer to feed a mesquite tree. It is not uncommon for plants to endure summer daytime temperatures of over 100 degrees Fahrenheit for more than three months at a time. In winter months, plants are subjected to temperatures that can fluctuate over 50 degrees between day and night. Hot blowing winds, lack of precipitation, and saline soils also challenge these desert magicians.

Amazing Adaptations

Over thousands of years, native plants have adapted to the harsh conditions of the desert. There are numerous fascinating mechanisms for reducing moisture loss. For example, plants must photosynthesize to create food for survival. As part of photosynthesis, all plants, including cacti, must capture carbon dioxide and release oxygen through pore-like openings called stomata. Most plants open these pores during the daytime. Some desert plants, however, open their pores at night when the temperatures are cooler. Thus, less moisture is lost as water vapor released through the stomata, a process called transpiration.

Reducing Moisture Loss

The tough, waxy leaves of creosote bush, the hairy leaves of brittlebush, and the thick outer coating and spines on cacti are adaptations to the environment. Cacti spines, which botanically are modified leaves, have limited surface area exposed to the sun. The fuzzy hairs on brittlebush reflect light from the surface of the leaf to keep it cooler. The hairs also act to hold moisture close to the leaf. Creosote leaves have pore openings that are sunk deeper in the leaf tissue. All of these mechanisms help reduce moisture loss.

Some desert trees and ocotillos can drop their leaves in times of water stress. In an extreme drought palo verde trees can go one step farther, cutting off the water supply to specific limbs, which will then dry up and break off. These adaptations reduce the amount of above-ground plant tissue to which the root system must supply water.

The leaves of the jojoba are angled vertically, minimizing the leaf surface exposed to direct sunlight, another method to reduce moisture loss. A plant's color is another adaptation: most desert plants are light green or grey to reflect sunlight.

These are just a few of the many examples of environmental adaptation by desert plants, which help them to survive the Southwest's challenging growing conditions. Let us now focus on three specific adaptations.

Faced with demanding desert conditions, how is it that a saguaro cactus can go many months without rain and still be a dependable food source for wildlife and people? How can an

Arizona queen of the night, a cactus whose blooms last for only one evening, rely on other *Peniocereus* cacti to cross-pollinate it on that same night? How do mesquite trees and other desert legumes obtain their nitrogen when desert soils are extremely low in organic matter and nutrients?

The Mighty Saguaro

The "desert sentinal" appears to be vulnerable standing alone in the desert's intense sunlight, but once it reaches maturity it can shade itself. Its pleated ribs and spines cast enough of a shadow to prevent sunburn. (As strong as it appears at maturity, the young saguaro begins life growing under the protection of trees and shrubs, which are called "nurse plants.") As stated earlier, the fruit of a saguaro cactus is always ready to harvest by the last week in June or the first week in July. It ripens at about the same time year after year, regardless of the amount of water it received that year. How can this be?

The saguaro has the amazing ability to store hundreds of gallons of water in its body. Rain is often brief and infrequent in the desert. Desert soils can also be very hard and slightly hydrophobic, meaning they repel water. During hard rains, water flows quickly away in a wash or arroyo, instead of being absorbed by the soil. Saguaros have a few critical minutes to lap up as much water as they can before it disappears. The saguaro uses its large network of shallow roots—most are within the first 12 inches of soil—to accomplish this feat. These roots can extend up to 100 feet in all directions and very quickly wick up enough water to sustain the saguaro until the next rainfall.

Queen for a Night

Another plant equally as mystifying is the Arizona queen of the night (*Peniocereus greggii*). For one night each year it absolutely rules the desert. Since this plant depends primarily on moths for cross-pollination and blooms last for only one night, it might appear that pollination is a game of chance. If it were not for one magical thing that happens, cross-pollination might not even occur. *Peniocereus* respond to temperature change. When the nighttime temperature reaches around 65 degrees, all these cacti in the same area will bloom. Once the flowers open, their heavy scent attracts moths and other pollinators.

Similar to the saguaro's ability to store water, the "queen" has its own "ace" for survival—a large, potato-like tuberous root that it uses to store nutrients and water. Some tubers can weigh as much as seventy pounds! This reservoir can carry it through

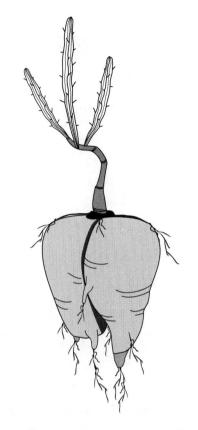

Arizona queen of the night stores water in its root.

extremely long drought periods. Native peoples also used this tuberous root as a food source.

Where's the Nitrogen?

Our vegetable and flower gardens will not perform well unless we physically add nitrogen to them in some form—either as fertilizers or composted mulch. All plants, whether in gardens or not, need nitrogen. Not only is nitrogen important for plant growth, it is an essential nutrient that supports all life.

Despite its significance, nitrogen is also the nutrient that is most commonly in short supply. This is even more startling considering our atmosphere is almost 80 percent nitrogen. The problem is that plants, or any living organism, can not use atmospheric or so-called "free" nitrogen. The nitrogen available in the atmosphere must be converted or "fixed" into a form available for plants to use.

In most non-desert areas plants obtain their fixed nitrogen from the soil. This useable nitrogen gets into the soil through the recycling and decomposition of organic material. For example, think of the forest floor as a large compost pile. Leaves and dead plant material containing both carbon and nitrogen fall to the ground. Animal excrement (another nitrogen source) also finds its way to the forest floor. This accumulation of organic matter is sometimes two feet deep. The bottom layer is decomposed by worms, insects, and soil microorganisms such as fungi and bacteria. As a result of decomposition, nitrogen and other nutrients once held within plant tissues become available to other plants.

Many desert trees and shrubs are legumes, a type of plant that produces a bean or pea pod. Examples of legumes include mesquite, palo verde, acacia, and ironwood trees, desert senna, and lupine. Where do mesquite trees and other desert legumes obtain their nitrogen since desert soils are extremely low in organic matter?

Two Ways to Fix Nitrogen
1. Lightning

In nature there are two ways of fixing nitrogen. Maybe you have heard that lightning is good for your garden? The reason is that the high energy of a lightning flash allows nitrogen and oxygen in the atmosphere to combine, creating nitric oxide. Nitric oxide is then converted to nitric acid, a form of nitrogen that is highly soluble in water and falls to the ground in rainwater.

Lightning, however, is an inefficient means of fixing nitrogen. Despite the large number of lightning flashes worldwide,

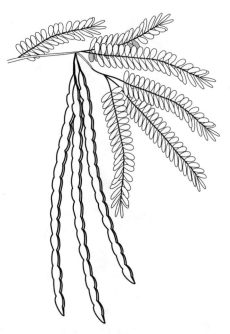

Many desert trees and shrubs are in the legume family, capable of fixing nitrogen in their root systems.

lightning produces a relatively small amount of fixed nitrogen. Between 60 and 90 percent of fixed nitrogen results from the activity of microorganisms living in the soil and water.

2. Legumes and Soil Bacteria

Here is another piece of magic: most legumes and a soil bacteria called *Rhizobium* have a symbiotic relationship to create useable nitrogen. For each species of host legume plant there is a specific type of *Rhizobium*.

Typically, nitrogen fixing is a two-step process in the soil. First, bacteria convert atmospheric or free nitrogen (N_2), which is inert and unuseable, into ammonia (NH_3). Next, bacteria convert the ammonia into nitrate (NO_3), which is useable by the plant.

In legumes, *Rhizobium* bacteria enter the roots and feed on the sap or juices flowing from the wound. The plant begins forming a scab over the wound, thus encasing the bacteria. If you have ever pulled up garden legumes, such as peas or beans, you may have noticed small, whitish nodules on the roots. These nodules enclose *Rhizobium* as they feed on the roots and provide nitrogen to the plant.

These bacteria have a symbiotic relation with the host plant. The host supplies the bacteria with energy for growth in the form of carbohydrates. In return, the bacteria produce nitrates that are dissolved in soil water and then absorbed by the roots of the host plant. Symbiotic nitrogen fixation is an essential process for plants such as the desert legumes, which are unable to obtain sufficient nitrogen from any other source. This is why most of our desert trees *are* legumes.

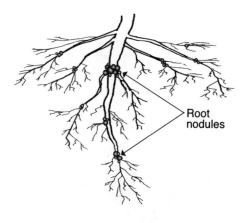

Root nodules

Tiny whitish bumps enclose soil bacteria that provide nitrogen to the plant.

How Plants Obtain Soil Moisture

Perhaps the most amazing adaptation of desert plants is their ability to extract moisture from seemingly dry soils. Even soils that appear parched still contain a certain amount of water. Plants must pull those water molecules from the soil. A problem for most non-desert plants is that they do not have the ability to retrieve the water tightly held in our desert soil.

Every soil particle is surrounded by a thin layer of water. Soil has the ability to hold onto this water with a certain force. As roots absorb water from the soil, the layer of water gets thinner around the soil particle, and "soil moisture tension" increases. In other words, there is less water so the soil particle tries harder to hang on to what is left. The availability of moisture for plants is related to the amount of force the soil exerts to hold on to the surrounding water. This force is measured in "bar units."

Most plants live somewhere on a scale of one-third of a bar unit to 15 bar units. As shown in the illustration, the smaller the bar unit number, the more moisture is available in the soil. Not all plants have the same ability to pull water from the soil. Most plants can easily pull moisture from the soil in a range between one-third and three bar units.

Because native and other drought-tolerant plants can extract water from the soil with more vigor than non-native plants, most desert vegetation can survive in soil measuring three to five bar units. The truly hardy souls, such as creosote, can live in extremely arid zones measuring 30 bar units.

Use Desert Plants in the Landscape

Desert-adapted plants have efficient structures that gather and store water to use as they need it. Other adaptations protect the plants from the sun, minimize water loss, enhance water storage abilities, and improve the plants' abilities to extract nutrients from the soil. These are excellent qualities for plants in any landscape, and they are particularly useful for beginning gardeners, as the plants require less care and maintenance. The Resource list contains many useful reference books that describe the characteristics of landscape plants in great detail. Include desert-adapted plants in your landscape and enjoy their magic!❀

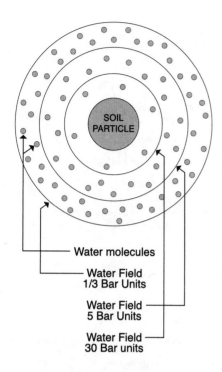

Water molecules

Water Field
1/3 Bar Units

Water Field
5 Bar Units

Water Field
30 Bar units

Desert plants have adapted
to survive in soil that has
very little available moisture.

Frank Martin is an organic farmer of Native American heritage. He volunteers hundreds of hours of service each year as a Master Gardener promoting the preservation of native crops through programs at the Maricopa County Cooperative Extension office, school gardens, and the Pima-Salt River Indian Reservation. Frank completed the University of Arizona Cooperative Extension Master Gardener training in 1993. In 1995 he received a Search for Excellence award for the Native Seeds Demonstration Garden he created. The award is given to individuals or organizations for demonstrating unique, creative, and innovative gardening projects that contribute to the community.

Chapter 2

Selecting and Transplanting Trees and Shrubs

By Shanyn Hosier

Many problems that homeowners experience with land-scape plants are a result of putting the wrong type of plant in a particular location. Spend a little time examining your landscape's characteristics and researching plants that will naturally thrive in that situation. Making appropriate plant selections will translate into less maintenance (pruning, fertilizing, troubleshooting) on your part once the plant is established. Equally important, fewer dead plants will need to be replaced. "Right Plant, Right Place" has become a guiding principle for gardeners and landscape professionals who understand that following that simple advice will save time and money as well as result in a more attractive landscape.

Choosing Landscape Plants

Answers to these three important questions will help you select appropriate plants.

1. *What do you want from your plants?* Many desert dwellers want shade. You can place plants on the south or west side of your home, which helps reduce temperatures by several degrees. Other things that plants can provide include color, food, wildlife habitat, fruit, screening, and noise abatement.

2. *How much landscape work do you want to handle?* Are you an avid gardener who enjoys digging in the soil and caring for plants? Or do you prefer a low-maintenance landscape that you can view from the comfort of an easy chair?

3. *What does your landscape have to offer plants?* Examine your site. What is the exposure: full sun, partial shade, full

shade? Don't put a sun lover in a shady northern exposure. Are you situated at the base of a slope where cold air will naturally sink? Choose cold-hardy plants that are less likely to suffer frost damage. Do you need to plant next to cement or stucco walls, driveways, and patios that will reflect heat and sunlight? Use desert plants that can withstand those conditions.

Is the soil sandy or clay-like? Sandy soil provides good drainage, but requires more frequent watering. Clay soil retains water longer, but some plants don't like their roots to sit in wet soil. Choose plants that will thrive in your conditions. Plants can become stressed if conditions aren't to their liking. Research shows that stressed plants are more susceptible to pest and disease problems than non-stressed plants.

It is essential to determine how much space a tree or shrub will need to grow to maturity. Trying to squeeze a plant that naturally grows too tall or too wide into an inappropriate space usually means that the poor plant will suffer repeated pruning to force it to conform. A general guideline is to plant a tree or shrub no closer to a structure than one-half its mature size. Don't plant a sprawling shrub or sharply pointed agave next to a sidewalk or tall trees underneath utility wires. Choose plants that won't outgrow their space and save yourself unnecessary maintenance.

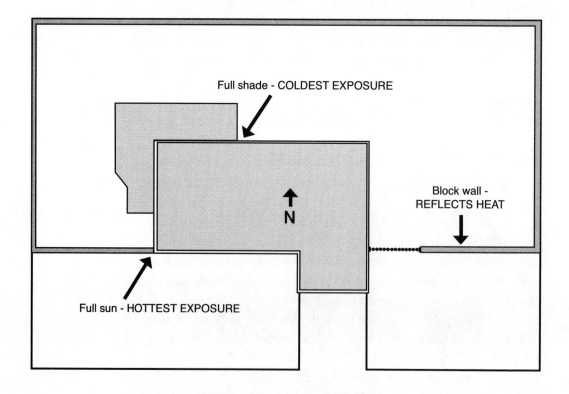

Situate plants in the landscape based upon their exposure needs.

After you've answered these questions, familiarize yourself with plants that will fulfill your requirements. There are excellent books available that can help you sort out the possibilities (see the Resource list). Visit demonstration gardens, botanical gardens, arboreta, and nurseries. Walk around your neighborhood and look at plants that interest you. Many community colleges, Cooperative Extension offices, and botanical gardens offer classes geared to the public.

It is easy to get carried away at the nursery and load up a cart, especially when plants are in bloom. But if you think about the above issues before purchasing, do a little research, and make a shopping list, you'll drive away with plants that have a good chance of survival in your specific conditions with a minimum of fuss on your part.

Select Healthy Plants

When you know what species will be a good match for your site, it is time to select a healthy candidate. Starting with a substandard plant increases the amount of work you will have to do and reduces your chance of success. Look closely at the plant, gently lifting leaves and branches. Be sure to look at the underside of the leaves. Avoid purchasing plants that have any obvious damage to the stems, branches, or leaves, or any evidence of insects (or eggs). Are there any pruning scars, and are they beginning to heal? If there are open wounds, skip the plant. Does this plant look unusually large in the pot, or are many roots escaping the pot from the bottom? Are roots encircling themselves horizontally rather than growing vertically? These are signs of a rootbound plant, so choose another specimen.

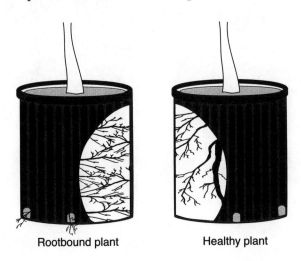

Rootbound plant   Healthy plant

Examine plant roots before purchase.

When buying a tree, find one that has a sturdy trunk that will stand without the stake. If there is a stake in the container at the nursery, ask them to remove it. If the tree leans or tips, pass it up. Native trees, such as desert willow, palo verde, ironwood, and mesquite, often have a multiple trunk structure that is extremely attractive in the landscape. It is acceptable to buy these with multiple trunks, although they are not always easy to find in the smaller container sizes. Many other trees, such as conifers and ashes, grow from one central trunk, called a leader. They should be purchased with just one strong, straight trunk.

Branches should be evenly distributed along the entire length of the tree. Half the foliage should be on branches that are on the lower two-thirds of the plant. Avoid trees that have been pruned into little puffs of foliage and shrubs that have been severely sheared into cubes or balls. Buy plants that have been allowed to grow into their natural shapes.

Preparing the Planting Hole

Once you've selected the right plant for the right spot, it is time to "lay the foundation" by preparing the planting hole. Time is well invested here and will produce great benefits to the plant, as well as save you from problems down the road.

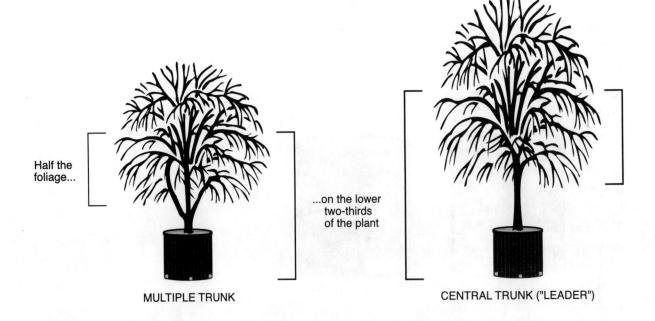

Half the foliage...

...on the lower two-thirds of the plant

MULTIPLE TRUNK

CENTRAL TRUNK ("LEADER")

Purchase trees with strong trunks and appropriately spaced foliage.

By preparing the soil in the planting area, you are helping to create an optimal environment for the plant's roots. Roots are a lifeline for the plant, harvesting water, nutrients, and minerals from the soil. You can help facilitate this process even before the plant is in the ground. The following information describing how roots grow will help you to understand the benefits of properly preparing the planting holes.

Roots Grow From Their Tips

As a plant's root system develops, roots appear to grow outward from the base of the stem. But actually, the thick, round roots found closest to the stem are the oldest roots, which no longer absorb water or nutrients from the soil. Instead, they act as pipeline connectors between the "feeder roots" and the green shoots growing above ground. Feeder roots are the thin, web-like, younger parts of the root system. They exist within the top one to three feet of the soil, growing out to and beyond the plant's canopy or crown, also referred to as the drip line.

Think of a young tree. When it is first planted, the roots only take up the space available in the container. But these roots will spread outward, just as the branches will. Preparing the soil in a small area immediately surrounding the roots will only temporarily help your tree, and may actually hinder its growth in the future. On the other hand, preparing the soil in a wide area equal to several years' growth (if not more) will be a great help to your plant as it grows.

For best results, till a circular area three to five times wider than the width of the container. For a one-gallon pot, that equals about one to three feet in diameter. A fifteen-gallon pot would increase to a circle about three to six feet in diameter. A 48–inch box needs a circle 12–20 ft. in diameter. As you can see, one of the benefits of selecting small transplant stock is less digging on your part!

When loosening the soil, it is best to do so only as deep as the original depth of soil and roots in the pot. Digging a deeper hole and backfilling it with organic matter is not recommended for two reasons:

1. Roots will generally not grow downward, but outward. You don't need to loosen the soil for a tap root, or to encourage deep, vertical "anchor" roots. The wide horizontal spread of roots will anchor the plant.

2. The backfill materials will quickly decompose or compact, allowing the weight of the plant to sink into the soil. The resulting depression will collect soil and water around the plant stem or trunk, creating an optimal environment for disease.

The Planting Hole

✔ 3 to 5 times wider than the pot

✔ Only as deep as the pot

✔ Roughen the side walls

✔ Do not amend the backfill with organic matter

So, digging deeper only makes more work for you and provides no benefit to the plant. Don't waste your time and energy doing it.

Roots Follow the Path of Least Resistance

Roots grow more easily through a uniformly light, loose, airy soil than through a dense, compact, heavy soil. When a growing root tip comes into contact with a hard object, like a stone, a cement footing, or the side of a container, it bends, redirecting growth in another direction (usually left or right, not up or down, contrary to popular belief). In the case of a pot, there's no place to go but around and around. This is why plants left too long in a pot will become "rootbound" or "potbound," with dense mats of roots wrapping around the root ball, eventually strangling the plant.

Tilling the soil in a wide circle around the planting hole helps to loosen up the soil. This lets in plenty of air for the roots to "breathe" and water for the roots to "drink." Roots growing in a dense or compacted soil (common conditions in clay soils) will find it difficult to spread outward from the trunk. Remember that these roots are a lifeline and help to anchor the plant. Give them lots of loose, airy soil to grow into.

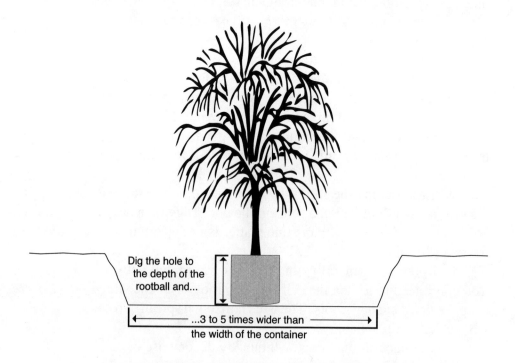

Dig the hole to the depth of the rootball and...

...3 to 5 times wider than the width of the container

The ideal planting hole provides plenty of space for roots to spread easily through the soil.

When digging and tilling heavy, clay soils, it's important to avoid leaving behind slick, smooth sides. A root coming into contact with this treats it just like the wall of a pot. When digging the planting hole, and tilling the planting area, be sure to roughen-up the walls of the undisturbed soil. Poke holes in it with a pick, or scratch it with a rake; do whatever it takes to avoid a slick, smooth wall. It also helps to slope the sides of the wall, so the bottom of the hole is slightly narrower than the top.

Roots Don't Appreciate Variety

Roots prefer a uniform soil: uniform density, texture, structure, composition, and moisture level. Soils that are irregular, with sandy patches or clay patches or rocky patches may be challenging for growing plants. For this same reason, roots seldom grow out beyond a heavily amended planting hole. So if you decide you must add soil amendments to your growing area, it is necessary to incorporate them uniformly throughout the entire area.

Should you amend the soil? Since roots don't like variety, it is generally not recommended that anything be added to the soil. Think for a minute about a native desert tree, such as a mesquite. It evolved to grow well in our native desert soils, despite conditions like salinity and alkalinity. When planting native or desert-adapted plants, there is no reason to amend the soil in an effort to change the root environment.

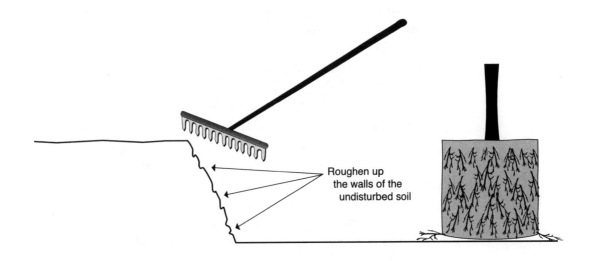

Roughen up
the walls of the
undisturbed soil

Roots can more easily penetrate disturbed soil, enabling them to grow beyond the planting hole to seek water and nutrients.

So what about non-adapted plants? Often, native desert soil is not optimal for plant growth in this case. Soil amendments might help improve the water-holding capacity, nutrient availability, or pH levels for these plants. However, in virtually every case, these improvements are temporary at best. The amendments break down and/or leach away within a year or two, leaving your plant back at square one, surrounded by native soil which is suboptimal for its growth. Once this happens, you are likely to begin noticing problems on this plant, like discolored leaves, stunted growth, or even dieback. It will be a constant battle with Mother Nature to keep these plants healthy.

What about plants that are intensely cropped, like annual vegetables and flowers? Again, native desert soil is not optimal for growth of many of these plants. But even though amending the soil is a temporary fix, these annual plants won't be around for long. Plus, they don't take up much room, so it's not necessary to amend a large area. If you're willing to put in the effort each growing season, annual vegetable and flower gardens are well worth the effort to amend the soil. (For specific details on soil improvement for growing annuals, see *Desert Gardening for Beginners: How to Grow Vegetables, Flowers and Herbs in an Arid Climate*. Roses and turf are other exceptions, performing better with amended soil. See Chapters 12 and 13 for more information.)

Do not fertilize or prune newly transplanted trees. Wait about one year for the root system to establish.

Transplanting Myths

Before detailing transplanting techniques, a word about some transplanting myths. Use of rooting hormones is only recommended in special cases when you are attempting to grow a plant from a stem or leaf, not one with roots already growing. Some B vitamins are marketed to improve transplant survival and growth. Most studies show that the main benefit may be the additional water that is applied when vitamin B is diluted for application.

Fertilizing of any kind at this point is not recommended. Fragile feeder roots that are beginning to grow are easily killed by very small excesses in fertilizer. It is best to wait until roots are well established, usually about one year, before fertilizing.

Also, resist the urge to prune the new plant. The plant itself will reach an energy balance between the root system and the shoot system. Let Mother Nature do the pruning for the first year! Following are six general steps that should bring you transplanting success.

Six Steps to Transplanting

Step 1: Dig the planting hole

The actual hole should be in the center of the tilled area you have already prepared as described above, and it will be the same size as the root ball of your transplant. Again, be sure the sides of the hole are sloped and rough, so as not to create a "pot-in-the-ground" situation that the roots won't grow beyond.

Step 2: Remove the growing container

If your plant was growing in a one-, five-, or 15-gallon plastic container, it should slip out fairly easily when you tip it slightly past horizontal. If not, set it on its side and gently roll it back and forth like a rolling pin a few times, then try again. Never try to yank the plant out vertically or pull on the stem. Placing your hand flat against the soil in the pot, with the stem between your thumb and the rest of your fingers, pull the pot off the root ball. Always carry the plant by the root ball, and place it in the ground immediately.

If you are transplanting a larger plant, you will need to wrestle with a wooden box to remove the root ball before placing it in the ground. Be forewarned that there is no gentle way to do this, and some damage is likely to occur. Your best plan is to minimize the damage. Using a dolly or crane (or many helpers), get the plant as close to the hole as possible, if not directly in the hole. You will likely need a hammer and crowbar to dismantle the box, and possibly metal cutting tools to cut wire bands sometimes used to secure the box. It is critically important that you remove all four sides and the bottom of the box. Some people falsely believe that these materials will quickly break down if buried in the soil with the plant. They do not! For the same reason, you should remove any cloth (including burlap) or plastic liners that surround the root ball.

The planting hole should be ready before removing the container. Put the root ball into the ground quickly so roots do not dry out.

Step 3: Fill the hole

Be careful when backfilling that you do not bury any part of the plant stem. A buried stem is likely to result in disease problems later on. Use leftover soil to build berms for a watering well around your plant (see step 4). Then, gently pat the soil down to ensure contact with the root ball. This is not the time for using your whole body weight to pack the soil into the hole. Doing this will result in compaction problems, even root damage. Just the strength of your arms will be sufficient.

Step 4: Water

It is vitally important that your plant gets watered immediately after transplanting. A deep, thorough watering helps the soil make contact with the tiny, fragile feeder roots of the plant. Without it, odds increase that those roots will die, resulting in a condition known as transplant shock. This can be fatal to your plant!

Now is a great time to build a watering well, especially for larger plants like shrubs and trees. The purpose of a watering well is to create a convenient space for a gardener to place irrigation water to effectively moisten the root zone, where the water is needed most. Use soil to build two circular mounds around the plant. The inner mound should be close to, but not touching, the stem, in order to prevent water from contacting the bark. The outer mound should be no closer than the drip line, or outer canopy, of the plant. Together, they look like the outline of a doughnut surrounding the stem of the plant. The height of the mounds may vary, depending on how quickly water is applied to your plant. If you apply a slow trickle of water each time, the mounds do not need to be very high.

For the next several days (or longer for larger transplants), keep the soil consistently moist, but not soggy. Moist soil will encourage root growth, while soggy soil will literally drown the plant's roots. Watch carefully for signs of wilting, yellow or brown

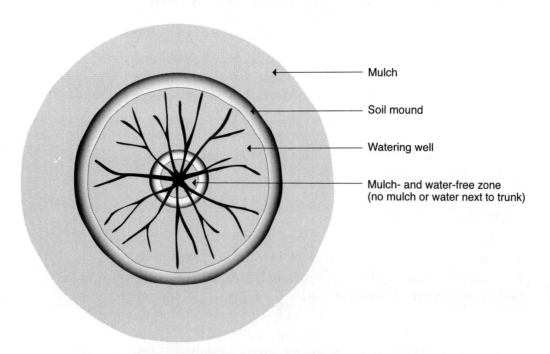

— Mulch

— Soil mound

— Watering well

— Mulch- and water-free zone
(no mulch or water next to trunk)

An inner and outer soil mound (like the shape of a doughnut) creates a watering well that keeps mulch and water away from the plant's stem or trunk.

leaves, drying out, or stress of any kind. Gradually increase the interval between waterings as the plant becomes established, but do not change the amount of water you give at each watering. Be sure the water penetrates as deeply as the roots are growing, if not deeper, and as far outward as the roots are growing, if not farther.

Step 5: Mulch

Mulching is the desert gardener's best friend! Mulching materials help to prevent water evaporation from the soil and help cool the roots in the summer. They are also great at preventing weeds from sprouting next to your plant. There are lots of things to choose from, ranging in price from expensive bark chips, to straw, to your own free lawn clippings and leaves. Whatever you choose, place the mulch all around the plant *except* up against the stem or trunk. Use enough to cover the entire root ball area, out to the drip line (as far out as the branches spread), several inches deep. For continued success, keep adding mulch as it breaks down (it's adding organic matter to your soil) and increase the soil area covered by it as your plant grows larger.

Types of Mulch
compost
bark chips
wood chips
straw
grass clippings
dried leaves
cottonseed hulls
pine needles
gravel

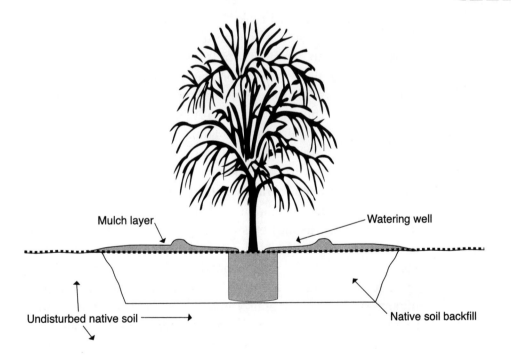

Mulch layer

Watering well

Undisturbed native soil

Native soil backfill

A properly planted tree in native soil at the same depth as it was in the container. It has a watering well over the root area and mulch to help maintain soil moisture. No mulch or water stands near the trunk.

Step 6: Protect your plant

You may need to take extra precautions to protect your plant from temperature extremes, animals, or human traffic. Also, remove any nursery stakes that are tied to your plant. Nursery stakes are usually attached very tightly to the stem and often damage the plant in the long run.

To Stake or Not to Stake

Is it necessary to stake your new tree or shrub? The answer is no, plain and simple. If a stem or trunk or root system is too weak to support the foliage, then it is inferior. In nature, these plants fall over, die, and become homes for decomposer animals and plants, recycling nutrients back into the soil.

However, in the gardening world there tends to be a lot of exceptions to this rule. When nurseries grow plants, they stake them. Why? Because consumers demand a product that looks like a miniature adult. For instance, a gardener shopping for a new landscape tree will select a plant with a tall, straight, clean trunk with no branches, and a sculpted round top knot of branches with foliage. Never mind that in nature, a "normal" tree of this age has a particular juvenile form, perhaps with irregular, scruffy-looking branches and ungainly foliage. No, this natural young tree is not attractive, and therefore won't sell.

Most gardeners will take home the pretty, mini-adult tree. They prepare the soil, plant the tree, then remove the nursery stake... and the tree promptly falls over! Now it seems obvious that some staking is needed on this particular specimen. But many gardeners fail to realize that the practice of staking is a therapeutic one, not a permanent crutch. Proper staking is a practice of constant monitoring and adjusting for a *short* time, with the goal being a self-supporting, upright tree.

Let's go back to our drooping new tree. In nature, young trees have many small branches that grow from the entire length of the trunk. These low branches help to increase the girth of the trunk for as long as they exist. This gives the trunk stability and strength as it grows. And yet, nurseries and gardeners often prune these low branches as soon as possible, denying the tree this advantage. In addition, the trunk has been firmly supported by a nursery stake for much of its young life, and never got the chance to grow strong on its own. To remedy this situation, gardeners must employ another aspect nature provides as therapy for the weak trunk—wind. As trees move in the wind, the wood fibers are strengthened. Gardeners should use stakes in such a manner as to provide just enough support to keep the tree upright, yet

A healthy tree should not require staking. Allowing it to sway lightly in the wind strengthens the wood fibers.

allow for free movement in the wind to build up the wood's strength.

If You Must Stake, Do It Right

First, choose your staking materials. The posts should be wood or metal and should be no taller than the lowest branch of the tree. Since the staked tree will be moving with the wind, care must be taken to prevent branches from hitting the stakes and being damaged. You will need a minimum of two stakes for each plant. Never use one stake alone—this does not provide proper support and often leads to trees bending or snapping off at the tie point.

When choosing tie materials, keep in mind that the less contact the tie has with the trunk or stem, the better. The best ties are soft but durable nylon straps. Wire that is inserted into a section of garden hose is acceptable. Never use bare wire. Remember, your staked tree will be moving with the wind, and care must be taken to ensure the ties do not bind tightly or rub the trunk, causing a wound. Only use one tie for each plant, but make sure the tie is long enough to attach to each of the stakes used.

Next, place the stakes properly around the plant. If using

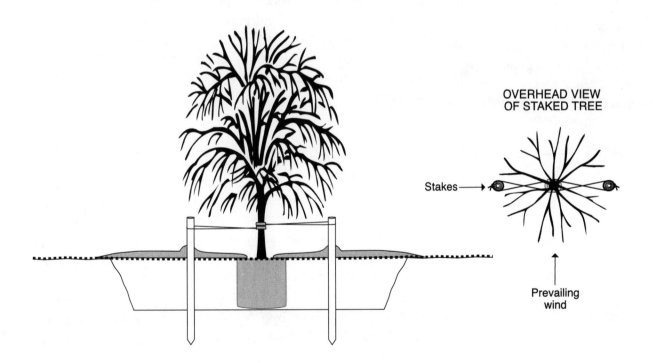

If staking is required, posts should be no taller than the lowest branch. Place them beyond the root ball to prevent damage to growing roots. Stakes should be perpendicular to the prevailing wind.

two stakes, place them in a line perpendicular to the prevailing wind direction. For example, if your plant is primarily exposed to winds blowing from west to east, place one stake to the north and one to the south of the plant. When using three stakes, place them in a triangular formation around the plant. The stakes should be put in the ground beyond the root ball area, so as to avoid damaging the roots. Sink them in the soil deeply enough so they do not move. Make sure that the top portions of the stakes are not higher than the lowest branches of the plant by sawing off the tops or burying the bottoms deeper.

There's a neat trick to determine where to place the ties on the trunk. First, let the tree or shrub droop with no support. Now make a ring around the base of the trunk with one or both hands, fingers and thumbs touching. Slowly and gently slide your hands together vertically up the trunk. The tree should be slowly righting itself with your help. Place the ties at six inches above the lowest point on the trunk where your hands can hold the tree upright.

And now the single most important part of staking: inspect the staked tree or shrub monthly! Are the stakes in good shape and still providing sturdy support? Have the ties done any visible damage to the trunk? Untie them regularly, and use your hands to adjust the proper tie point. As the tree builds trunk strength, the tie attachment point should move lower down the tree. Eventually, you will untie the stakes and your tree will remain upright. At this point, remove the stakes. The therapy was successful—congratulate yourself with a cool glass of lemonade!❀

How to tie the knot?

Consider looping the tie material around the stakes, never touching the trunk. If this is too loose, try a modified figure-eight setup, where the ties gently loop around each stake and the trunk. Try to avoid tying any knots that contact the trunk. Be creative, keeping in mind that a tight tie attachment will rub away bark and damage the trunk where it touches, and may reduce the movement of the trunk in the wind.

Shanyn G. Hosier worked for the University of Arizona Maricopa County Cooperative Extension Urban Horticulture program for four years, helping to train Master Gardener volunteers and citizens. She has a Bachelor's degree in biology from Indiana University and extensive botany and horticulture training from Arizona State University. She is an International Society of Arboriculture Certified Arborist and University of Arizona Cooperative Extension Master Gardener.

Chapter 3

Watering Desert Landscapes

By Donna DiFrancesco

In a temperate or non-desert region where precipitation averages 30 inches or more annually, most landscape plants perform quite well on natural rainfall. These regions may experience periodic dry spells that can be remedied by watering with a hose or sprinkler. In contrast, our Southwestern desert climates are characterized by low humidity and little rainfall. (The Sonoran Desert receives only seven to 14 inches per year on average, depending on elevation.) The low humidity combined with high heat and drying winds causes over six feet of water to evaporate from soil and water surfaces each year.

Because of these climatic conditions, landscape watering is needed to help plants establish a root system and to keep them healthy and beautiful. Your goal should be to provide the plants with adequate water, while not using more water than is needed.

An alternative title to this chapter could be "Watering Desert Landscapes: A Theory" because there is probably much that is unknown about soil, plant, and water relationships. A theory might be defined as an assumption based on available knowledge or information. Although much research has been conducted across the country on plant water use, it typically concentrates on agricultural crops or temperate climate plants. There has been little research to date on the many adaptations that desert plants utilize to survive in desert climates. Seeing a healthy, attractive palo verde tree perched on a desert mountain, growing in rock, during an extended dry spell demonstrates that there is still much to learn about desert plants and their true water needs.

Perhaps due to the lack of adequate research and knowledge, landscape watering provokes the most conflicting advice of all landscape maintenance activities. Ask five "experts" how to water a tree, and you'll likely get five different answers. It is difficult to provide a single answer because there are so many factors that can affect plant water needs. This chapter will explain these factors and provide you with the knowledge to determine how much water to apply to your plants, in your local conditions.

Why Watering Correctly is Important

Landscape plants probably suffer more from problems related to watering than from any other cause. Water is truly the life substance of plants and accounts for over 90 percent of plant weight. Not only does water form a continuous liquid pipeline in the plant for growth, but large amounts are also used to cool the plant through transpiration. Plants definitely need water. However, too much water in the soil means too little oxygen for plant roots. This condition may slow the uptake of nutrients and/or encourages disease organisms to attack. Overwatering can also cause excessive growth that will require more pruning.

Shallow watering is another problem. Although plants may survive, it encourages the roots to stay close to the surface of the soil. This can subject plants to water stress, especially during hot, windy days. It may also cause trees or shrubs to have poor root development, making them more susceptible to blowing over in strong winds.

Salt Problems

Salt build-up in the soil is another consequence of shallow watering. The problem starts with the high concentration of salts naturally present in desert water and soil. As plants are watered, these salts move through the soil. They stop wherever the water stops penetrating. Since irrigation cycles are usually repeated many times, it is easy to understand how salt may build up in the same location if the water never penetrates deeply past the root zone.

Salt burn may show up as yellowing leaves or brown leaf margins. It kills the tissue and the entire leaf dries out and turns brown. To alleviate this problem, irrigate twice as deeply two to three times each summer to leach—or push—those salts past the root zone. Soaking or heavy summer rains may also leach the salts away.

Watering Tip

A drip system with a one-gallon per hour emitter and a 15-minute run time only puts out one quart of water.

A garden hose running only two or three seconds puts out one quart of water.

Would you handwater a plant for only three seconds?

Drip systems must run long enough for water to penetrate to the appropriate depth.

How to Water Correctly

Delivering Water

There are a number of ways to deliver water to plants. How you water depends on such factors as where you live, type of landscape, need for convenience, and budget. You may live in an older neighborhood that still offers flood irrigation, where water is delivered once or twice a month in great quantity, "flooding" the entire landscape. Or, you may have a new home supplied with a drip irrigation system. Table 1 covers some of the characteristics of different watering methods.

When to Water

For sprinkler systems, early morning (between 3 and 6 a.m.) is the best time to water. Just make sure that you don't set the irrigation controller to sprinkle the grass at the same time your family is trying to shower. Sprinklers can take away a great amount of water pressure.

TABLE 1 Watering Methods				
Method	Description	Pro	Con	Tip
Rainwater harvesting	Capture rainwater on property with proper grading	Free, high-quality water	Must provide water during dry spells	Fall planting is a good time to establish plants
Watering hose, soaker hose	Apply water directly to plants by hand	Less likely to overwater; less salt build-up occurs	Not fun dragging hose around in summer	Use timers to remind you to turn off water
Flood irrigation	Untreated water from canals floods the landscape	Very inexpensive; waters entire root zone and more	Landscape needs borders or berms to contain water	To grow fruit or nut trees, live in these neighborhoods
Bubblers	Flood plant wells or bordered areas, 0.5-2 gallons/minute	Wet root areas very well; good for citrus	Must build and maintain a basin around plants	Increase basin size as plants grow
Drip emitters	Apply water slowly to plant roots, 0.5-10 gallons/hour	Apply water only where needed; reduced evaporation	Can lead to salt build-up; difficult to see problems	Add emitters as plants grow to wet expanding root zone
Above-ground sprinklers	Apply water in patterns to large surface areas	Most effective way to water grass areas	Water lost to evaporation and misdirection	Check system frequently

Watering early in the day gives plants plenty of time to dry, reducing the chance of developing leaf diseases. Watering early will also minimize water loss from evaporation. As much as 30 percent of water evaporates if lawns are watered under the hot midday sun with sprinklers; adding wind to the equation increases the evaporation rate to 50 percent.

With drip irrigation, you can water at almost anytime since it does not wet plant foliage. Drip irrigation is at ground level, so little is lost to evaporation. It also requires little water pressure. It is still recommended to water early in the morning when you are more likely to see irrigation problems, such as leaks. If you water in the evening, the evidence may be dry by daylight.

Where to Water

The soil surrounding a plant's roots serves as a storage tank from which the plant draws moisture. The goal is to water the root zone where most water-absorbing or "feeder roots" are found. This is usually within the top one to three feet of the soil and they spread one and one-half to four times as wide as the plant's canopy. Apply water in this zone.

How Deep: The 1-2-3 Rule

Typically, the smaller the plant, the smaller the root system. Therefore, a basic guideline is to water small perennials and annual flowers and vegetables to a depth of one foot; shrubs and large groundcovers to a depth of two feet; and large shrubs and trees to a depth of three feet.

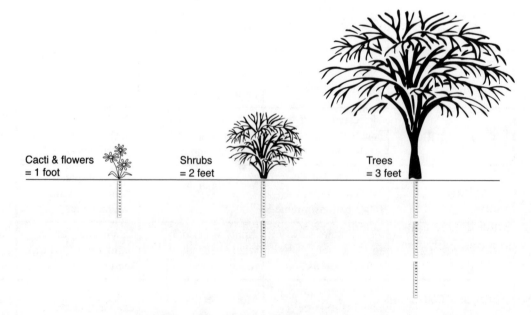

Cacti & flowers = 1 foot

Shrubs = 2 feet

Trees = 3 feet

Water should soak far enough to moisten a plant's entire root system.

How Wide: The Pizza Principle

An easy way to understand how far out water should be applied to wet the root zone is "The Pizza Principle." This principle simply states that it is usually a better bargain to buy the bigger pizza. The rationale is that a two-inch increase in diameter translates to a 44 percent increase in area. As plants grow, a small increase in diameter translates to a much larger increase in the root zone. The Pizza Principle is useful for understanding how a plant's water needs dramatically increase as it grows.

Near or Far: The Doughnut Principle

Another visual food analogy helps explain where water should be applied. Most of a plant's feeder roots, which take up water and nutrients, are located around the outside edge of the plant (the drip line) and beyond. Therefore, it is unnecessary to significantly wet the area surrounding the plant stem or tree trunk. Imagine a doughnut: water would be applied to the outer edge and beyond, not to the inner circle. The illustration on the next page demonstrates this concept.

How Much Water to Apply

To monitor how deeply you have watered, use a soil probe (a piece of sharpened wood or metal, such as rebar). The probe will slide easily through moist soil but will become difficult to push when it reaches dry soil. Once you have determined how long it takes to fill a root zone, try to irrigate that same length of time each watering session. The time this will take depends on the following three factors:

Type of watering method used

Drip emitter sizes vary, providing anywhere from one-half to 10 gallons of water per *hour*. Bubbler systems can deliver between one-half to two gallons per *minute*. Garden hoses deliver four to six gallons of water per *minute*.

Type of soil

Soils can be predominantly sand, clay, or a mixture called loam. Most desert soils are sandy or clay-like. One gallon of water covers approximately two square feet of clay-type ground to a one-inch depth. However, water penetrates faster and three times deeper in sandy soil than in clay.

Size of each plant's root zone

(See the previous section on Where to Water.)

Pizza Principle
The larger pizza is usually the better buy.

10" pizza = 3.14×5^2 =
78 square inches
12" pizza = 3.14×6^2 =
113 square inches

A 2-inch diameter increase provides 44% more pizza!

Watering Principle
As plants grow in diameter, a much larger root zone area should be watered.

*Area of a circle = πr^2. π = 3.14. r = radius of a circle. Numbers have been rounded.

The author would like to credit Terry Mikel for the intellectual creation of The Pizza Principle.

For guidelines recommending how many gallons will be needed to wet the root zone of different types and sizes of plants, see Table 2. Some of these numbers may seem large to you, especially if you use a one-gallon-per-hour emitter on a four-foot diameter palo verde tree. A 47-hour run time does seem excessive, but it also makes it clear that you need to add emitters to a larger plant. Remember that drip systems apply water at a slow rate.

Factors that Influence Watering Frequency

Plant type and maturity, weather, soil type, and many other factors determine the frequency of watering. Table 3 examines some of these factors.

A good rule of thumb is to apply water when the top one-third of the soil in the root zone is dry or when plants begin to appear water stressed. Be observant and look for signs of stress such as those listed in Table 4. The following information describes how different factors can influence watering frequency.

Plant Type

Whether the plant is a tree or shrub affects how deeply the

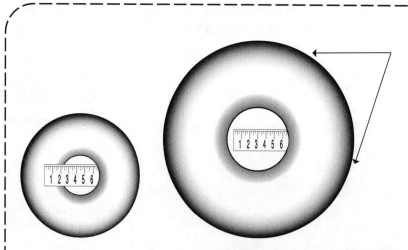

As the plant grows, apply water near the outer canopy, not near the stem or trunk.

Doughnut Principle
The bigger the doughnut, the bigger the doughnut hole.

Watering Principle
As the plant grows, water more around the edge of the plant canopy and less near the center of the plant.

roots may grow and how deeply water should penetrate (recall *The 1-2-3 Rule*). The deeper the roots, the less frequently you will need to water and the better buffered they will be against weather changes. Your plants will be more likely to develop a deeper root system if you water to the recommended depth. The plant type or species is also a major factor that influences watering frequency. Native plants or plants from other desert regions are adapted to withstand long dry periods. Temperate or tropical plants will need to be watered more frequently than desert plants.

Plant Maturity

Young plants should be watered more often than older plants. Table 5 provides guidelines for watering new plantings. As plants become established, allow a longer drying period between waterings.

Soil Type

The type of soil determines the availability of water and oxygen to your plants. It also governs how easily water penetrates the soil and how long it stays there. If your soil is shallow, compacted, or sandy you will need to irrigate more frequently; however, less water will be needed to wet the entire root zone. One inch of water applied to the surface of a sandy soil will penetrate about 12 inches, in loam about seven to eight inches, and in clay soil about five inches.

Watering Tip

Time required to apply 47 gallons of water to a tree using different watering methods:

✔ 47 hours with a one-gallon-per-hour drip emitter

✔ 24 minutes with a two-gallon-per-minute bubbler

✔ 8 minutes with a garden hose.

If you place four separate four-gallons-per-hour emitters around the tree, the system will output 16 gallons per hour. You can reduce the run time from 47 hours to three hours.

TABLE 2 Gallons of Water Required to Wet Root Zone Based on Plant Type and Size											
Plant type: Depth water must soak	Plant diameter in feet										
	1'	2'	3'	4'	5'	6'	8'	10'	12'	14'	16'
Flowers: 1 foot	1	3	6	10							
Shrubs: 2 feet	2	8	20	35	50	78					
Trees: 3 feet	3	12	26	47	74	105	188	294	425	575	750

NOTE: Figures based on typical Phoenix-area clay loam. Sandy soils require less water; heavy clay or compacted soils require more. Assume that larger plants are receiving water from surrounding plants.

Weather

The soil will dry more rapidly during warmer summer months and less rapidly during cooler winter months as illustrated in the graph below. Heat, sun intensity, wind, rainfall, and humidity all play a role in how much water plants lose. Adjust

Typical water-use curve for a plant through the year shows a sharp increase when temperatures rise.

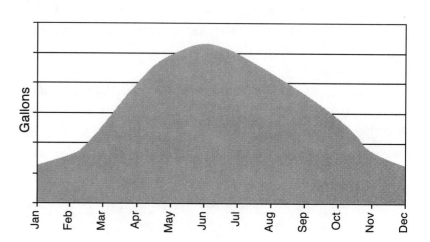

TABLE 3		
Factors That Influence Plant Water Needs		
Factors	Example Less water needed	Example More water needed
Plant type	Desert plant such as a palo verde tree or Texas sage	Non-desert plant such as an ash tree or hibiscus
Plant maturity	Newly planted or small plants need less water, but applied more often	Large or well-established plants need more water, but applied less often
Soil type	Sandy soil needs less water to wet root zone, but applied more often	Clay soil needs more water to wet the root zone, but applied less often
Season/climate	Water less when cool, when high humidity, or during rainy season	Water more when warm, during hot dry winds, or if no rainfall
Microclimate/exposure	Northern or shaded exposures stay moist longer	Hot and sunny southern or western exposures dry out quickly
Soil cover/mulch	Organic or inorganic mulch helps retain soil moisture	If leaf litter or mulch is not on the surface, soil dries more quickly

your watering schedule to the season and significant changes in the weather.

Watering Schedule Guidelines

With all of the factors that influence plant watering, it is easy to see that appropriate watering involves both science and art. Observations of your plants, checking the soil moisture, and a little practice will keep your plants healthy without overwatering. The watering schedule guidelines in Table 6 provide some basic recommendations for established plants. Copy this chart and post it as a reminder to change your irrigation controller seasonally. Laminate a copy and place it inside the controller box for easy reference. *You can save 30-50 percent annually on landscape watering by adjusting the irrigation controller seasonally.*

Making the System Work

If you have an existing irrigation system, it will be up to you to determine how to apply the water as efficiently as possible and to modify it as plant needs change. An irrigation system will also require routine maintenance to continue functioning properly and running efficiently. Checking the system one or two times each year will help ensure that the parts are working correctly. The ideas on the following pages may help.

TABLE 4 Symptoms Observed from Underwatering or Overwatering	
Underwatering	Overwatering
Soil is dry	Soil is constantly damp
Older leaves turn yellow or brown; drop off	Leaves turn lighter green to yellow
Leaves are wilted	Young shoots are wilted
Leaves are drooping	Leaves are green yet brittle
Leaves curl	Algae and/or mushrooms appear
Stems or branches die back	Presence of soft, smelly rotted tissue

Modification

Modify irrigation systems as plants grow to accommodate larger root systems. Move emitters out towards the plant canopy edge and add emitters to soak larger areas, especially on trees. If you have a bubbler system, you may have to increase the size of the basin that contains the water.

It is often standard practice to install irrigation systems that combine trees and shrubs on the same valve or watering zone. Although inefficient for watering, this design is faster and less expensive to install, so unfortunately, it is common in landscapes especially when homeowners are unaware of alternatives. If you have this situation, you may want to consider making adjustments to the existing irrigation system. Ideally, for plant health and water efficiency, you would water trees on one line and shrubs on another because they have different water requirements. If you don't want to go through the labor and expense of adding a valve and trenching in some irrigation line, here are some methods to mitigate the situation:

✔ Add emitters with greater flow rates to trees so that more water is applied in the same amount of time.

✔ Add extra organic mulch around shrub roots so that soil will stay moist longer.

✔ Spot water areas that need more water than the rest of the landscape with a water or soaker hose.

TABLE 5 Watering Frequency to Establish New Desert-Adapted Plants		
Weeks since planting	Summer	Fall, winter, and spring
1 & 2	Every 1 - 2 days	Every 3 - 4 days
3 & 4	Every 3 - 4 days	Every 6 - 7 days
5 & 6	Every 4 - 6 days	Every 7 - 10 days
7 & 8	Every 7 days	Every 10 - 14 days
9 and beyond	Gradually extend time between irrigations until plant is established. Check position of drip emitters and move them to the outer edge of the root ball. Water no more than once per week after the first summer.	

The Irrigation Controller

Don't just set it and forget it! A common mistake made by homeowners is never changing the initial establishment schedule on the irrigation controller. Manage your irrigation controller by adjusting the irrigation schedule seasonally. The controller controls the irrigation system and you control the controller. The right controller, properly scheduled, can result in significant water savings and lower water bills. Always keep in mind that you are the "brains" behind your irrigation scheduling system.

If you have an opportunity to select your own controller make sure it is one you find relatively easy to use. If you are uncomfortable with programming the controller, you are unlikely to adjust the watering as much as is necessary.

Information Needed to Program the Controller

1. What day is today?

2. What time is it now?

3. What days do you want the irrigation to run?

4. What time of day do you want the irrigation to start?

5. How long do you want the stations to run?

TABLE 6 Watering Schedule Guidelines for Established Plants (Days Between Watering)		Spring Mar-May	Summer May-Oct	Fall Oct-Dec	Winter Dec-Mar	Watering Depth
Trees	Desert-adapted	14 - 30	7 - 21	14 - 30	30 - 60	3 feet
	High-water-use	7 - 12	7 - 14	7 - 12	14 - 30	3 feet
Shrubs	Desert-adapted	14 - 30	7 - 21	14 - 30	30 - 45	2 feet
	High-water-use	7 - 10	5 - 7	7 - 10	10 - 14	2 feet
Groundcovers & Vines	Desert-adapted	14 - 30	7 - 21	14 - 30	21 - 45	1 foot
	High-water-use	7 - 10	2 - 5	7 - 10	10 - 14	1 foot
Annual Flowers		3 - 7	2 - 5	3 - 7	5 - 10	1 foot

Adapted from *Guidelines For Landscape Drip Irrigation Systems.*

Instructions to input information should be located in the inside panel of the irrigation controller. If your instructions or manual have been lost, try to find a toll-free phone number for technical support from the manufacturer. Wholesale irrigation stores may also be able to assist you. You will need to know the make and model of the controller, so have that information handy before you call.

Troubleshooting

Here are two common occurrences that are easy to remedy.

Problem: Irrigation runs frequently and/or at times you didn't program.

Solution: Check for power failure and loss of program. The controller may have reverted to a factory default program. Exchange the old "dead" battery with a new one.

Problem: Irrigation keeps starting over after it has finished.

Solution: Make sure that there is only one start time per program.

Irrigation Maintenance Checklist

✔ Check sprinkler heads for proper operation or clogging.

✔ Check that the wetting pattern is consistent. In other words, all areas are being watered evenly, without major dry or wet spots or spray landing on sidewalks.

✔ Check for leaks and breaks as evidenced by flooding, standing water, or water holes.

✔ Check valves for leaks and malfunctions. Valves will stick open or closed if debris is caught in the diaphragm.

✔ Check controllers for correct timing and smooth operation. After an electrical storm check to see if your irrigation program is still intact.

✔ Check drip systems for clogged and malfunctioning emitters; check for leaks along points of connection; bury exposed tubing or wiring; flush out lines periodically.

✔ Check garden hoses and faucets for leaky connections.

Water Conservation

Watering plants is like feeding goldfish. The more you give them, the more they grow. If you don't overwater your plants, they grow less, require less pruning, and look healthier. Don't assume that because you have an automatic system plants are being watered correctly. Recent studies from both The University of Arizona and Arizona State University have found that landscapes with automatic irrigation systems tend to be overwatered. Homes with in-ground sprinkler systems used 35 percent more water than those homes without in-ground sprinklers. Homes with automatic timers used 47 percent more water than those without timers. Arizona landscapes are being watered two to five times more than is needed.

Become water conscious in your garden in other ways, too. A large part of household water use (50–70 percent) goes to watering landscapes. Look for a variety of ways you can save water or eliminate waste. The added bonus is that you'll save money.

Tips to Save Water

✔ Use a soil probe (as described earlier) to determine that you are watering only to the depth needed.

✔ Control weeds that compete for the plant's water; do not lay plastic over the soil.

✔ Prevent runoff or misdirection of water; retain water in a basin around plants or water at a slower rate if necessary.

✔ Choose low-water-use plants when you plant or renovate your landscape.

✔ Place organic mulches on the surface of plant roots to keep soil cooler and retain moisture longer. As the mulches decompose, they add nutrients to the soil. Cover with granite if you prefer.

✔ If you slowly soak plants with a hose, install a faucet timer to automatically turn water off, or use a kitchen timer as a reminder.

✔ Incorporate rainwater harvesting into landscape design whenever possible. Contour your yard by constructing small berms, channels, or swales to direct water runoff to your plants.

Much of the Southwest's water travels hundreds of miles from the Colorado River. Water conservation should always be practiced when gardening.

✔ Place a rain gauge in your yard. If you receive at least one-half-inch of rain, skip the next irrigation cycle.

✔ Consider not overseeding lawns with winter rye grass. Dormant bermuda only requires watering once every three to four weeks in the winter.

✔ Don't overfertilize plants and lawn. They will require more water and more frequent pruning and mowing.

✔ Monitor your water usage. Learn how to read your meter or check your monthly water bills.❀

Donna DiFrancesco is a Horticulturist with the City of Mesa Water Conservation office where she educates Mesa residents and landscape professionals about Xeriscape and water conservation. She worked four years as a Horticulture Program Coordinator for the University of Arizona Maricopa County Cooperative Extension and worked two years as a Revegetation Ecologist (overseeing maintenance of arid landscapes) for the Flood Control District of Maricopa County before taking her current position.

Donna has served as an Arizona Master Gardener since 1991 and is a Certified Arborist and Certified Pesticide Applicator. She has an A.S. in Applied Plant Science from the University of New Hampshire and a B.S. in Horticulture from the University of Missouri-Columbia.

She dreams of someday taking on a superhero persona as Xeriscape Woman, wearing a large "X" on her chest, and carrying an ironwood branch magic wand that will turn dull landscapes into beautiful Xeriscapes.

Chapter 4

Pruning for Healthy Trees and Shrubs

By Lucy K. Bradley

Many of us aren't sure why to prune, which plants to prune, when to prune, and more importantly, when *not* to prune. This chapter will provide you with the essentials to help you become an effective and confident pruner. It will examine how plants grow and how that should impact your decisions about how and when to prune. Other topics include basic pruning methods, pruning specific plants, and the selection, use, and care of pruning tools. Tips on when and how to hire a pruning professional will also be covered.

Why Prune?

Each time you make a pruning cut, you are opening up a wound on your plant that will provide easy access for pests and diseases. This wound requires energy from the plant to heal. So before you make the first cut, identify a specific goal and a plan for achieving it with the minimum number of cuts. Good reasons to prune include promoting the plant's health and eliminating potential hazards by removing branches that are dead, weak, crowded, crossed, or damaged. Never prune your trees or shrubs just because neighbors or landscape maintenance workers are pruning.

The most common reason gardeners start pruning is because a tree or shrub is growing out of bounds, encroaching on sidewalks, driveways, or patios. If the only reason you are pruning is to reduce the size of a plant, it's likely that you have the plant in the wrong place. Select a plant that will be able to grow to its full mature size in the space you have available. There are many excellent reference books that provide guidelines for the height and width of mature plants (see Resources). Enjoy an excursion to area botanical gardens, parks, and demonstration gardens to observe plants in natural settings. A little time spent in plant selection translates into reduced pruning chores over the lifetime of the plant. If you have inherited a plant that is in the wrong place, remove it and replace with one appropriate to the available space.

A plant's natural form is usually the most desirable. Thus, tree care professionals recommend that most pruning should occur only to correct growth defects. However, another common reason that gardeners prune is to change the shape of the plant. If you want a tall narrow tree, select a tree whose natural form is tall and narrow. Do not try to force a tree that grows naturally as wide as it is tall into a pyramid shape. Unnecessary pruning damages the health of the plant and overburdens the landfills with trimmings. Of all the materials sent to the landfills, 40 percent is plant matter.

In this chapter we will be discussing how to prune for the improved health and long life of the plant. Another reason that some people prune is to increase flower and fruit production in roses and deciduous fruit like apples and peaches. That involves a very different strategy which we will not address in this chapter.

How Plants Grow

Understanding how plants grow will enable you to make better decisions by predicting how the plant will respond to either pruning or no pruning.

Future Growth Builds Upon the Existing Framework

New growth begins at the tip of the previous year's growth and lengthens from there. A small twig that branches out from the trunk two feet off the ground may grow into a mighty limb twenty feet long, but it will always be attached to the trunk two feet off the ground. Therefore, it is important to choose appropriate primary "scaffold" branches that will be the framework upon which the plant will grow. On young trees, choose branches evenly spaced up, down, and around the tree trunk. Keep branches that have a wide angle of attachment, which will be stronger.

On young trees, select scaffold branches 4–6 inches apart. As the tree grows, you can remove some of the scaffold branches to allow for wider spacing. It is helpful to be familiar with the

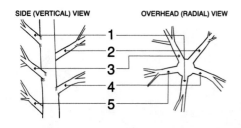

Retain "scaffold" branches that are evenly spaced to form a framework for the tree's future growth.

maximum size of a mature tree's branches. For example, branches that are 12 inches in diameter should be 12–18 inches apart. A smaller tree may have thinner branches spaced 6–12 inches apart and a really large tree may have branch spacing 2–3 feet apart.

Plants Elongate From The Tips

You can redirect the growth of a plant by selectively removing the tips that are not headed in a desired direction. So prune back to a bud or a branch pointing in the direction you want the plant to grow. Prune spreading branches back to upright stems to increase height. Alternatively, remove upright limbs (not the terminal leader) to encourage spreading. With your overall purpose in mind, make each cut a calculated decision.

Cut back to a side branch or a bud that follows the general flow of the main branch. The side branch should be at least one-third the diameter of the branch that is removed. If a branch is cut back to a twig that is less than that size, the branch will sprout many new shoots that will each be weakly attached.

Apical Tips Dominate

The tip of the branch produces growth-inhibiting hormones called auxins that are sent back down the branch to keep other buds from breaking and growing thus insuring that all the energy is channeled into supporting the growth of the tip. This is called

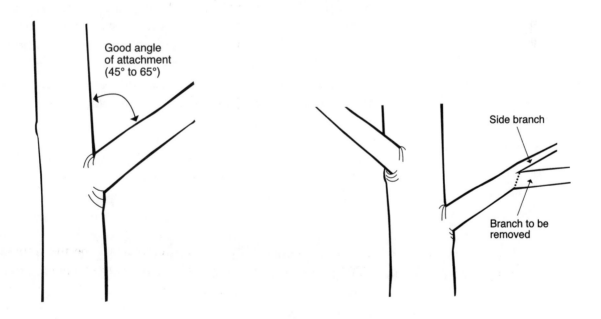

Keep branches with strong angles of attachment, which are less likely to break.
Cut back to a side branch that follows the flow of the main branch.

apical dominance. For shrubs, if you want dense branching it is important to cut back the tips, eliminating the production of growth inhibitors and stimulating the development of lateral buds. For trees, apical dominance is what gives them their form so this practice is not recommended.

Leaves Are "Factories" That Produce Food

Leaves, through photosynthesis, produce the food for the plant. While plants do take up some nutrients from the soil, it is similar to humans taking vitamins. Just imagine if a giant oak tree was getting all its "food" from the soil. By the time it was mature it would have "consumed" so much soil that it would have created a valley all around it. This doesn't happen because the leaves are "factories" converting sunlight into the nutrients for plant growth. So when you remove leaves, you stress the plant by reducing its ability to feed itself. Pruning is basically "dwarfing" the tree. Therefore, do not remove more than one-fourth of the canopy per year. If too many leaves are removed, the plant can literally starve. In addition, heavy pruning can open up leaves and branches not previously exposed to sunlight, making them vulnerable to sunburn.

Dormancy

It is a good idea to postpone extensive pruning until the plant is dormant. When dormant, the bark is more tightly affixed so it is less likely to tear when cut. In addition, the plant is more likely to successfully seal off the pruning wound prior to disease or pest damage. A further advantage of pruning during dormancy is the ability to clearly see the structure of the tree without leaves obscuring the view. Deciduous trees and conifers that are native to cold climates are usually dormant in the winter, so prune these plants in January in the low desert.

Trees that evolved in hot climates tend to be dormant or slower growing in summer. Prune trees native to the desert in the early summer, usually May or early June. The trees are able to more quickly seal a pruning wound at this time.

Most pruning is done when the plant is dormant or right after flowering. However, it may be necessary to do light pruning at other times, to remove dead or diseased branches or for safety. If you must prune in the summer, it is essential to not expose the plant to sunburn, which can damage leaves and bark tissue permanently.

Some arborists prefer to do all pruning in the low desert in the early summer since rot and disease pathogens are less active during the hot, low-humidity season. In the low desert, pruning in fall is not recommended as late summer thundershowers create conditions that promote the spread of fungi, and plants with open wounds are more easily infected.

Meristematic Tissue

Plants have a special protective tissue where branches and offshoots meet, called meristematic tissue. Should a branch break off, this tissue enables the tree to quickly grow over the wound and seal it from diseases and pests. A proper pruning cut will leave this area of meristematic tissue intact so that it can generate new tissue to grow over the wound.

Pest and Disease Susceptibility

Dead, injured, and diseased branches attract pests and more diseases. Remove these branches to prevent the buildup of pest populations. Prevention and early intervention are key to maintaining the health of trees.

Weakly Attached Buds

Trees have very strong survival strategies. Hidden just beneath the bark are adventitious buds. Unlike the normal buds that occur at the base of leaves and are anchored deep within the

Best Time to Prune*

Native trees	Early summer (May-early June)
Non-native deciduous trees	During winter dormancy (January)
Conifers	During winter dormancy (January)
Spring-blooming shrubs (bloom on last season's wood)	After bloom is finished
Summer-blooming shrubs (bloom on new wood)	During winter dormancy (January)

*While these are optimal pruning times, if done correctly and no more than 25 percent of the canopy is removed it is possible to prune anytime of year in the low desert. However, pruning outside the recommended guidelines may jeopardize bloom the following year.

Prevent Overpruning

Once you get started pruning it is often difficult to stop. Try these ideas to prevent overpruning.

✔ Begin with a plan and stop when you have accomplished your goal.

✔ Never prune a plant you love when you are angry.

✔ Begin with your fastest-growing, toughest plants, and work your way through to your most expensive, slowest-growing plants after your enthusiasm has worn off.

✔ Don't clean up clippings from beneath a plant until you are done pruning. Leave them as a visual reminder of how much of the canopy you have removed.

✔ Stop every 20 minutes to assess what has been done and what is left to do.

✔ Have someone come over every half hour and ask if you have finished yet.

stem, these adventitious buds are weakly attached to the bark of the branch. They remain dormant unless the tree is wounded. When a tree loses lots of leaves, adventitious buds can open and grow into stems and leaves to produce food for the plant. The problem is that these weakly attached buds grow into weakly attached branches that are likely to be torn off in a wind storm. Or, as they grow larger, they may become unable to support their own weight, and break.

To avoid the growth of weak adventitious buds do not remove more than one-fourth of the canopy in a year. It is also important not to leave stubs. The adventitious buds along the stub will begin to grow to try to compensate for the leaves that were lost in pruning. Always remove branches at their point of origin, or prune back to a lateral side branch at least one-third the diameter of the branch being removed.

Limited Resources

The more flowers and fruit a plant produces, the smaller each flower and fruit will be. Pruning reduces the overall number and so concentrates energy into the production of larger, though possibly fewer, flowers and/or fruit. Most flowering shrubs will bloom either on new wood or on one-year-old growth. Properly timed pruning will increase the production of wood that will bear flowers.

Before Pruning

Here's a quick review of some of the key points to keep in mind before making a pruning cut. Always have a purpose and base your pruning decisions on achieving it. Every cut you make opens up a wound on the plant, making it more vulnerable to disease and pest problems. Every leaf you remove reduces the plant's ability to produce food for itself. Every branch you remove creates green waste. Don't prune unless you have a specific reason that outweighs the potential risks. You may be pruning to remove diseased and damaged branches, to eliminate hazards or obstacles, or to direct growth. Note that pruning to encourage new growth to head in a specific direction is different from heavy pruning to reduce a plant's size.

Examine The Plant From Every Angle

Begin with a thorough inspection of the tree or shrub from all vantage points. Look at the structure and identify damaged branches that will need to be removed.

Based On Your Goal, Select Branches To Remove

Visualize what the plant will look like when those branches have been removed. Be sure that you have mentally traced each branch to all its tips. Many tree workers find it helpful to tag the branches to be removed with bright tape or yarn and then step back to imagine how the plant will look after pruning.

Basic Pruning Methods

How to Make a Pruning Cut

It's essential to make proper pruning cuts that leave the plant's meristematic tissue to seal off the wound. An effective cut is made along a line connecting the "branch bark ridge" and the outer edge of the "branch collar." The branch bark ridge is a raised furrow of bark found on the topside of the branch, in the angle where the branch and the stem or trunk that it is attached to meet. The branch collar is a raised furrow of bark on the underside of the branch where it meets the stem or trunk. The plant's meristematic tissue is found within this collar. Find the ridge at the top and the outside tip of the collar at the bottom. Make your cut in a direct line between the two. Sometimes you may need to cut from the bottom up (rather than top down) if the angle is too tight.

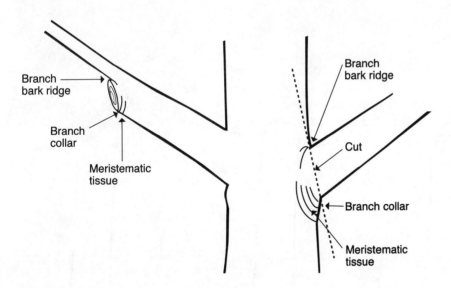

Cut in a straight line from the branch bark ridge to the branch collar. This allows the plant's meristematic tissue to remain intact and generate new tissue to cover the pruning wound.

To protect this collar of tissue, do not make flush cuts. Flush cuts remove a branch as close to the trunk as possible. For many years flush cuts were recommended, but research now shows they are dangerous to the tree. In flush cuts the meristematic tissue found in the branch collar is cut off with the branch. This results in a large oval wound that may never be sealed off. On the other hand, a proper pruning cut will result in a smaller, round wound with the branch collar still attached to the trunk. Within six to 12 months new growth from the meristematic tissue will begin closing off the wound.

Pruning Small Branches

Remove the branch at its point of origin (where it attaches to its parent branch or trunk) or cut back to a bud facing in the direction that you want future growth to expand. *Do not leave a stub.* The stub will eventually die back, attracting pests and preventing the plant from sealing off the wound. In addition, diseases that start in the stub can spread back into the main trunk. Even if the stub doesn't die, it may develop new, weakly attached stems.

When cutting back to a bud, make the cut at a 45-degree angle, one-quarter inch above the desired bud, angled toward the bud. If the cut is made too close or the angle too steep, the bud may be wounded. On the other hand, don't cut too far away,

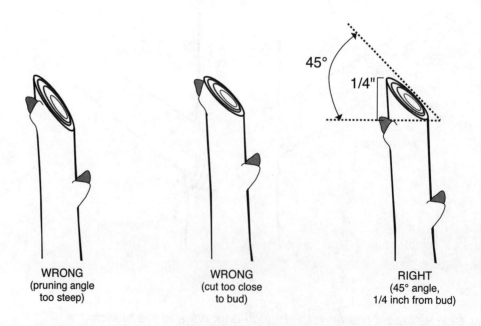

WRONG
(pruning angle
too steep)

WRONG
(cut too close
to bud)

RIGHT
(45° angle,
1/4 inch from bud)

45°

1/4"

If the pruning cut is too steep or too close, the growing bud may be damaged.

leaving a stub. Place the cutting blade under the stem, cutting upward. This has several advantages: it reduces the possibility of tearing the bark; it requires less effort; and it allows a closer cut.

Shearing is generally not recommended, especially for native plants. This is the practice of indiscriminately cutting off all stems and foliage at one length, creating a "flat" surface. Shrubs that have been shaped into cubes and balls have been sheared. Shearing increases the number of wounds to the plant, making it vulnerable to insect, disease, and frost damage. It causes the plant to generate new growth all in the same plane (along the line of the shear), which destroys the natural branching pattern. If done at the wrong time of year, it eliminates flowering and it is very expensive to maintain.

Pruning Large Limbs

Remove branches where they attach to the parent branch or cut back to a side branch at least one-third the diameter of the branch to be removed. The side branch should follow the same general direction as the original branch. Avoid creating sharp angles, which are unattractive and unhealthy. There are three important steps to removing large limbs to prevent the bark from ripping down the side of the trunk when the branch is cut.

First, undercut one-quarter of the way through the branch at a point six to 12 inches out from where the final cut will be. This will prevent the bark from ripping.

Second, make a top cut just beyond the first undercut, sawing all the way through the limb. This removes the weight of the limb, leaving a shorter, lighter section to prune off.

Third, make the final cut at an angle connecting the tip of the branch bark ridge with the outside of the branch collar. Once you start, saw through completely and smoothly. Don't saw partially from the top and then some from the bottom. This protects the tissue, enabling the tree to seal off the wound efficiently.

No More Stubs

It is important to emphasize that just as with trimming small branches, do not leave stubs when pruning large limbs. The tree only has meristematic tissue capable of sealing off the wounds at the joints. When a stub is left, the tree is unable to seal off the wound and it becomes an entry point for diseases and pests. In addition, weakly attached buds on the stump may grow into hazardous, weakly attached branches.

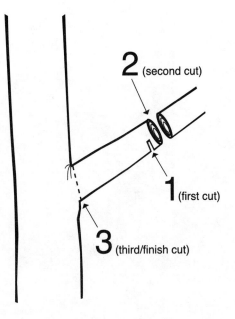

A series of three cuts will prevent bark from ripping down the main trunk when pruning large limbs.

No More Topping

Do not top trees! Topping hacks off all limbs at the same height. Most people say they top trees to reduce the size of the tree, to improve the view, or to eliminate danger, but topping doesn't achieve this. It destroys the natural branching pattern of the tree, creates unattractive stubs, makes the tree dangerous, shortens its life span, and eventually kills it.

Topping will not result in a smaller tree. It merely exhausts the tree as it expends all its stored energy to regain its original size to replace the missing leaf area. Rather than making a tree safer, topping actually makes a tree hazardous. Topping opens the tree to invasion by rotting organisms, it starves the tree by removing the leaves that produce food, and it results in weakly attached limbs formed on sucker or shoot regrowth. It causes the tree to become top heavy due to thick regrowth, increasing the likelihood that the tree will be blown over. Topping stimulates growth. Crown reduction pruning (discussed below under Special Circumstances) is much more effective at reducing size. If necessary, completely remove the tree and replace it with one more appropriate to the space available.

The initial cost of topping is expensive and once a tree has been topped, it requires constant maintenance. In addition, trees that would add thousands of dollars to the value of your property drop in value by one-third or more as soon as they have been topped, and may actually be considered a liability rather than an asset.

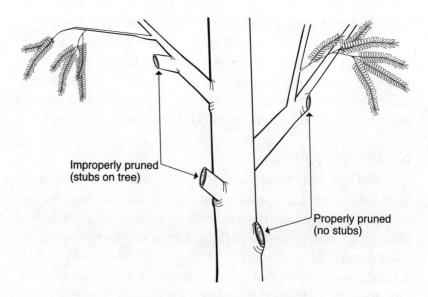

Improperly pruned (stubs on tree)

Properly pruned (no stubs)

Stubs are unsightly and don't allow the tree's natural mechanisms to close the pruning wound.

Do Not Paint Wounds

Do not use pruning paint or sealant. Although once recommended, research shows that these products inhibit the tree from sealing off the wound and may actually lock in moisture creating an ideal climate for disease. (Note: Rose canes are painted with wood glue after pruning to prevent entry by the rose cane borer. This is the only time wound dressing is recommended.)

How to Prune Specific Plants
Young Trees

Do not prune during the first year except to remove dead, diseased, damaged, or crossing branches. Think of every leaf on the plant as a mini-factory producing food for the plant to direct toward root and shoot growth. Each branch you remove reduces the amount of food produced and limits growth.

In the second year, begin to develop the structure by selecting strategically located scaffold branches that are evenly spaced around the tree and up and down the trunk. Keep branches with a wide angle of attachment. Leave the lower, small branches on young trees to increase the trunk girth and taper and to develop strength and stability. Removing too many of these lower branches reduces the tree's ability to make food for itself. After three or four years, gradually remove low branches over a two- to three-year period. When in doubt, leave it. You can always remove it later, but you can never put it back.

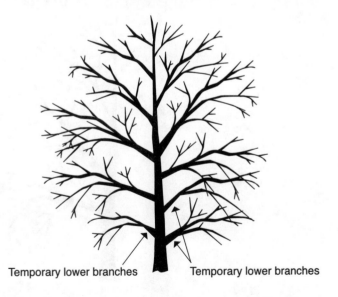

Temporary lower branches   Temporary lower branches

Leave lower branches for several years, as they help the tree develop strength and girth. They can be removed later.

Mature Trees

Begin by removing the dead, diseased, damaged, and crossing branches. The wind can cause crossing branches to rub against one another creating a wound through which disease and insects can enter. Next, remove branches that will become a nuisance if not managed carefully. This would include those destined to interfere with the house, a walkway, or a view. If two branches are parallel to each other in the same plane, remove the weaker one, as the lower branch will be shaded out by the upper one. Never remove more than one quarter of the canopy in a year. Be prepared to protect the tree from sunburn if pruning has exposed tissue that was previously shaded.

Native Trees

Many low desert native trees naturally grow with a multiple branching structure. Ironwood, palo verde, and mesquite are a few examples of trees that can develop this attractive effect when allowed to grow with minimal pruning interference. However, these natives also grow codominant leaders and stems. These codominant branches are of similar size and grow from the same point. They head off in the same direction and as they mature, there won't be enough room for both to develop. They often cross or rub against each other. Try to remove obvious codominant stems when choosing the scaffold, or framework, branches for the tree when it is still young.

BEFORE

Remove branches that are:
• dead
• crossing
• interfering
• in the same plane

AFTER

Begin pruning by removing these branches for the long-term health of the tree.

Deciduous Shrubs

For spring bloomers, prune immediately after flowering in order to minimize disruption of the next year's blooms and to prevent the litter from fruit and seed pods. For summer bloomers that flower on new wood, prune during winter dormancy, usually January. The goals for pruning shrubs are to maintain a natural appearance at a given height and width and to have evenly spaced branches that do not crowd each other. Thin out by cutting the oldest and tallest branches back to their points of origin or to a lateral side branch. These "thinning cuts" keep the plant open for air circulation and prevent excessive top growth.

Refrain from pruning shrubs into geometric circles and cubes. Once done, it becomes a constant maintenance chore to retain these shapes. It usually results in a weakened plant that is seldom in bloom as flowering wood has been regularly sheared back. To rejuvenate these shrubs into a more natural appearance, prune them back severely every few years.

Deciduous Hedges

Select fast growing, multiple-stemmed young trees or shrubs with small foliage for hedges. Prune back to six to eight inches at planting time to promote branching. Late in the first season, prune off half of the new growth. In the second year, again prune off half of the new growth. In the third year, begin to shape to a slightly rounded or pointed top (not flat) with sides slanting to a

BEFORE

AFTER

 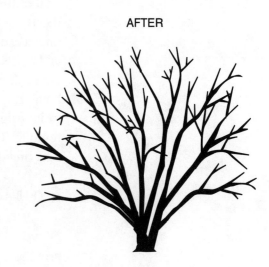

Thinning cuts remove old branches at their point of origin, opening up the interior to air and sun.

wide base. Maintain the top narrower than the bottom to insure that sunlight reaches the lower leaves. When to prune depends on whether it is a spring- or summer-blooming plant. Follow the guidelines above in Deciduous Shrubs.

Evergreen Hedges

Use a similar, though less severe, pruning strategy than with deciduous hedges. Trim lightly in the winter after a year or two.

Palms

People remove dead palm fronds to reduce potential litter from storms; to remove nesting sites for pigeons, spiders, and scorpions; and to eliminate a fire hazard. The fronds do not need to be pruned for the health of the tree. Removing too many live fronds may starve the tree causing it to weaken and the trunk to narrow dangerously at the top. Prune the fronds no higher than 10 o'clock and 2 o'clock (like hands gripping a steering wheel).

Removing the flowering/fruiting stalks will prevent the mess that comes when they ripen and reduce the number of unwanted seedlings that sprout each year. On the other hand, the fruits are a source of food for birds.

Don't prune palm trees from a ladder. If you can't prune it from the ground, hire an arborist.

Special Circumstances

In the following situations, continue to adhere to basic pruning guidelines whenever possible. Remove no more than 25 percent of the canopy in one year so the plant's ability to photosynthesize is not drastically reduced. Removing too much wood in one season can also result in sunburn, weak branching habits, and soft sucker growth. Prune stems at their point of origin, or cut back to a side branch at least one-third the size of the branch being removed. Be sure to follow a branch visually all the way to its origin to see what effect pruning it will have. Promptly remove from the premises or compost all debris to help eliminate breeding grounds for insects and diseases.

Frost Damage

When a plant has been damaged by frost, wait until new growth starts in the spring before pruning. The dead wood will provide a supporting framework for draping frost cloth or other protection if there are more frosts during the season. In addition, the dead wood will help to create an insulating air space around the plant to further protect it from frost. Pruning tends to stimulate new growth, so pruning before the last frost date could cause the plant to send out tender new shoots that would be extremely vulnerable to repeat frost damage.

Finally, frost damage often initially looks much worse than it actually is. Frequently in the spring, new growth is initiated way out on a branch that appeared to be dead. By waiting until the plant begins to grow in the spring, you can see exactly how far back the plant was damaged and remove only the dead tissue.

Storm Damage

Treating storm-damaged trees requires wise decisions and prompt action if maximum repair is to be achieved. Consider hiring a professional certified arborist. Repairs come in two stages: first aid for immediate attention; and follow-up work to be distributed over a period of several months to several years. If you decide to repair the tree, remove only the branches necessary for immediate repair. Gradually prune and reshape the tree for balance and general appearance over a period of three to five years.

Storm Damaged Tree: To Save or Not to Save

✔ **Severity of damage**
If over 30–50 percent of the main branches or trunk are severely split, broken, or mutilated, it may be advisable to remove the tree.

✔ **Desirability of species**
This may provide a good excuse to replace a tree that you did not have the heart to remove earlier.

✔ **Location**
If too close to power lines, buildings, or other structures, the tree may need to be removed.

✔ **Soundness**
Extremely old trees of low vigor might not be able to recover.

✔ **Special values**
Consider the rarity of species or variety and any sentimental or historical value.

✔ **Purpose of tree**
Does it serve a true landscaping purpose or value?

Crown Raising

The goal here is to raise the canopy of the tree by removing lower limbs to provide for vertical clearance below a given point. It may be necessary to walk underneath a tree or clear a sight-line for traffic. Crown raising should be done gradually and co-incide with the tree's regular pruning. If you must raise the tree's canopy, selectively remove lower branches at their point of origin (near the crotch), or cut back to a side branch at least one-third the diameter of the branch being removed.

Occasionally, and particularly if a tree is planted in the wrong place, crown raising may have to be done at the wrong time—both in terms of the life of the plant and time of year. In this case, a "temporary cut" may be used. A temporary cut resembles a stub cut, but it is performed with the knowledge that the stub will be properly removed, usually within a year. This allows the tree to maximize its potential to photosynthesize while at the same time providing for necessary clearance underneath the tree.

Crown Reduction

The intention here is to reduce the height or width of the tree's canopy. Selectively remove branches that extend furthest out from the canopy. The goal is still to cut back to a branch bark ridge and collar (not just hack off a section of the tree that sticks

BEFORE   AFTER

Crown raising removes lower limbs at their main point of origin to provide clearance under a tree.

out too far). Protect the tree's internal structure to maintain its beauty. Crown reduction is also called "drop crotching." It should not be confused with topping, which leaves stubs and is not recommended.

Crown Thinning

Examine the appearance of native trees in desert settings. Branches sweep the ground in a broad canopy that prevents strong winds from getting underneath the tree and literally lifting it out of the ground during thunderstorms. The canopy naturally directs the wind around the tree. On the other hand, frequently in landscape situations, the trunks are stripped of branches and a topheavy canopy is formed. Crown thinning is sometimes done to prevent trees from being uprooted and blown over when the canopy becomes particularly dense. The goal is to open up the canopy to allow light and wind to pass through by selectively removing branches at their point of origin, or by cutting back to a side branch at least one-third the diameter of the branch removed.

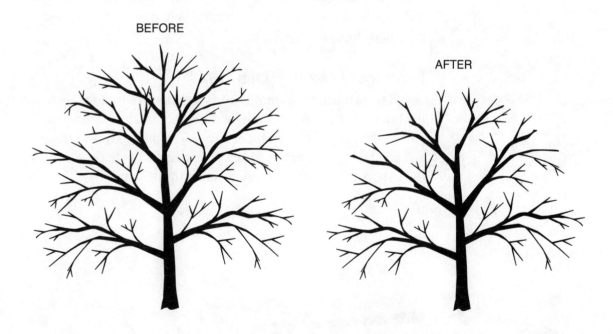

BEFORE

AFTER

Crown reduction reduces the height of a tree by selectively removing branches at their point of origin. It is not the same as topping a tree, which is never recommended.

Tools of the Trade

The two most important things about pruning tools is that they be clean and sharp. There are many different types of tools and they each have a purpose. It is important to use the right tool for the job. When the wrong tool is used on too large a stem, you can damage the branch, ruin the tool, and injure the operator.

Small Stems/By-Pass Pruners

Use by-pass hand pruners for cutting small stems that are less than one-half inch in diameter. These pruners have a sharp blade and work like scissors to make a clean cut. Another type of hand pruner is the anvil. Anvil pruners have one blade and a flat surface (the anvil) that the blade crushes the stem against. Do not use anvil pruners to cut live wood as they have a tendency to smash plant tissue. If the stem seems too thick, use loppers or a saw.

Large Stems/By-Pass Loppers

Use by-pass loppers for larger stems that are one-half to one-and-one-half inch in diameter. Like by-pass pruners, they use a scissors action to make a clean cut. Anvil loppers are also available; however, like the anvil pruners, they crush the stem and should not be used on live wood. When in doubt, use a saw instead of loppers.

Branches/Razor Tooth Saw

The razor tooth pruning saw is an effective tool for removing branches that are over one-and-one-half inch in diameter. It cuts on the pull stroke (turbo-cut saws cut on pull and push strokes) and can be kept extremely sharp. The narrow blade fits easily in tight spots to get the appropriate angle for the cut.

By-pass pruner

By-pass lopper

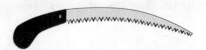

Razor tooth saw

Tools to Avoid

In addition to anvil shears and anvil loppers, don't use hedge trimmers and hedge shears for natural target pruning (removing selected stems and branches to create a natural appearance). Hedge trimmers do not allow the pruner to make selective cuts at specific locations to redirect growth. They cut each branch at the same distance, stimulating new growth at the same place all along the plant, which is neither healthy nor attractive. Bow saws are another tool that should not be used for pruning. The handle often damages branches you would like to keep and the angle of the blade is difficult to control.

Anvil pruner

Hedge shears

Hedge trimmer

Bow saw

Tool Care

✔ Disinfect tools after use

An easy method is to screw a trigger-type sprayer on a bottle of rubbing alcohol. To remove sap and sawdust, simply clean with soap and water. When pruning a diseased plant, clean pruning tools between each cut to prevent spreading disease with the tool. (Humans are the number one transmitter of many plant diseases, spreading them on tools, gloves, etc.)

✔ Keep cutting edges sharp

Dull tools are dangerous. They lead to frustration, increased use of force, and poor safety decisions. Several passes with a good oil-stone will usually suffice on smooth blades. Saw blades are replaceable, and if dull, it's usually easier to replace than sharpen. The cost difference is negligible.

✔ Clean and oil tools regularly

Coat with machine or motor oil to prevent rust. Wipe an oily cloth on blades and other surfaces after each use. Wooden handles should be painted, varnished, or regularly treated with linseed oil.

✔ Use tools properly

Don't twist or strain pruners or loppers. Keep the branch to be cut as deeply in the jaws and near the pivot as possible. Don't cut wire with pruning tools.

Hiring a Professional

Tree experts, known as arborists, provide a variety of services to help you care for the valuable investment you have made in your trees. At first glance a well-pruned tree often looks as if no work was done at all, even after an arborist has spent a good amount of time removing numerous carefully selected branches. Just as with a good hair cut, good pruning leaves plants looking better than before.

When to Seek Help

✔ If a tree is near any kind of phone, cable, or power line, don't risk working on it. Each year people are electrocuted while pruning.

✔ If the tree is a hazard and falling limbs could injure people or damage property.

✔ If the tree is of great sentimental or monetary value.

✔ If there has been extensive storm damage and decisions will need to be made on what to remove now and what to leave for later.

✔ If work is needed high above the ground.

What Arborists Do
Pruning

An arborist can determine what type of pruning is necessary to maintain or improve the health, appearance, and safety of your trees. These techniques include removing diseased, insect infested, damaged, and dead limbs; eliminating branches that rub against each other; removing limbs that interfere with wires, buildings, sidewalks, streets, and views; and selectively removing branches to create better tree structure and reduce wind resistance and potential for storm damage.

Removal

Although removal is a last resort, it is recommended when the tree is dead or dying; irreparably hazardous; causing an obstruction that is impossible to correct through pruning; or to be replaced by a more suitable tree.

Emergency Tree Care

Storms may cause limbs or entire trees to fall and possibly

land on buildings, cars, or other trees. An arborist can assist in the safe removal or trimming of hazardous trees, while reducing further risk of damage to your property.

Other Services

Many arborists also provide a variety of other tree care services including tree selection and planting; preventive maintenance; fertilizing and determining nutritional needs of trees; cabling or bracing for added support to branches with weak attachments; aeration to improve root growth; installation of lightning protection systems; and spraying or injecting to control certain insect and disease problems.

Selecting Arborists

In selecting someone to care for your trees, review insurance, references, certifications, education, experience, and prior work. Before hiring, obtain estimates from several companies. Before any work is done secure a signed contract, specifying what work will be done, and how much will be paid.

Reputable Firm

Beware of people soliciting work door-to-door without identification on their vehicle or uniform or an I.D. card. "Door knockers" are especially common after storms when there is an opportunity for "quick money." Often, storm damage creates high-risk situations for both workers and homeowners. There is potential for even more damage to trees and shrubs if work is not done correctly. You may want to determine if the firm carries Workers' Compensation. You may also wish to call your state's Department of Revenue to assure that the company is legal and paying proper taxes. More than one person working on your property constitutes a "business operation and employment of employees" and therefore, the company must carry all state required insurance, as well as pay taxes.

Insurance

Request to have a certificate of insurance (including proof of liability for personal and property damage) sent to you directly from the insurance agent. This does not cost either party any money. Be sure to call the insurance company to verify that the policy is current, even if the certificate has not expired. Under some circumstances you can be held financially responsible if an uninsured worker is hurt on your property or damage is done to a neighbor's property.

References

Ask for and verify local references. Go by and look at some of their work. Talk to previous clients. Experience, education, and a good reputation are signs of a good arborist.

Certifications

Ask for proof of membership in professional organizations and professional certifications. Certification does not guarantee high quality work, but it does demonstrate a basic level of professional capability and commitment to the field. Contact the associations in the Resources to request a list of certified professionals practicing in your area.

Estimates

Have more than one arborist provide an estimate. You may be required to pay for the estimate but two or more opinions are worth the extra effort. Remember that pruning is both an art and a science. The arborist's skill and professionalism may be more important than a low bid.

Responsible Practices

While some arborists are not equipped to service every aspect of every job, a good arborist can advise and direct in all areas of tree care. If reducing the height of the tree is a goal, a good arborist will use drop crotching or crown restoration techniques. They will not simply chop off the top of the tree at the desired height. A good arborist will not use climbing spikes, except in emergencies, if the tree is to remain in the landscape. Beware of an arborist who is eager to remove a living tree. Removal should be a last resort.

Cost

Well-cared for trees can contribute up to 15 percent of your property value, so the expense of proper care is an excellent investment. Commercial arborists have large investments in equipment and training. Trucks, hydraulic booms, chippers, sprayers, stump cutters, and chain saws represent major capitol investments and maintenance costs. Labor, insurance, safety training, and continuing education add to the overhead. The price charged for the job reflects all of these costs as well as a reasonable margin of profit. You may cut down on the cost by scheduling your work well in advance. By coordinating with your neighbors you may be able to obtain a group discount.

Contract

A contract prevents misunderstandings and assures the work is performed to the standards you expect. Most companies have their own forms, and conditions vary widely. Read the contract carefully and check with your attorney if you have questions.

What A Contract Should Include

✔ The date that work is to begin and end.

✔ Exactly what will be done, such as "Prune all dead, dying, diseased, and weak branches 1.5 inches or greater in diameter."

✔ Specify that the work will be done according to *Pruning Standards* (obtain a copy from the International Society of Arboriculture, Western Chapter, Certification Committee, P.O. Box 3118, Napa, CA 94558), and *Tree, Shrub and Other Woody Plant Maintenance—Standard Practices* (obtain a copy from the American National Standards Institute, 11 West 42nd St, New York, NY 10036. Ask for publication ANSI A3001995.)

✔ If your tree is to be sprayed, get a written statement detailing the specific insect or disease to be treated, the chemical to be used and how much, and what you need to do (cover lawn furniture, keep pets inside).

✔ If fertilizing is to be done, specify type, amount, and method of application. A rough map of the property identifying trees to be serviced or a clear written description of location.

✔ Specify what clean up work will be done and when.

✔ Clarify who will get any firewood, and if it is you, will it be cut into 16-inch lengths and stacked by the garage?

✔ Clarify if removal of tree includes grinding out the stump and surface roots, filling with topsoil, and restoring to grade or to matching conditions.

✔ What is the absolute total dollar amount you will be charged? Leave no room for confusion over whether the price is per tree or for the whole job. Work is usually priced as a single fee for the whole job or on an hourly basis plus materials. When using the latter, be sure to include the wording, "but not to exceed...".

Types of Tree Workers

Certified Arborist. Certification by the International Society of Arboriculture. Exam on tree identification and care. Thirty hours of continuing education required every three years.

Certified Horticulturist. Certification by the American Society for Horticultural Science. Minimum qualifications are a B.S. in horticulture and five years of experience. Intended primarily for agricultural consultants or expert witnesses.

Certified Tree Worker. Certification by The International Society of Arboriculture. Two exams include an oral test on all aspects of tree care, and a practical exam covering climbing skills and aerial rescue procedures. Requires 18 months of experience. No college training but continuing education is required.

Consulting Arborist. Anyone may call themselves a consulting arborist. Membership in the American Society of Consulting Arborists is not required.

Forester. B.S. in Forestry. Focuses on management of forests and wild lands to produce wood, water, forage, recreational opportunities, and wildlife habitat.

Landscape Architect. B.S. in Landscape Architecture; state license. Specialize in landscape planning, design, and construction. Expertise in horticulture and tree care is not required.

Landscape Designer. No license or certification required. General knowledge of landscape design, construction, and species selection.❧

Lucy K. Bradley is the Urban Horticulture Agent for the University of Arizona Maricopa County Cooperative Extension in Phoenix, Arizona. She works with home horticulture, school gardens, community gardens, the Master Gardeners, and other urban gardening programs in the County. Lucy has a Masters degree in Botany from Arizona State University. She is a Certified Arborist and has served on the board of the Arizona Community Tree Council.

Information on pruning techniques was adapted from the The University of Arizona Cooperative Extension Arizona Master Gardener Manual chapter on arboriculture authored by Lucy K. Bradley. Information on hiring tree care workers was adapted from The University of Arizona Cooperative Extension Publication AZ 1003, *How to Hire a Tree Expert*, also by Lucy K. Bradley.

Chapter 5

Plant Problems

By Lucy K. Bradley & Shanyn Hosier

Well-meaning humans are responsible for most plant deaths in urban settings! We tend to select plants that are not well adapted to this environment, or disregard the plants' needs for sun and space. We don't follow proper procedures when transplanting, and either through over attention or lack of attention (inappropriate water, fertilizer, and pruning) we allow the plant to become stressed and thus vulnerable to pests and diseases.

An Ounce of Prevention

A little thought and planning up front will prevent most problems over a plant's lifetime. If problems do crop up, correcting poor cultural practices will alleviate most of them. Start by thinking "Right Plant, Right Place" when purchasing plants. Select those that are well adapted to an arid desert environment and are resistant to known pests. Place them in locations that meet their need for sunlight or shade and have room to accommodate their mature size so excessive pruning will not be necessary.

Prepare the planting hole as described in Chapter 2. Follow the appropriate schedule for that plant's care, irrigation, and fertilization. Healthy plants resist pathogens that would damage or kill a stressed plant.

Pay attention to the condition of your plants. Intervene early when you first start to see signs or symptoms of stress or disease. If the problem continues, the following information can help you diagnose the cause.

Diagnosing Problems

There are three essential elements to a plant problem: the Plant, the Environment, and the Pathogen (a pathogen is an agent able to cause disease). These three elements make up the "Plant Disease Triangle." Understanding each of these components and how they interact holds the key to preventing and solving plant problems.

Plant Disease Triangle

The Plant

Individual species have specific strengths, weaknesses, and needs. They are adapted to thrive in a particular type of environment and may become stressed if their environmental needs are not met, e.g., inadequate or too much water, not enough or too much sunlight, temperature that is too warm or too cold. Specific types of plants are susceptible to certain live pathogens and not susceptible to others.

The Environment

The place where the plant grows has specific characteristics including the type of soil, irrigation, sunlight, and weather. The plant may or may not be well adapted to these characteristics. The environment may be conducive to the action of certain pathogens and inhospitable to others.

The Pathogen

Pathogens may be living organisms or non-living factors. Some examples of living organisms include insects, animals, nematodes, plant parasites, fungi, bacteria, and viruses. Gener-

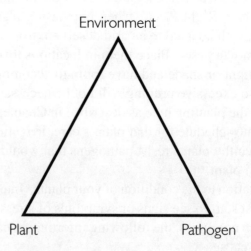

Plant Disease Triangle

ally, living pathogens are selective about the type of plant they feed upon, the damage they cause is progressive over time, and they frequently leave evidence of their presence (fungus, tunnels, droppings, or dead insects).

Some examples of non-living pathogens include: mechanical or chemical injury, nutrient deficiency, weather (lightning, hail, sunburn), and pollution. In most cases non-living pathogens cause a sudden onset of symptoms, the symptoms appear on a variety of plant types, and the damage does not usually spread.

A Method to Diagnose Problems

The three elements of the disease triangle can be used to identify the best method of managing the problem. For example, modify the environment to have it better meet the needs of the plant or to make it inhospitable to the pathogen. Remove or directly manage the pathogen. It may be necessary to replace the plant with one better adapted to the environment and less vulnerable to the pathogen.

Diagnosis can be a complicated process requiring horticultural knowledge, experience, common sense, intuition, good judgment, and sometimes, good old-fashioned luck. There are specific strategies that you can use to successfully diagnose plant problems. Even if you are unable to determine the cause yourself, following the step-by-step system in Appendix A will enable you to provide the information necessary for professional diagnosis.

Plant Nutrient Deficiencies

Plants need the right combination of nutrients to live, grow, and reproduce. Too little or too much of any one nutrient can cause problems and the plant will show symptoms of being unhealthy, such as yellow leaves or stunted growth.

Plant nutrients fall into two categories: macronutrients and micronutrients. Macronutrients are those elements that are needed in relatively large amounts. They include nitrogen, potassium, sulfur, calcium, magnesium, and phosphorus. Micronutrients are those elements that plants need in small amounts (sometimes trace amounts), including iron, boron, manganese, zinc, copper, chlorine, and molybdenum. Both macro- and micronutrients are naturally obtained by roots from the soil.

Plant roots require certain conditions to obtain these nutrients from the soil. First, the soil must be sufficiently moist to allow the roots to take up and transport the nutrients. Sometimes simply correcting improper watering methods will eliminate nu-

Macronutrients			
Nutrient	Deficiency symptoms	Comments	Fertilizer source
Nitrogen (N)	General yellowing of older leaves (bottom of plant). The rest of the plant is often light green.	Most plants absorb nitrogen in the form of ammonium or nitrate. These forms readily dissolve in water and leach away.	Anything with the words "ammonium," "nitrate," or "urea." Also manures.
Phosphorus (P)	Leaf tips look burnt, followed by older leaves turning a dark green or reddish-purple.	Plants absorb phosphorus in the form of phosphate, which dissolves only slightly in water, but pH strongly affects uptake.	Anything with the words "phosphate" or "bone." Also greensand.
Potassium (K)	Older leaves may wilt, look scorched. Interveinal chlorosis (yellowing) begins at the base, scorching inward from leaf margins.	Plants absorb potassium as an ion, which can be readily leached from soil. Desert soils and water generally have plenty of potassium, so deficiency is rare.	Anything with the word "potassium" or "potash."
Calcium (Ca)	New leaves (top of plant) are distorted or irregularly shaped. Causes blossom-end rot.	Desert soils and water generally have plenty of calcium so deficiency is rare. Excessive calcium can limit the availability of other nutrients.	Anything with the word "calcium." Also gypsum.
Magnesium (Mg)	Older leaves turn yellow at edge leaving a green arrowhead shape in the center of the leaf.*	Plants absorb magnesium as an ion, which can be readily leached from soil. May be readily leached from soil if calcium is not present.	Anything with the word "magnesium." Also Epsom salts (magnesium sulfate).
Sulfur (S)	Younger leaves turn yellow first, sometimes followed by older leaves.	Plants absorb sulfur in the form of sulfate, which readily leaches from the soil. Sulfur may acidify the soil (lower the pH).	Anything with the word "sulfate."

How to Use the Nutrient Tables

→   Know the characteristics of the plant when healthy to identify symptoms of distress. For example, some plant varieties have been bred to have variegated leaf patterns that contain more than one color.

→   Identify where the symptoms are appearing (new leaves, old leaves, edge of leaf, leaf veins). Note that many deficiencies may look similar.

→   Identify any pattern of symptoms. Compare the symptoms to the Tables.

→   If fertilizer is warranted, follow directions on the product's label.

Micronutrients			
Nutrient	Deficiency symptoms	Comments	Fertilizer source
Boron (B)	Terminal buds die; witch's broom (a spray of multiple shoots) forms.	Plants absorb boron in the form of borate. Problems are seen in intensely cropped areas.	Anything with the words "borax" or "borate."
Copper (Cu)	Leaves are dark green, plant is stunted.	Plants absorb copper as an ion. Desert soils generally have plenty of copper, so problems are rare.	Anything with the words "copper," "cupric," or "cuprous."
Iron (Fe)	Yellowing occurs between the veins of young leaves.**	Plants absorb iron as an ion through their foliage as well as their roots. Uptake is strongly affected by pH. Chelated iron is readily available for use by the plant; other forms of iron may be tied up in the soil.	Anything with the words "iron chelate."
Manganese (Mn)	Yellowing occurs between the veins of young leaves.** Pattern is not as distinct as with iron. Palm fronds are stunted and deformed, called "frizzle top." Reduction in size of plant parts (leaves, shoots, fruit) generally. Dead spots or patches.	Plants absorb manganese as an ion through their foliage as well as their roots.	Anything with the words "manganese" or "manganous." Often required with zinc application.
Molybdenum (Mo)	General yellowing of older leaves (bottom of plant). The rest of the plant is often light green.	Plants absorb molybdenum in the form of molybdate. Problems are rare in desert soils but are occasionally seen on legumes where it mimics nitrogen deficiency.	Anything with the words "molybdate" or "molybdic."
Zinc (Zn)	Terminal leaves may be rosetted, and yellow occurs between the veins of the new leaves.**	Plants absorb zinc as an ion through their foliage as well as their roots. High pH (alkalinity) may limit availability.	Anything with the word "zinc."

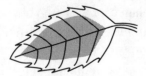

*Magnesium deficiency symptom appears as yellowing at the edge of the leaf. The center remains green.

**Interveinal chlorosis, a symptom of iron, zinc, and manganese deficiencies, appears as yellowing between the veins. Veins remain green.

trient deficiency symptoms. Second, the soil's pH—a measure of acidity or alkalinity—must be within a certain range for nutrients to be releasable from the soil particles. (A soil test will determine pH level.) Third, the soil temperature must fall within a certain range for nutrient uptake to occur. The optimum range of moisture, pH, and temperature varies for different species of plants. Thus, nutrients may be physically present in the soil but unavailable to plants.

Many micronutrients are used by plants to process other nutrients or work together with other nutrients, so a deficiency of one may look like another. For example, molybdenum is required by legumes to complete the nitrogen fixation process that was described in Chapter 1. Thus, the symptoms of nitrogen deficiency and molybdenum deficiency appear similar.

Too much of any nutrient can be toxic to plants. This is most frequently evidenced by salt burn symptoms on foliage. These symptoms include browning on the leaf edges. The browning is separated from green leaf tissue by a slender yellow halo. The browning pattern, called necrosis, begins at the tip and proceeds to the base of the leaf, along the leaf edge.

Nitrogen, phosphorus, and iron are the only nutrients that are commonly lacking in Arizona soils. Most of the others may be lacking under certain conditions, but deficiencies are quite rare. The tables on the previous pages list nutrients that may be lacking and what deficiency symptoms *usually* look like. However, each plant variety is different and may display different symptoms.

IPM Steps

✔ Prevention is key
✔ Identify the pest
✔ Monitor plants
✔ Decide how much damage is okay
✔ Determine how to control
✔ Keep records
✔ Evaluate results

Integrated Pest Management (IPM)

Integrated pest management is a fancy term for simply practicing all of the available methods for controlling problems, including doing nothing at all. Prevention is the most important component of IPM. Many insect and disease problems are a result of improper plant care. In addition, those *symptoms* of poor plant care are often blamed on pests or diseases. Then, pesticides are applied needlessly, to "solve" a problem that doesn't exist. Understanding the components of integrated pest management will help you maintain strong, healthy plants.

Controlling Problems with IPM

1. Identify the Symptoms and Pest

Your best defense against excessive plant damage is to monitor your landscape. Look underneath leaves and on fresh tender shoots where pests are often found. Gardeners frequently blame any insect found on the plant at the time symptoms are discovered. Don't leap to conclusions: try to observe the culprit in action.

Examine the insect and the plant it was on carefully. You may need a magnifying glass. Insect identification often starts by determining what type of damage (if any) was inflicted on the plant. For example, insects with sucking mouth parts, such as whiteflies, aphids, and leafhoppers, cause the leaves to turn yellow and will leave sticky honeydew secretions. Ragged edges and holes in the leaves show that chewing insects, such as caterpillars, beetles, or leafcutter bees, have been on your plants.

Learn which insects are beneficial and which are destructive. It is also an excellent idea to learn the different life stages (egg, larva, pupa, adult) of insects, both beneficials and pests, that appear seasonally so you don't mistakenly destroy useful insects. This isn't as difficult as it might seem and can be quite fascinating, especially for children. The Resources contain some useful references to get you started.

2. Monitor Your Plants

Go out into the yard regularly to check for signs of pest damage or disease. Look on the bottom of leaves and at tender new growth, both places where insects are often found. Vigilance on your part can contain a situation before it gets out of control. Learn to recognize the symptoms of problems that regularly occur on your plants.

3. Decide How Much Damage is Acceptable

Decide what, if anything, needs to be done. If it is too late for control to be effective, or if the damage is minor and doesn't threaten the plant's health, consider taking no action. A few holes in a few leaves will not influence an otherwise healthy plant.

4. Determine Control Options

An IPM program starts with the most benign control method. If it doesn't work, move on to the next. Control methods are categorized as cultural, mechanical, physical, biological, or chemical. Chemical pesticides should be the method of last resort.

Cultural Controls

Maintaining healthy plants with good cultural methods should be your first control method.

✔ Water appropriately

Underwatering and overwatering are common causes of plant stress and easy problems to remedy. Apply water to the soil; don't sprinkle water on foliage, which promotes the spread of diseases.

✔ Fertilize only as needed

Too much fertilizer stresses plants. It is not effective to overapply fertilizer to "speed up" the growth of plants.

✔ Clean up the landscape

Weeds and plant debris attract pests by providing food and shelter. Pull weeds as soon as they appear. Prune dead, diseased, or damaged limbs. After pruning, remove all trimmings and rake up debris. Pick up fallen fruit. If plant material has any disease or insect problems, destroy it; otherwise, it can go into the compost pile.

Mechanical Controls

These methods use your labor or materials and devices other than pesticides to deter problems or to remove them.

✔ Handpicking

This method works well for larger insects such as tomato hornworms and cabbage loopers. It is more efficient to pick off a few caterpillars than to spray an entire plant, and it doesn't cost anything. It also puts you in close contact with your plants so you can spot other potential problems before they get out of control. Squash the insects or put them somewhere the birds will quickly find them for a tasty treat.

✔ Water sprays

Common pests such as spider mites, whiteflies, and aphids can be kept under control by spraying off the plant with a blast of water from the hose. Make sure you hose off the plant completely, including underneath leaves. Spray early in the morning to prevent sunburn. Early spraying also allows foliage to dry before cooler evening temperatures. This method can be repeated as often as needed to control pests. If plain water has not been effective, step up to a soapy water spray.

Soapy Water Spray

Use one teaspoon to two tablespoons of liquid detergent soap per gallon of water. Start with the lowest amount and slowly increase if results are not seen. Use regular soap, not concentrated or lemon. (The citric acid in lemon can burn plant tissue.) Test on a few leaves and wait a day before spraying the entire plant. Spray early in the morning so leaves won't burn in the hot sun.

✔ Barriers

Prevent pests from reaching seedlings and plants with obstructions, such as floating row covers to deter leafhopper insects or birds.

✔ Traps

Sticky traps can be purchased or handmade. Cover yellow cardboard with petroleum jelly or a sticky substance such as Tanglefoot®. Place near susceptible plants. Whiteflies land on them and are stuck. Whiteflies can quickly become too numerous for traps to control their population; however, the traps provide a warning that the insects are present so other control measures can be taken. Beer traps work for snails and slugs.

Physical Controls

The plant's physical environment (temperature, humidity, sunlight) can be altered to prevent or control problems. For example, powdery mildew thrives if air circulation is poor. Allow space between plants to reach their mature size without crowding.

Frost- or sun-damaged plant tissue is susceptible to other problems. Protect cold-sensitive plants if freezing temperatures are predicted. Place non-adapted plants where they will receive afternoon shade in summer, reducing the chance of sunburn.

Biological Controls

Living organisms can be used to control pests. Biological controls include predator insects, parasites, and even diseases.

✔ Predators

Predator insects consume other insects. They usually arrive in your landscape shortly after pest populations start building. The best way to attract these beneficial predators is to refrain from spraying pesticides. If you have used chemicals frequently in the past, it may take some time for beneficial insect populations to build up.

✔ Parasites

Parasites are living organisms that lay eggs on or in another living organism, which acts as the "host." This is usually a highly specific relationship with a parasite going after a particular species as host. After eggs hatch, the insect feeds on the host, which will ultimately die. (Note: There is no threat to humans or pets from these parasitic insects.)

For example, a female parasitic wasp lays eggs within an

Snail & Slug Traps

Sink small plastic containers of beer below the surface of the soil. Slugs and snails are attracted and fall in. A mix of sugar, water, and yeast can be used in place of beer.

Refrain from using pesticides in your landscape and beneficial insect populations will increase over time.

Beneficial Predator Insects

Assassin bug. Long antennae will help you recognize this insect. It is brown, about one-half inch long, and seeks out caterpillars.

Big-eyed bug. These bugs are aptly named with their protruding eyes. They are only about one-eighth inch long and will consume whiteflies and caterpillars.

Damsel bug. These slender bugs are less than one-half inch long and range from grey to pale tan. Like assassin bugs, they have an impressive set of antennae.

Dragonfly and damselfly. Fascinating to watch, these insects capture mosquitoes and flies while in flight. They live near water sources.

Green lacewing. These pretty insects are pale green and about one-half inch long. Their wings are veined, almost lace-like, and they resemble delicate moths. Their pale green eggs can be found under leaves, attached to "threads." Lacewing larvae are pale brown or grey and are voracious consumers of aphids.

Ladybeetle. Most people recognize the adult beetle, with its reddish coloring and black spots. The adult lays clusters of orange eggs on plant foliage near aphid populations. When they hatch, the larvae feed on aphids.

Minute pirate bug. Smaller than the big-eyed bug, but both the immature and adult form will consume spider mites and thrips. Pirate bugs are often found in flowers.

Praying mantis. This fascinating creature has large front legs held in a "prayer" position while it waits for an insect to capture. Some people mistakenly destroy its egg case, confused by its unusual appearance. The round to oval-shaped egg case has a brown, papery covering and is usually one to two inches long. The adult attaches it to plant stems or underneath boards. Dozens of tiny praying mantises will hatch from the egg case in spring.

aphid. The larvae mature inside, leaving behind a dried aphid "mummy." Leave the mummies alone, as adult wasps will emerge to lay more eggs inside other aphids.

✔ Diseases

Certain disease organisms are used to kill insect pests. Probably the most commonly known is the bacteria *Bacillus thuringiensis* (Bt). Caterpillars feed on plant parts that have been treated with Bt, which destroys their digestive system. There are over 30 types of this bacteria, targeting different species of caterpillars.

Chemical Controls

Chemical pesticides are usually classified by what type of problem they are designed to control, such as insecticides (insects), miticides (mites), or herbicides (weeds). They are also classified by the material their active ingredient is derived from. Pesticides can be made from inorganic, biological, or synthetic materials but they are all toxic to some degree.

✔ Inorganic

Made from naturally occurring substances that do not include carbon, such as minerals (sulfur dust or Bordeaux) or insecticidal dusts (diatomaceous earth).

✔ Biological

Made from once-living organisms that do include carbon, such as rotenone and pyrethrum.

✔ Synthetic

Manufactured substances, often petroleum based, such as horticultural oil or malathion.

Know exactly what an insect is before attempting to eliminate it. You may be killing a beneficial insect or using the wrong method.

Before using any pesticide, try all the other control methods. They are often more effective over the long-term. Read the label to ensure that the product is formulated for your problem and appropriate for use on specific plants. Follow product instructions exactly. Using the wrong pesticide or applying it incorrectly may damage plants and do more harm than good.

Chemical pesticides often seem like a quick and easy solution, but they also create problems. They are indiscriminate, killing natural predators that keep pest populations under control. They may also adversely effect other living creatures in the food chain, including amphibians, fish, and birds. When widely used, insects develop resistance to them. Since the development of chemical insecticides in the 1940s, over 200 insect species have developed resistance, so their application is no longer effective. Most chemical insecticides are petroleum based, which means they are costly to produce and consume an important natural resource. This doesn't mean that chemical insecticides should never be used, but it is important to use other control methods first. A combination of cultural, mechanical, physical, and biological controls will handle most pest problems.

5. Keep Accurate Records

Keep a log of all insects you find, what plants they were on, and the time of year. Use this information to monitor plants and nip problems before they get out of control.

6. Evaluate Results and Modify as Needed

If you keep careful records, it will be easy to determine what worked and what didn't. If for several days you tried a spray of water to get rid of aphids but their numbers increased, you may want to start with a low dose of soapy water. If that doesn't work, you might increase the amount of soap. Maybe you have counted an increase in the number of beneficial insects and will wait to see if they control the pest.

In conclusion, most plant problems can be prevented by choosing well-adapted varieties and caring for them appropriately. If problems do occur, there are numerous solutions that can be tried before applying chemicals. The next chapter describes some of the insects or diseases that you might encounter in the low desert.✿

Don't be so quick to sweep away those spider webs. There are many types of spiders and all are predators of a wide variety of insects.

Some material in this chapter is adapted from *Desert Gardening for Beginners: How to Grow Vegetables, Flowers and Herbs in an Arid Climate*, co-authored by Cathy Cromell, Linda A. Guy, and Lucy K. Bradley and The University of Arizona Cooperative Extension Publication AZ1106, *Guide to Symptoms of Plant Nutrient Deficiencies*, co-authored by Shanyn Hosier and Lucy K. Bradley.

Chapter 6

Seasonal Pests

By Terry Mikel

I t is important to understand how pests and plants interact to manage pest problems in the landscape. Pests, here referring to insects, mites, and/or diseases, interact with plants frequently; however, they rarely cause severe damage.

There are always pests in the environment, but specific types of pests are active only during certain seasons. Thus, the insects or mites found in the spring are not the same ones found in the fall. Similarly, different diseases tend to be active in different seasons, each adapted to specific temperature and moisture levels. At almost any time of year there might be a potential problem from one or another of the enormous collection of insects, mites, or diseases, but rarely are all of the potential pests a threat at the same time.

Pests will thrive in an environment where they can get the most food with the least amount of effort. On the other hand, they will decline in settings where they must work hard for a minimal amount of food. This explains why sometimes pests flourish and must be controlled, while at other times, only a few are seen and they do little if any real damage. *The overriding factor that helps pests gain the upper hand is a stressed or weak plant.* Healthy, vibrant plants contain built-in mechanisms developed over eons to survive the onslaught of pests. Without this ability, the plants would not have survived in nature. (Note that overly vigorous plants, such as those watered and fertilized excessively in a landscape environment, are not healthy and would have a weakened ability to withstand attack.)

Pests attack and encounter less resistance by choosing weaker plants. The pests' inherited genetic intelligence teaches that stressed plants are easier targets. It is perhaps simpler to view the insects, mites, and diseases in the same image as predators. Lions, tigers, and sharks—just like plant pests—search out the weak, injured, or lame.

Healthy plants can also be attacked by pests but they will react quickly by sending various metabolized chemicals coursing through their veins to stop the attack and begin the repair. Unhealthy plants have lost this ability in their weakened state.

The most effective way to reduce the impact of pests is to maintain healthy plants. Actually there only a few pests in the low desert that do real damage. For some of these, if you have not successfully prevented the pest before it overwhelmed the plant, there is not much, if anything, that can be done but to accept it as a part of the natural cycle.

Pests in the Landscape

The information on the following pages provides a list of insects or diseases that may occur in the low desert including the seasons they are most active, the plants they typically attack, the type of damage that appears, and suggested control methods. *Note that some of these insects may appear in large numbers, but they inflict little, if any, damage to plants.*

Scorpions

Scorpions are active year around but they do not damage plants. They are efficient and tenacious predators of all arthropods (anything with jointed feet, including insects, arachnids, crustaceans, centipedes, and millipedes). Outdoors they are considered beneficial because they control large numbers of crickets and nuisance pests. If a scorpion wanders indoors, it becomes a pest mainly because of the fear of being stung. It is probably slowly starving to death because there is no food source. If seen during the day, stun with a flyswatter and sweep it outdoors as food for other scorpions. Because scorpions become iridescent in the presence of ultraviolet light, they can be seen at night with a blacklight, when they are more active.

Agave Snout Weevils

Season: Adult seen in May; damage appears in September.

Plants: Agave (sometimes yucca)

Damage: The weevil attacks the hearts of agaves and sometimes yuccas. The plants usually experience three to four years of reinfestation before the final collapse of the plant that occurs in September. The insects primarily attack old, mature plants that, in the case of agaves, would probably bloom and die in a couple of years anyway.

Control: In May, look for the black, three-quarter to one inch long adult walking around the plants and stomp on all that are seen. (For a possible chemical control, see Chapter 8.)

Aphids

Season: Spring and Fall when temperatures are in the range of 70–80 degrees Fahrenheit; typically February–April and October–November.

Plants: Milkweed, oleander, yucca flower stalks, roses, and many others.

Damage: These are tiny (one-sixteenth inch), soft-bodied insects that suck the juices from tender foliage. They may be green, greyish-black, or other colors depending on their preferred plant. There is little damage although the plant can become messy underneath with sticky honeydew residue.

Control: Don't control. Keep aphids around to feed beneficial predator insects, such as ladybeetles and lacewings. Remember: if the predators have a lot to eat with little work, they will thrive. Aphids are the buffet lunch for spring predators. If you don't want predators or can't stand aphids, hose them off the plant with a strong blast of water.

Bacterial Rot

Season: Year around, but rot typically appears in May–June.

Plants: Saguaro cacti.

Damage: There is usually some type of mechanical damage, sometimes caused by humans, to the skin of the plant. This is not the same as bird holes, which the cacti have developed adaptations to so the bacteria can't get started. Bird holes in saguaro are a natural part of the desert ecosystem and are not a cause for alarm. Ideal entry wounds for bacterial rot are caused by planting too deep, a puncture from a stick or rock, or spines being scrunched together, for example if a cactus was propped against a wall. The bacteria rots the interior tissue over time, usually four to five years. A black ooze may seep out of the wound. The final collapse reduces the saguaro to a sad monolith of dried brown skin draping on the skeletal ribs.

Control: To prevent, do not plant them any deeper than the natural soil line. Avoid any practice that will create a hole in the skin. (For treatment for existing rot, see Chapter 8.)

Cicadas

Season: Early Summer.

Plants: All plants, mostly trees.

Damage: The males are noticed because of the cacophony of buzzing they produce while attempting to attract females. There may be small scars on young twigs resulting from the adult insect laying eggs. At worst, the tip of the branch may die.

Control: There is no control because the adults don't feed (thus, won't ingest an insecticide), and after the eggs hatch, the larvae spend the next two or three years in the soil. They emerge as adults, ready to repeat the cycle.

Cotton (Texas) Root Rot

Season: Fall, typically September–October.

Plants: Most broadleaf plants are susceptible. Plants that are desert-adapted have proven to be the least susceptible to this disease. Monocots (grasses, palms, yuccas) are immune.

Damage: Quick collapse or death of the plant caused by a soil fungus that is indigenous to the desert.

Control: There is no control.

Darkling Beetles

Season: Appear seasonally in early or late summer, May or September.

Plants: They do not feed on plants.

Damage: These are ground denizens that feed on and recycle dead organic matter. When soils heat up and dry out, these insects may roil out of the earth in huge numbers, migrating randomly for more favorable soil conditions.

Control: No control is needed. If they get indoors, vacuum them up.

False Chinch Bugs

Season: When the desert dries or when weeds in vacant lots dry, usually May–June.

Plants: Any plants, especially those with foliage touching the ground.

Damage: Small crawling insects leave their feeding sites when plants dry, migrating into neighborhoods. They may be noticeable because of their high numbers, but damage is very minimal and extremely seasonal.

Control: None needed.

Flat-Headed Wood Borers

Season: May–December.

Plants: Any plant with dead, diseased, or damaged wood.

Damage: A cream-colored, wide-headed grub about one to one-and-a-half inch long tunnels or bores under ruptured bark. It may be seen in the fall if you carefully peel back the bark. The adult lays eggs in April or May, selecting dead, diseased, or damaged plant parts, such as sunburn, cracks, broken branches, and improper pruning cuts.

Control: No control is necessary. They should be considered as a sentinel to examine why/where the plant is not healthy.

Flea Beetles

Season: Spring, April–May.

Plants: Mexican evening primrose.

Damage: A teeny, shiny black beetle (resembling a black onion seed) with very small mouth parts chews on plant leaves. The insects have strong back legs and can jump like fleas. An extensive population can lead to temporary defoliation.

Control: No control is needed, as its preferred plant usually spreads readily, even invasively.

Ganderma Root Rot

Season: The fungus lives year around, but the conchs typically appear in September–October.

Plants: Since the late 1990s, this fungus has been accepted as a true plant pathogen of many desert landscape trees, including citrus and mesquite. It appears as a growth, called a conch, at the base of the trunk. When fresh, it is tannish-yellow, drying to a burnt umber with an underside that resembles maroon varnish.

(It is sometimes called varnish fungi.) Individual conchs may be six inches or less in size, but they often arise in clusters, which makes them appear larger.

Damage: Over several years the fungus eats away at the large buttress roots. Eventually the mature tree declines.

Control: None, except to enhance the plant's growing conditions to keep it healthy.

Harvester or Leafcutter Ants

Season: Spring through Fall, March–December.

Plants: Any with leafy foliage.

Damage: Colonies of these nocturnally active ants will climb all over selected plants and remove leaf tissue. Many times the evidence is barren branches and bits of leaf tissue forming a trail back to the ant hill.

Control: The following method works best on sunny, warm days. Make a slurry of orange peels and water in a blender. Immediately pour it into the ant hill's entry hole. Fumes from the orange rind will spread through the colony, killing the ants. It may take more than one application. Note that other ants are considered beneficial because they recycle vast amounts of organic matter, and should be left alone, if possible.

Mistletoe

Season: Year around.

Plants: Any desert tree.

Damage: In the low desert, mistletoe is mostly visually unappealing, although some people find it attractive when the berries ripen. (Note that this is not the same mistletoe that is used as festive decor during the holidays.) It is a parasite, obtaining nutrients from the host plant. It appears as a bundled mass of small twigs hanging on a branch or propped in the crotch of a branch.

It easily spreads within one host by seeds and over time might shorten a tree's life expectancy by a few years. Over a life-span of 75–100 years, it is really not much of a pest. It rarely moves from plant to plant because the birds that feed on the sticky seeds in April get them stuck to their beaks. They readily wipe their beaks clean on the branches they are standing on. They rarely fly to another tree with their beaks loaded with the berries. (And why should they fly to a tree that doesn't have the mistletoe seeds?) In nature it's common to see two trees close together— one loaded with mistletoe and the other with none.

Control: None in the low desert.

Mites

Season: Late Spring through Fall; typically May–October.

Plants: Italian cypress and juniper trees, aloe, yucca, and aloe flower stalks, and pyracantha.

Damage: Mites pierce and suck juice from foliage. They are extremely tiny and may be difficult to see without a magnifying glass. Their bodies are round and they have eight legs. They cause witch's broom (a spray of multiple shoots) in trees; odd growths on the blades of aloes; twisted, flattened or distorted flower stalks; and browning of foliage associated with fine webbing.

Control: A forceful spray of water knocks them off the foliage. If that doesn't work, try a mild soapy water spray. When the damage is seen, the mites may no longer be around. This is especially true for witch's broom. It shows up in the spring but the damage was done the year before.

Palm Flower Caterpillars

Season: During palm bloom period, usually April–June.

Plants: Fan palms most commonly affected.

Damage: Minimal damage, which may even be considered beneficial because the caterpillar is feeding on the unwanted flower stalk. This cream-colored caterpillar is one to one-and-a-half inch long and has a pink stripe down the top if its body. After pruning, and sometimes after strong winds, many caterpillars are flung from the palm to the ground. They crawl to get out of the sun, sometimes getting indoors. Their natural tendency is to pull fibers from a palm tree to make a cocoon. Indoors, that tendency may appear as pulling fibers from carpet.

Control: After pruning, watch for crawling caterpillars and keep doors and windows closed.

Palo Verde Root Borers

Season: Summer; typically June–August.

Plants: Palo verde trees are the preferred target although it has been found on most deciduous trees in the low desert.

Damage: The whitish grub is five inches long by one inch wide and it feeds on tree roots. The enormous dark brown beetle that lays the eggs is three to four inches long, with exaggerated long antennae. It is sometimes called the long hair beetle. On older and stressed trees they can do some damage. Due to the unusually large size of the insect, more damage is usually attributed to it than it actually inflicts. The first symptom on the tree is general die-back starting at the tips.

Control: Due to their size and the fact they live two to three years below ground on roots, chemicals have proven ineffective. If this pest is suspected, efforts to enhance the tree's vigor with appropriate water and fertilizer pay more dividends.

Palo Verde Webworms

Season: Spring; typically April.

Plants: Palo verde and mountain laurel trees.

Damage: Small colonies of half-inch caterpillars feed on young leaves and shoots during the night. During the day they huddle within the protection of silken webs that are strung between shoot tips.

Control: Prune off the branches that contain the webbing. A nighttime spraying with *Bacillus thuringiensis* (Bt) is also effective.

Phyllostica Rot

Season: Appears after heavy rainy periods.

Plants: Prickly pear cacti.

Damage: A rot spreads on the pads usually in a circular pattern. The circle can rot completely through the pads. It is seen only after years with extra rain or on cacti that get wet repeatedly from sprinkler spray on their pads.

Control: Keep cacti dry. Dust spots with sulfur. The affected pads will show the damage forever. New pads, if kept dry, are healthy and unaffected until the next overly wet rainy season.

Psyllids

Season: Spring; typically April–May.

Plants: Desert trees, primarily ironwood and palo verde.

Damage: This slender insect is about one-quarter inch in size. It is rounded on both ends, somewhat shaped like a gel capsule. Its greenish-tan coloring blends in with twigs and leaves. In cyclic years of high numbers they spread all over the tree and suck the sap from foliage. This leads to a glistening coat over the branches from the honeydew. There can be minimal defoliation.

Control: Forcefully spray off with water. Spraying chemicals up into the tree is not a safe technique, as the chemicals will drift widely.

Slime Flux

Season: Summer, usually May–June.

Plants: Many trees including mesquite, cottonwood, sycamore, ash, elm, mulberry, willow.

Damage: A bacterial infection causes runny black sap to drip down the trunk.

Control: There is no control. Maintain healthy trees to withstand infection. The sap may stain so remove objects near trees and hose off sidewalks.

Spittle Bugs

Season: Summer, May–September.

Plants: Most common hosts are rosemary and bean-producing desert trees (legumes), such as mesquite, ironwood, and palo verde.

Damage: Noticeable globs of a white frothy (spit-like) substance appear on branches. It is caused by this small insect with piercing mouth parts. Damage to the plant is minimal.

Control: Hose off the bug with water.

Springtails

Season: Appear seasonally in early or late summer, May or September.

Plants: They do not feed on live plants.

Damage: Like the darkling beetle, springtails feed on and recycle dead organic matter. They may appear in large numbers when soils heat up and dry out.

Control: No control is needed.

Whiteflies

Season: Fall, typically September–October.

Plants: Many, including lantana, lisianthus, hibiscus, mallow, and vegetables.

Damage: Whiteflies are about one-sixteenth inch long and pale colored. They tend to prefer certain families of plants. Symptoms include leaf wilt, some defoliation, and stickiness. There may be hundreds simply resting on some plants, but not feeding. (If you tap the plant, a cloud of white will rise from it.) Be sure to check the underside of leaves for the immature and non-moving stage of the pest, which is sucking sap. It resembles a dew drop at this stage.

Control: Because of the whitefly's potential for extremely high numbers there is not an effective single-shot control. A soapy water spray kills the current batch. They usually reappear a couple days later. Keep monitoring and treating as needed.❀

Termites

Termites only feed on dead wood, not live plant tissue and hence cause little damage to plants. If you suspect termites on any structures, including fences and outbuildings, call a professional.

Being the child of starving graduate students and then school teachers, Terry grew up in Flagstaff, Yuma, Gadsden, Roll, Luepp, and Tucson. He and his sister wandered for hours in the surrounding areas, entertaining themselves by grazing, touching, smelling, and feeling the plants. This childlike fascination with plants was barely tempered by getting a B.S. and M.S. from the University of Arizona and working for the Cooperative Extension for 20 years in Yuma, Pima, and Maricopa Counties. As Area Horticultural Agent, he teaches for the Certified Arborists Training; Master Gardener Program in Maricopa County and statewide; Arizona Certified Nursery Professional Program; Advanced Certified Nursery Certification; and private and public entities' landscape employees.

Terry has been recognized with the following awards:
1995 - Arizona Nursery Association Distingushed Service
1996 - Xeriscape Person of the Year
1997 - University of Arizona Extension Faculty of the Year
1998 - Phoenix Home and Garden Magazine's 'Master of the Southwest'
1999 - American Nursery and Landscape Association's Extension Person of the Year.

Chapter 7

Frost Protection

By Lucy K. Bradley

First and last frost dates can differ considerably from region to region depending on various factors such as differences in elevation or population density, which influences the amount of heat absorption by concrete and pavement. To adequately protect plants from frost damage it is helpful to understand cold weather, how plants respond to cold, and how to prevent frost damage. It is also useful to recognize symptoms of frost damage and know how to care for plants that have been damaged by frost.

Understanding Cold Weather

The coldest temperatures occur about daybreak. The sun warms the soil surface during the day; the heat is then radiated into the cool atmosphere during the night. Nighttime clouds can absorb and reflect heat back to the earth. Calm, clear nights pose the greatest danger of frost since there is no wind to mix the ascending warm air with the descending cold air, and no clouds to radiate heat back to the soil. Also, humidity slows temperature change, which is why extremes between night and day temperatures occur so quickly in dry desert climates.

To understand your own yard's climate, take temperature readings in your yard daily and compare them to the temperature reported by news stations. Then use this information to predict the impact for forecasted freeze warnings. For example, your comparisons will let you know if you are generally four degrees colder or three degrees warmer than the temperature reported at the local airport. Remember, cold air settles downward, flowing like water, to the lowest point. Hot air rises. Thus, cold air may collect at the bottom of a slope, so take the topography of your yard into account. Also, cold winds compound temperature loss, so plants affected by these winds could be experiencing more cold than plants in protected areas.

Understanding Plant Response to Cold

The effects of temperature vary with plant species, age, general health, whether the plant is dormant or growing, and the plant's water content. Dormant plants are less susceptible to frost damage. Young, actively growing, flowering, and/or dehydrated plants tend to be most vulnerable.

The lower the temperature, the longer the exposure to cold, and the faster the temperature drops, the greater the damage to the plant. If a freeze occurs when there has been no prior cold weather to "harden off" a plant, the damage will be more extensive. Therefore, the heaviest damage from low temperatures generally occurs in late spring, early fall, or any time cold temperatures occur after a warm period in winter.

Preventing Frost Damage

Plant selection and placement are key steps in preventing frost damage. Selecting frost tolerant plants will ensure less winter

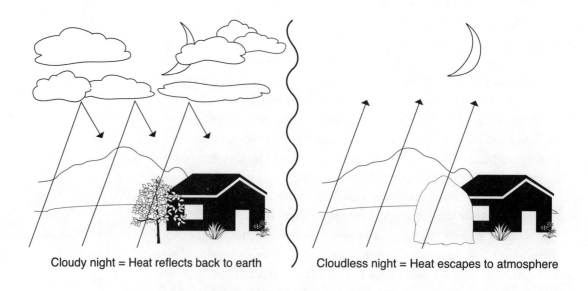

Cloudy night = Heat reflects back to earth   Cloudless night = Heat escapes to atmosphere

Clear nights pose greater danger of frost damage to plants than cloudy nights.

preparation and maintenance for you and a better chance of surviving winter freezes for your plants. However, even frost-tolerant plants may blossom too early, thus risking flower and fruit damage. Place them in cold spots in your landscape to prevent a premature break of dormancy.

If you have plants that are not cold-hardy, you can take measures to protect them. Situate frost-sensitive plants in sheltered locations. Block walls, rocks, and patios collect and reflect the heat of the sun, and western and southern exposures tend to be warmest. Areas that receive full sun are obviously warmer than shaded locations.

Caring for Plants

Maintaining healthy plants that are appropriately watered is the next step in lowering the possibility of frost damage. Frost injury occurs when ice crystals form on the leaf surface, drawing moisture from the leaf tissue. The damage from this dehydration will be less severe if the plant is not already drought-stressed. Throughout winter manage irrigation carefully, keeping the soil's moisture level as even as possible. Keep in mind that plants will require less total water during their dormant periods.

Also, use a layer of mulch to help insulate against soil temperature fluctuations. Firm, bare, moist soil absorbs more heat and loses it more rapidly than soil that is loose, dry, or covered with mulch or vegetation. Mulch is useful if you are trying

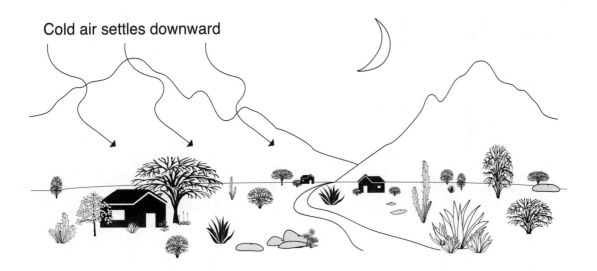

Cold air settles downward

If you live at the base of a slope, temperatures may be colder than nearby flat areas.

to keep a deciduous fruit tree from breaking dormancy too early, but it prevents the capture of heat that could be harnessed to protect a frost-sensitive plant such as citrus.

Don't overprotect your plants! They will be more frost resistant if kept hardened to cold weather.

Reducing Heat Loss

If frost is predicted, take steps to reduce heat loss and physically protect your plants. Cover plants with cloth or paper (not plastic) for insulation. You can use sheets or blankets for minimal protection or purchase a frost cloth. A properly applied frost cloth can protect plants at temperatures from 20 to 30 degrees Fahrenheit, depending on the fabric and the weave of the cloth.

Completely drape the plant from top all the way to the ground. Do not allow any openings for warmth to escape. This procedure will trap the heat radiating from the soil and maintain a more humid atmosphere around the plant foliage. Optimally, the drape will be supported by a frame that does not allow it to touch the foliage. Do not gather the drape around the trunk of the tree or

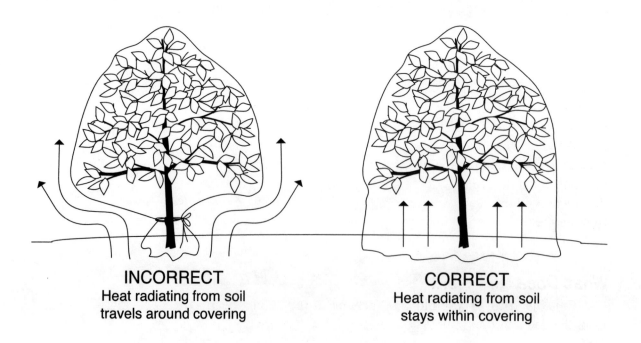

INCORRECT
Heat radiating from soil
travels around covering

CORRECT
Heat radiating from soil
stays within covering

Cover citrus and other cold-sensitive plants if frost is predicted.
If possible, the covering should not touch the foliage.

plant. The goal is to trap heat being radiated from the ground, so ensure that the drape touches the ground at least as far out as the drip line or canopy.

If you use sheets or blankets, remove the coverings every morning when the temperature under the covering warms to 50 degrees F. Permanently covering plants with sheets or blankets for the duration of the winter can be harmful and is not recommended in the low desert. Even if the temperature under the drape does not warm up enough to "cook" the plant, it is likely to warm up enough to cause the plant to break dormancy, begin actively growing, and thus become more susceptible to frost damage. Many of the frost cloths available may be left on for extended periods without risk of harming the plant.

You can also wrap the trunks of young citrus and other frost-sensitive trees to help prevent serious frost damage to the vital trunk. A tree can lose foliage or a branch or two, but if the trunk is badly damaged, the plant can die. Multiple layers of weather-proof paper or cloth provide good insulation against cold. Looser wrapping provides better insulation than tight wraps and should extend completely to the ground and at least up to the lower branches or limbs. This wrapping may be left on all winter (mid-November through mid-February).

Loosely wrap trunks of frost-sensitive trees from the ground up to the lowest branches.

Using Supplemental Heat

Walls and benches exposed to the sun during the day are good sources of supplemental heat at night. You may wish to add heat with 100-watt electric light bulbs. Use them to provide extra heat to covered plants, if needed. Be sure to hang bulbs below the foliage, allowing the heat they generate to rise (within the covered area) and warm the plant. Take care that the bulb is not so close to the trunk or a branch that it could burn.

Another way to add heat is to apply running water (just a trickle) to the ground at the base of the tree late night and early morning for no more than three nights in a row (after that the detrimental effects of drowning the plant's roots cancel out any frost protection benefits). When water is cooled, energy in the form of heat is released.

What Does NOT Work

Smudge pots. These block 90 percent of the radiant heat from the sun and trap only 20 percent of the heat stored by the earth.

A large fire. This creates an updraft sending hot air above plants, while sucking in cold air from surrounding areas.

Chemicals. A variety of chemicals have been marketed with claims of changing the freezing point of the plant tissue, reducing the ice-nucleating bacteria on the crop (thus inhibiting ice and frost formation), or affecting growth (extending dormancy). To date, no commercially available material has withstood scientific scrutiny.

Common Symptoms and Treatment of Frost Damage

If plants do experience frost damage, you'll see some combination of dead fruit, flowers, and dormant flower buds or dieback of leaves, shoots, and stems. In dieback, growing tips turn brown or black as if they had been scorched.

Do not prune frost-damaged plants until they begin growing in the spring. Pruning might stimulate new growth which would be vulnerable to late frosts. The frost-damaged leaves and stems will continue to help trap warm air within the canopy. In addition, the damage is often not nearly as bad as it initially looked. New growth may come out of tissue that looked dead. Only after new growth starts in the spring is it safe to prune out dead wood.

Realize that in grafted plants (many citrus and roses), if the plant dies all the way back to the bud union (the initial graft), then the regrowth will be of the root stock and not the desired variety. Regraft to the root stock or replace the plant.❀

Information in this chapter was adapted from The University of Arizona Cooperative Extension Publication AZ 1002, *Frost Protection*, authored by Lucy K. Bradley.

Chapter 8

Cacti & Other Succulents

By Kirti Mathura

Succulents are plants that are able to store water in their tissues for prolonged periods. This ability evolved in response to challenging environmental conditions. Succulents may have fleshy water-storing stems, leaves, or roots, in addition to other adaptations which help the plants to conserve water and withstand high temperatures. Almost all cactus plants are considered succulents, but not all succulents are cacti. Succulence is exhibited by many different families of plants, including the sunflower, cucumber, and geranium families.

Succulent-type plants (including cacti) that do best in low-desert regions are those that are adapted to fairly dry, harsh environments. Succulents are found in deserts throughout the world, and many of them adapt well to the Southwest. However, some succulents are native to mountainous, tropical, or seashore areas and don't perform as well under desert conditions.

Succulents offer an incredible diversity of textures, colors, and shapes, often in striking sculptural form. They provide wonderful accents for any landscape. Many also feature stunning blooms. Some people may think of cacti as boring, not having seen their dazzling flower displays. Some succulents offer exotic, or even bizarre, appearances. Spines or leaves can create artistic patterns. Various succulents also provide food, nesting, or shelter areas for wildlife. Night-blooming cacti and other succulents give evening entertainment. Flowers of some succulents have a wonderfully alluring fragrance, enticing both pollinators and people.

General Growing Requirements
Sun Exposure

Bright light is required by succulents, with some preferring full sun exposure. For succulents that cannot withstand all-day sun, it is ideal to plant them in locations to take advantage of native trees or shrubs that provide filtered sunlight. Contrary to common belief, not all cacti perform well in full sun. Some are native to Mexico or Central or South America, where temperatures are not as extreme and sun may not be as intense. In addition, some of our Southwest native cacti naturally grow within the light shade of a desert tree or shrub.

If a succulent plant is exposed to too much sun, the surface tissue will yellow. Provide shade, or move the plant to a more appropriate location. If left without relief, the tissue will turn brown, indicating permanent damage.

Soil

For the majority of succulents, soil does not need to be organically rich, but it must have good drainage. Soil amendments are typically not necessary, except to enhance drainage.

If the soil drains poorly because of heavy clay, work coarse mineral material (sand or gravel) into the soil to a depth of about two feet. You can also add composted mulch, up to 25 percent of the soil amendment. Avoid the use of peat moss, which does not work well for our desert plants.

Water

Many succulents, especially cacti, could survive on nothing more than rainfall once established with a good root system. However, for landscape purposes, we usually prefer our plants to look better, so we provide supplemental water in addition to rainfall.

Most cacti will do well with a good soaking, in which water penetrates about two feet deep, once a month during the summer (typically from April to September). This is their season of active growth. If your plant is looking shriveled or wilted, it is usually an indication that it needs water, the same as with perennials in your garden. Natural rainfall usually provides enough water for the cooler months, if we are not experiencing drought conditions.

A general guideline for other succulents is a deep watering every one to two weeks in the summertime. Our tougher natives that typically grow in full sun might be all right with a soaking

Watering Schedule
During Active Growing Season
(April-September)

Every 1— 2 weeks
Agaves
Euphorbias
Ice Plants
Slipper Plant
Elephant Food

Every 2 weeks
Aloes

Every 3— 4 weeks
Desert Milkweed
Red Yucca

Once a Month
Cacti
Yuccas

once every three to four weeks. Be aware that some succulents slow their metabolism or become dormant during the summer, and require less frequent water during these months than actively growing succulents. These dormant plants may look "sad," but resist the temptation to overwater them, as they may rot.

For your cacti and succulents, allow the soil to dry between deep soakings, at least a few inches deep into the soil. You can test the soil moisture with your finger, a stick (moist soil will stick to it, dry soil will not), or a moisture meter. For most succulents, avoid the combination of wet soil and cold temperatures. This condition can cause rot in many plants.

Fertilizer

As with supplemental water, fertilizer is typically not necessary, but an application or two of mild fertilizer during the growing season for your succulents will yield more appealing plants. Organic fertilizers are good for steady, long-term growth. Synthetics are good if you want quick-growth results. You can use organic type fertilizers full strength, but it is advisable to dilute most synthetic fertilizers to half-strength. If using a synthetic fertilizer, choose one that is lower in nitrogen content (the first of three sequential numbers on the label, such as 10-30-20).

Planting

Spring or fall months are usually the best time to plant most succulent plants. Summer conditions may be too harsh on a plant trying to establish a root system. In the winter, you can risk rotting plants and roots if they get too wet and cold. Plants will become established more rapidly when they are in an active growth phase.

If a plant is being transplanted from a pot with a fairly rich, organic soil mix, gently shake or tap the soil from the root system and discard it. This is easily done when the soil is dry. Removing the old soil prevents roots from growing in two different soil types after it is planted, a situation that is difficult to water correctly.

This is also a good opportunity to trim away damaged roots. Place the plant in a location out of direct sun, with good air circulation, and allow the root system to heal (callus) for about a week. This will help prevent infection of roots when you replant. If the plant is coming from a container of mineral soil similar to your planting area, simply remove the plant from the pot with soil/root ball intact, and gently rough up the outer surface of the soil ball.

Watering Schedule During Cool-Season and Dormancy (October-March)

Once a Month
*Aloes
Agaves
Ice Plants
Slipper Plant
Elephant Food
Desert Milkweed
Red Yucca
Most Euphorbias**

Every 6—8 weeks
*Yuccas
Cacti**

*Depending on temperatures. Check soil moisture.

Dig a planting hole only as deep as the root mass, and about twice as wide as the root system. Backfill the hole with the soil that was dug from the hole. Gently firm it around the roots as you go, keeping the soil around the plant at the same level it was in its container.

Wait a few days for damaged roots to heal before watering the plant thoroughly. If it is hot and you are planting in a sunny location, you may need to provide the plant with temporary shade until it gets established. Do not place shade cloth directly on the plant as good air circulation is necessary to prevent heat buildup and contact burning of the plant tissue.

For cacti or other prickly succulents, use heavy gloves, thick layers of newspaper, or old carpet pieces to handle them safely. For larger plants, old pieces of garden hose can be handy for leverage, used in sling fashion. It is also wise to wear long-sleeved shirts and eye protection.

Maintenance

In addition to the interesting effects that succulent plants provide in the landscape, another reason to include them in your plan is their ease of care. In general, they are as close to maintenance-free as you can get!

Pruning

Pruning is not necessary for most succulents. In fact, it usually detracts from the overall appearance of the plant. It is much better to be familiar with the potential mature size of a particular type of plant and locate it accordingly in your landscape. This will eliminate the need for pruning to maintain size or to keep a prickly plant at a safe distance from traffic. This way, you will only need to prune to remove dead or damaged parts. Even this isn't always necessary or desirable, as with yuccas, for instance. Removing the lower dead leaves of these plants detracts from the natural look. Desert spoons or agaves can end up looking like pineapples if their lower leaves are pruned away.

Always use clean, sharp pruning tools, making smooth cuts to reduce the chance of bacterial or fungal infection. Be careful when working with euphorbias, which exude an irritating milky sap when the stems are cut.

Periodically, clumping-type succulents (such as some aloes) may need to be divided if the clump becomes too large. Once the clump is dug up and thinned, follow the general planting procedure for succulents.

Tip

When planting your cacti or succulent, try to orient it in the same direction towards the sun as it was growing previously, if this is known. This will help prevent sunburn of the sides of the plant that are not accustomed to intense afternoon sun exposure.

Frost Protection

Many succulents are frost sensitive. For example, plants from Africa (such as some aloes or euphorbias), Mexico, or Central America (some agaves) may be native to areas that do not normally experience freezing temperatures. Columnar cacti can be damaged when temperatures reach the mid-20s Fahrenheit. Protect plants by covering them with frost cloth (available in nursery centers) or by placing styrofoam cups on the tips of columnar cacti. Do not use plastic to cover plants, as contact with plant tissue can cause damage.

Pests and Diseases

Pest and disease problems in cacti and other succulents are generally minimal. Insects, such as mealy bugs and aphids, can usually be controlled by organic methods such as insecticidal soap. Cochineal scale insects, which appear as white, cottony masses on cacti, can usually be removed by a forceful spray of water.

Agave Snout Weevils

Agaves may be attacked by snout weevils. Initially, you might notice a wrinkling at the base of the leaves. If you wriggle a bottom leaf loose from the plant, you will find a perfectly round hole eaten by the weevil larva. At a later stage of infestation, the entire agave will collapse. To treat this problem, choose an insecticide for beetles and grubs. If using a liquid insecticide, drench each agave and the surrounding soil. If using a granular insecticide, work it into the surrounding soil. (Follow product instructions exactly when using an insecticide.) Treat all agaves in the area. This is important to control the spread of the weevil. If caught at a very early stage of infestation, an infested agave may be salvaged with a liquid application (drench the plant and soil at its base). To prevent infestation, apply a chemical treatment every March, before the weevils become active.

Mites

Internal mites may attack aloes and agaves, creating distorted growth. In aloes, areas of the leaves, stem, or flowers may look like the inner tissue has exploded out of the plant. You can use a clean, sharp knife to cut the affected tissue off the plant, and allow the wound to heal in the open air. Badly affected plants should be destroyed.

Agave mite infestations first appear as discoloration of the leaf tissue, almost like a darkened waterspot. Next, brown corky

Tip

Damage from mammal pests, such as rabbits or javelina, can be controlled by fencing around individual target plants. Chicken wire works well for rabbits, but heavier material, secured deep in the soil, is needed for javelina. Another tactic is to fence the critters out of the area.

lesions develop on the leaf. Finally, you will notice distorted growth of the leaves. Agave mites are very difficult to eradicate and can be prevalent in potted plants. Try a treatment of dimethoate, an insecticide. As with the aloes, heavily infested agaves should be discarded.

Bacterial Diseases

In addition to pests, disease can also become a problem. Wet rot, caused by a bacteria, can affect the stem tissue of cacti. Initially there is a softening of the tissue, which may be slightly darker than the healthy tissue. Infected tissue may become black, brown, red, or orange, and continues to soften. A bleeding or oozing of a dark substance will follow. Treatment involves cutting away the affected tissue with a clean, sharp knife, down to healthy tissue (which resembles a raw potato). Rinse off the area with a 10 percent chlorine bleach solution (9 parts water to 1 part bleach). Allow the area to air dry and heal.

Dry rot on cactus plants is caused by a fungus. Initially it resembles the wet rot, but the affected tissue becomes hard and dry instead of soft and oozy. Dry rot can be controlled by cutting away all the dried, discolored tissue, treating with a bleach solution, and allowing the cut to air dry and heal.

Crown rot may affect aloes (especially the tree aloes) and agaves. The attack usually begins in July or August, caused by the weather (increased humidity and rain) or by overhead watering, where water collects and sits in the crown of the plant. Initially the base of a few mid-section leaves will appear blackish-brown, with the rot eventually extending the length of the leaves. You will notice the bad smell of the affected tissue. If crown rot is caught early enough, it can be treated with a bacteriocide/fungicide (streptomycin/benomyl or metalaxyl) mixture, or the tissue can be carefully cut away (leaving the growing point). If the rot has greatly affected the main stem, or attacked the growing point, the plant cannot be saved.

Propagation

Cacti and many other succulents are wonderfully easy and fun to propagate. You can share cuttings and offshoots with neighbors and friends, enhancing your collection for landscape or containers. You will be most successful working with plants when they are actively growing (for most, during the warm season).

Propagating Cacti

Cactus cuttings can be made from columnar cacti or jointed

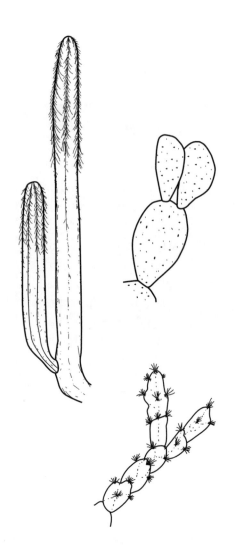

Many cacti are easy to propagate by cutting a pad or section off at the joint, where it connects to the main trunk or stem.

cacti. For a columnar cactus, make a clean cut with a sharp knife, or a saw if the stem has a woody skeleton. If the cactus has branches, you can cut at a branch junction (for cosmetic purposes). If not, cut anywhere on the stem. For jointed cacti, such as prickly pears or chollas, make a cut at a joint (again, for cosmetics). Place the cutting in a well-aerated, shady location (direct sunlight will burn it) and allow the cut to dry and callus. This may take a week or longer, depending on the time of year.

After the cutting has callused, it is time to root it. Place it in a pot of pumice or sand, or a very light, well-draining soil mix, just deep enough for it to stand upright. Place it in light shade so it does not burn. Water well, and let the rooting medium dry out some before watering again. Do not keep it too wet, or the stem could rot. Check every couple of weeks for root development by gently rocking the stem in the soil. If there is resistance, it has begun rooting. Swelling of the cutting due to water uptake, and new growth are two other indicators that rooting has occurred. Once well rooted, your new plant is ready to go in its intended growing place.

Propagating Agaves

Many agaves form pups, or offshoots, around the base of the parent plant. Gently dig the soil away and cut the runner stem from the parent to remove these. Place the pup in a shaded location and allow the cut to dry for a few days. Plant the pup in pumice or light, well-draining soil, at the same soil level it was originally. Water as directed for the cactus cuttings. A few aga-

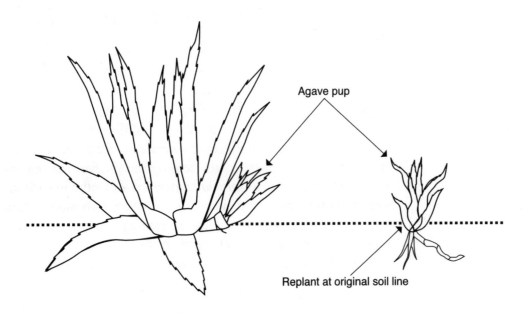

Agave pup

Replant at original soil line

ves develop bulbils, or plantlets, on their bloom stalks. These can be gently pulled or twisted off the stalk and set upright in pumice for rooting. Water as directed for the cactus cuttings.

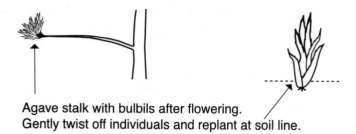

Agave stalk with bulbils after flowering.
Gently twist off individuals and replant at soil line.

Propagating Aloes

Many aloes form clumps of offshoots. The offshoots can be gently separated from the parent plant. Often they will already have roots and can be planted where you like. If not, place the offshoot in a shaded location and let any separation wounds heal for a few days to a week. Then place it in pumice for rooting. Water as directed for the cactus cuttings.

Container Gardening

Many cacti and other succulents can be grown in containers. Make sure that any container used has a drainage hole (about the size of a nickel) in the bottom to allow excess water to drain out. Due to the shallow nature of succulent plant roots, shallow containers may be used. Soil needs to be well draining, so avoid using peat moss in the mix, which can hold too much moisture or dry out too much between waterings. Pumice, a volcanic material, is a wonderful soil amendment because it holds a small amount of moisture and keeps the soil loose, enhancing drainage.

Cacti and succulents should be dry planted. Allow the soil in the old container to dry before transplanting to a new container. If the soil in the old container is different from the new soil you will be using, it is best to "bare-root" the plant. Remove the plant from its pot and gently remove the soil from around the roots. Set the plant in a shaded location and allow the roots to dry and callus for about a week. Plant in the new container at the same soil level at which the plant was growing previously. Wait a week before watering to allow the roots to heal.

All succulent plants need to be watered during their growing season; frequency depends on weather conditions and light exposure. Actively growing plants may need to be watered once a week during warmer times of the year or only once a month during the cooler season. The soil needs to dry out some between waterings. Test the upper inch or two of soil (with a finger, stick, or moisture meter) for moisture. When dry, give the plant a thorough watering, allowing excess water to drain off. If there is a saucer under the pot, excess water needs to be emptied from it. Water-soluble fertilizer can be used about once a month during the plant's growing season. If you prefer to fertilize more frequently, dilute the fertilizer accordingly.

Most succulents in containers will grow well in bright light, but may burn with full sun exposure. Too little light (more than 50 percent shade) will cause abnormal elongated growth. Some container cacti may be grown in full sun, but many will do better with up to 50 percent shade.

Container Soil Mixes

Cacti
Most cacti are best grown in a mineral-based soil mix. Use sand, silt, and gravel.

Agaves and Yuccas
Use equal parts light potting soil, mineral soil, and pumice.

Aloes and Other Succulents
Mix 4 parts organic-based cactus mix, 2 parts pumice, and 1 part grit (such as #12 silica sand).

Most container-grown succulents cannot tolerate as much sun exposure as those grown in the ground.

Plant Selection

Choosing the right cactus or other succulent for your landscape requires just a little forethought. Here are a few things to consider in making your selection.

Consider the soil drainage, light exposure (including reflected light), heat and cold exposure, and access to a water source in deciding where to place a particular plant. Knowing the needs of the plants, combined with your site assessment, will ensure proper placement for happy, healthy plants.

Some plants have harmful spines or irritating or toxic exudates (sticky substances that seep from cuts in plant tissue). Many people have a rash-like reaction to chemicals found in agaves, which can be exposed when leaves are cut or if you are poked by a sharp leaf tip. Euphorbia plants exude a milky sap from the stems when they are damaged or cut. Exposure can cause minor to severe skin irritation, depending on the type of plant, and can be toxic if ingested. Some aloes can cause skin irritation if there is exposure to broken leaves. These types of plants are best planted away from activity and/or a young person's reach.

Know the mature size of the plant. Succulent plants range in size from minute to majestic. Some plants become extremely heavy and/or "gnarly" with age, making them next to impossible to transplant if they become too large for the area in which they were planted. There is a range of plants to fit any need, from groundcovers to shrub-like forms to tree-like specimens. The following information provides some choices to help get you started.

Cacti

Saguaro (Carnegiea gigantea)

This stately cactus, with stout arms on the upper portion, can reach 30–40 feet in height, but it takes years as they are extremely slow growing. Mature plants grow in full sun, but younger ones need at least afternoon shade or filtered sunlight until they get established. Beautiful white, night-blooming flowers appear in April and May, followed by ripe fruits that are enjoyed by many birds in June and July. Birds will nest in holes in the main trunk or arms of the more mature plants. Bird holes generally do not damage the cactus and no controls should be taken.

Organ Pipe Cactus (Stenocereus thurberi)

Organ pipes grow 10–15 feet tall, with many upright branches developing from the base. Mature plants can be 10–12 feet wide, but growth is slow. They grow in full sun. Cream and pale pink flowers open at night, April through June, followed by round fruits. This is another cactus that can certainly be a focal point in a landscape.

Night-Blooming Cereus or Peruvian Apple Cactus (Cereus hildmannianus, syn. C. peruvianus)

This is another tall cactus, reaching about 10 feet, which branches from both the base and higher up. It is a fast grower and is not nearly as spiny as the organ pipe or other cacti. Numerous large, trumpet-shaped, white flowers open at night through the summer, followed by colorful fruits with red exteriors, gray interiors, and black seeds. The fruit is also quite tasty. This cactus grows best in full sun but can withstand light shade. Plant this cereus where you can enjoy the flowers in the evening.

Hedgehog Cactus *(Echinocereus engelmannii)*

Slowly, with age, this low-clumping cactus can develop up to thirty stems from its base. The overall size is usually about 1 foot tall and 2–3 feet wide. The stems are covered with 2- to 3-inch spines. In spring, bright magenta flowers adorn the stem tops, followed by red oval fruits. This cactus grows in full sun but can tolerate light afternoon shade.

Golden Barrel *(Echinocactus grusonii)*

This slow-growing globular cactus is covered with golden yellow spines. At maturity, it takes on a more elliptical form, reaching 4 feet tall and 2–3 feet wide. With age, the cactus will have yellow flowers in the spring, but with the spination color, the blooms don't stand out much. It is best to give these barrels some afternoon shade or filtered sun in the low desert, but if gradually acclimated, they can be grown in full sun. The spines make a dramatic scene when backlit by the late afternoon sun.

Compass Barrel *(Ferocactus cylindraceus, syn. F. Acanthodes)*

This barrel begins life as a rounded or globular plant, taking on a cylindrical form as it matures. It typically grows 3–5 feet tall, but can potentially reach 8 feet at maturity, with a width of a foot and a half. Because plants often lean toward the south or southwest, they took on the reputation of being compasses. The thick, often hooked central spines add yellow, pink, red, or brown coloration to the plant. In spring and early summer, yellow to orange funnel-shaped flowers open in a ring at the top of the plant. Yellow oval fruits develop afterwards, which are eaten by wildlife. This barrel is best grown in full sun.

Pincushion Cactus *(Mammillaria grahamii)*

This small cactus is often a single stem but may branch towards the base. It grows to about 6 inches tall and is covered with clusters of spines, with the center spines hooked. For such a small plant, it can put on quite a display. During the spring and summer, it will produce rings of .75- to 1-inch wide bright pink blooms. This gem is best grown in filtered sunlight, as it grows tucked under bushes in its native habitat.

Beavertail Prickly Pear (Opuntia basilaris)

This prickly pear has a very attractive bluish-gray cast to the pads. This makes a striking contrast to the bright magenta flowers that appear in clusters along the pad edges in the spring. Low-branching pads form clumps about 1 foot tall and 2–3 feet wide. Since there are no large spines, this plant looks innocent, but watch out for the tiny, hairlike spines called glochids. Grow beavertail in full sun.

Purple Prickly Pear (Opuntia santa-rita)

As with other prickly pears, this one is fairly fast growing, reaching a height of about 4 feet and a width of 4–6 feet. The rounded pads have a purplish color, which is more pronounced in response to cold or drought. In spring, yellow flowers contrast nicely with the purple of the pads. Plant this prickly pear in full sun for best color.

Teddy Bear Cholla (Cylindropuntia bigelovii)

This cholla looks cuddly, but don't be fooled! Pale yellow barbed spines cover the joints of this cactus. The plant can reach 4–5 feet tall, with the upper branching giving it a width of about 2 feet. Spring blooms are a somewhat inconspicuous greenish yellow, followed by green fruits. Plant teddy bears in full sun to enjoy the glow of the spines as they are backlit by early morning or evening sunlight.

Other Succulents

Agaves, or Century Plants (Agave spp.)

The selection of agaves that we can use in our landscapes is tremendous. They range in height from just a few inches to seven feet. Leaf coloration varies from pale grey-green to bright green to purple-tinged. Leaf margins can be viciously toothed or smooth, with tips that are needle-like or soft and flexible. Some prefer full sun, while many need filtered sun or afternoon shade in the low desert. Most have a moderate to slow growth rate. Some are solitary growers, while others form clumps of offshoots. Remember that most agaves die when they send up their tall bloom stalk (this usually takes several years, depending on the species). The difficulty lies in trying to choose just one, or a few!

Cow's Horn (Agave bovicornuta)

This agave has wide, bright green leaves that are margined with reddish curved teeth. It grows to 3 feet tall and 4–5 feet wide. Grows best in filtered sun, with protection from frost.

Agave desmettiana

This more "friendly" plant reaches 4 feet in height and width with flexible, bright green arching leaves with smooth margins. Plant in filtered sun and protect from frost.

Octopus Agave *(Agave vilmoriniana)*

This is another friendly agave. Its gracefully twisting flexible leaves are light green and smooth edged. This agave grows 3–4 feet tall and 4–6 feet wide. Very adaptable, they can be located in full sun or light shade and withstand light frost.

Black-spined Agave *(Agave macroacantha)*

It has beautiful blue-gray leaves tipped with dark red or blackish spines. The plant grows to about 18 inches tall, forming a clump of many offshoots. Provide this one with some shade or filtered sun. It may be frost sensitive.

Parry's Agave *(Agave parryi)*

This agave has grayish-green leaves with dark teeth and tips. The plants are fairly compact, growing 2 feet tall and wide. Grow in full sun or light shade. There are also very attractive varieties of this agave.

Queen Victoria Agave *(Agave victoriae-reginae)*

A very sculptural agave with thick stiff leaves arranged in a tight rosette. White markings and margins of the leaves add to its attractiveness. Queen Victorias grow about 18 inches tall and 2 feet wide. They can grow in sun or light shade.

Aloes (Aloe spp.)

The range of aloes is as great as that of the agaves. Some are quite small and can be tucked into niches among rocks. Some form clumps, while others are solitary in growth form. Many are stemless or only have short stems. A few even have tree-like growth habits, growing very tall with a main trunk. The flowers they produce can be dazzling oranges, reds, or yellows, or muted creams or greens. They usually bloom in the cooler season, and unlike most agaves, they bloom annually without dying. The flowers are hummingbird magnets. Most aloes prefer filtered sunlight in the low desert, or at least afternoon shade. Many are frost tender.

Medicinal Aloe *(Aloe vera, syn. A. barbadensis)*

A must in every yard as it is handy for treating burns. Since it is a clumping aloe, you can probably get a plant from a friend! This aloe usually grows to about 2 feet tall and can become very wide if the clump isn't divided periodically. Flowers are yellow.

Tree Aloe *(Aloe ferox)*

Although it doesn't reach the height here that it does in its native Africa, it is still interesting in its growth form. It is slow growing. Leaves atop the trunk are toothed on the top and bottom. The deep orange-red flowers add a burst of color to a winter garden. Plant in sun or light shade.

Euphorbias (Euphorbia spp.)

This is another diverse group of plants that can be very fun in the landscape. Be aware that broken stems of euphorbias exude a milky substance that can be very irritating to the skin of some people. Protective clothing and glasses should be worn when working with them. Some euphorbias do well in full sun; others need some shade provided. Cold hardiness also varies.

Candelilla *(Euphorbia antisyphilitica)*

It gets its name from the slender gray-green stems that grow in a clump. A plant can reach 2 feet tall and 3 feet wide, with fairly slow growth. If planted in a wet area, candelilla can spread vigorously and become invasive. Minute leaves are present only on new growth, dropping in response to drought. During the warm season, small pinkish flowers develop on the upper stems. Candelilla is fairly cold hardy.

Moroccan Mound *(Euphorbia resinifera)*

An interesting clumping plant with stout, erect stems. Pale green mounds grow to 2 feet tall and 3 feet wide. It prefers full sun or light shade. In spring, inconspicuous yellow flowers develop.

Ice Plants

Ice plants offer some wonderful groundcover selections. Most of them are low growing, hugging the ground or only reaching a foot high. Some will stay compact, while others will spread for many feet. Flowers often appear in brilliant masses, with colors ranging from yellow or orange to deep magenta or more subtle pinks. A good number of ice plants will perform well in direct sun, but others will need filtered sunlight conditions. Sometimes birds will present a problem with these plants, pecking at the irresistibly succulent leaves.

Yellow Ice Plant *(Malephora luteola)*

This pretty bloomer grows to about 8 inches tall and spreads 3 to 4 feet wide. Sunny yellow flowers dot the bright green foliage mass most of the year, occurring on new growth. This ice plant can be grown in full sun, but might look healthier during the summer if placed in light shade.

Yuccas (Yucca spp.)

Yuccas present yet another wonderful group of landscape plants. There are single stemmed species and those that branch, either at the base or higher up. Some are quite large and treelike. Yuccas have attractive cream-colored, bell-shaped blossoms arranged in clusters.

Banana Yucca *(Yucca baccata)*

This plant usually has a clumping habit, reaching 4 feet tall and up to 6 feet wide. The stiff leaves are about 2 feet long and 1–2 inches wide, arranged in a rosette. The large flower clusters bloom in the spring, followed by fruits that look like short green bananas. Plant banana yucca in full sun.

Soaptree Yucca *(Yucca elata)*

This is a taller yucca, reaching 10–12 feet in height. The trunk can be single or branched. Soaptree yucca's leaves are narrow and grasslike, with attractive filaments curling off the margins. In spring, the flower clusters rise tall above the top of the stems. Plant this yucca in full sun.

Other Interesting Succulents

Desert Milkweed *(Asclepias subulata)*

This fascinating plant draws in the butterflies. A clump is formed of many slender gray-green stems, reaching 4 feet tall and 4–5 feet wide. Narrow leaves are only present on new growth and don't persist for long. Clusters of pale yellow flowers appear during the warm season. This milkweed has a better form when grown in full sun and is very drought tolerant. Stems exude a milky latex when broken.

Red Yucca *(Hesperaloe parviflora)*

With a slow to moderate growth rate, hesperaloe can form a grass-like clump 3 feet tall and 3–4 feet wide. It grows best in full sun. The long, narrow stiff leaves are deep green. From late spring through fall, deep pink, bell-shaped flowers on tall stems attract hummingbirds. This is a great plant for areas with hot reflected sun, or around pools, as it doesn't drop much litter.

Slipper Plant (Pedilanthus macrocarpus)

This interesting plant grows vertical succulent stems from a woody base, reaching a height of 3 feet and about the same width. The half-inch thick, bright green stems temporarily have small leaves on new growth. In the spring and fall, slipper-shaped orange-red flowers develop on stem tips, attracting hummingbirds. This is another good plant for sunny locations.

Elephant's Food (Portulacaria afra)

Elephant's food is a fast growing succulent shrub that typically grows 2–6 feet tall and wide in the low desert. It seldom blooms in the low desert, but the small, rounded, bright green fleshy leaves shimmer in the sun. *Portulacaria* is versatile, working well in sunny as well as shaded areas.❀

Kirti Mathura grew up in muggy Michigan. As a young girl, she started gardening with her mother, growing roses, flowers, vegetables, and herbs. Kirti left behind the Midwest's humidity, receiving a Bachelor degree in botany and environmental biology from the University of Montana. Kirti moved to arid Arizona in 1987 to take a job in the cotton fields of Maricopa. She had to forget everything she learned about gardening as a child and start over from scratch. She began volunteering at the Desert Botanical Garden and developed a love for desert plants, especially the natives. Kirti hung up her cotton pick sack and became an employee at the Garden in 1994. Kirti is a University of Arizona Cooperative Extension Master Gardener and a member of the Arizona Herb Association, the Central Arizona Cactus and Succulent Society, and the Arizona Native Plant Society.

Illustrations in this chapter were recreated from the author's original drawings.

Chapter 9

Growing Wildflowers

By Michelle Rauscher

The Southwest is known for its spectacular wildflower displays. They are part of our identity, providing us with a sense of region or place. We pause and take notice when coming across a flower growing in the wild that is tended only by nature. To duplicate this experience in our own yards can be a pleasurable and simple endeavor if we take note of how nature accomplishes its colorful wildflower shows.

Millions of seeds rest dormant in the soil, waiting for the right combination of rainfall and soil temperature to germinate. In the wild, this combination may only come about every seven to ten years. In our landscapes, we have the advantage of supplementing the water at the appropriate time to ensure a colorful bloom period.

When to Plant

Here in the Southwest desert, spring is the biggest wildflower season. The fall and winter rains that occur typically from October through December bring on the spring flowering. These soft drizzly rains soak the soil, and with fall's cooler nighttime temperatures, the dormant seeds spring to life. Sowing wildflower seeds in early October will enhance your chances of success, as the seedlings will benefit from winter rains.

Optimum soil germination temperature will vary greatly from one species to another. Typically, spring bloomers germinate when the evening temperatures fall below 70 degrees Fahrenheit. For summer wildflowers, germination begins when the nighttime temperatures are consistently over 70 degrees F. In nature, summer

Spring Bloomers
Annuals

Coulter's or Desert Lupine
(Lupinus sparsiflorus)
violet-blue

Desert Bluebells
(Phacelia campanularia)
blue

Mexican Gold Poppy
(Eschscholtzia mexicana)
gold to orange

Owl's Clover
(Orthocarpus purpurascens)
purplish-pink

Scarlet or Red Flax
(Linum grandiflorum 'Rubrum')
scarlet

Scorpionweed
(Phacelia crenulata)
violet-purple

Toadflax
(Linaria macroccana)
assorted colors

germination may be as late as the thunderstorm season, which is usually July and August. You can certainly speed up that process in the landscape by supplementing the water. Prepare for early summer color by simply mixing wildflower seeds together in the fall—both spring and summer bloomers. As the spring flowers are finishing up their last cycle of color for the season, summer flowers are germinating and developing in the moist soil shaded by the spring bloomers. When you clear out the spent spring flowers, summer plants are up and ready to go!

Selecting a Planting Site

It is best if you know the history of your site. Does it support vegetation now? If nothing grows in the area, chances are wildflowers won't either. Perhaps a soil sterilant has been used there in the past. You may need to have the soil tested. Is it where the weeds sprout up after a rain? This can be a positive and a negative. First of all, if weeds will thrive in a given location, so will wildflowers as they have similar characteristics and growing requirements. But if weeds have gone unchecked for a number of years, it means that there are most likely millions of weed seeds lying dormant, waiting for the right conditions to germinate, and your efforts to grow wildflowers will provide those conditions. Be prepared to weed out the undesirables for the first few years until your wildflower display becomes established.

Eliminate Weeds Before Planting

If you know the site to be contaminated by weeds, there are a few things you can do to reduce the weed seed bank before planting. Thoroughly water the area until the weed seedlings appear. At this point, hand pull the seedlings or use a herbicide to kill them. (With any herbicide use, follow product instructions exactly.) Continue to repeat this process, each time reducing the weed seed bank in the soil. As weeds germinate, be sure to take samples and press them on index cards or in your gardening journal. This provides a reference of what the weed seedlings look like once the flowers have been sown. It will greatly reduce the chance of unwittingly pulling up wildflowers, believing them to be weeds. Begin eliminating weeds early so that there is still time to plant wildflower seeds.

Start Small

It is a good idea to start out small with wildflower displays and develop more areas as your beds become established and require less maintenance. Select sites that will provide the greatest impact: along walkways, near front entrances where people can pause to admire them, or close to a patio where you can sit and enjoy the fruits of your labor. Many gardeners start out with grand ideas of vast meadows of wildflowers. It is important to understand that there is a level of maintenance involved. If you begin with a large area, and find that you are spending all of your weekends weeding until the bed becomes established, it will take away the joy of growing wildflowers. However, your established bed of wildflowers will eventually choke out the potential weeds, greatly reducing the amount of time you will need to invest.

Sunshine and Water

Look for sites with full sun. Most wildflowers require a minimum of eight hours of sunlight a day. If you have a shady location that you have your heart set on, you will need to seek out the species that will thrive in that type of environment. If you attempt to grow sun-loving flowers in shady locations, it will be at the expense of the blooms and ultimately you will end up with spindly plants.

Locate your wildflower display near a water source. In a good year, you can rely on what nature provides. Unfortunately, good years tend to be few and far between. To ensure a colorful and reliable display, you will need to supplement the rain. It will quickly become a tedious task if you have to drag a hose a long distance or make numerous trips with a watering can.

Soil Conditions

Well-draining soil is ideal for wildflowers. It may be tempting to select areas that are low-lying or poorly drained, with the hope that wildflowers will thrive in these moist conditions. Most often the opposite is true. Moist locations are usually the deposit site for weed seeds as water drains through the area, leading to extra work for you. Also, wildflowers need well-drained soils so that their roots do not drown.

An ideal planting situation is one where a fresh layer of decomposed granite has been laid. It allows you to simply sprinkle the seeds on the surface, hose them in, and they are ready to go! The granite acts as an inorganic mulch, which helps to retain soil moisture and regulate soil temperature. It also gives wildflower seeds little niches to protect them from scavenging birds.

If soil is heavily compacted, you will need to do some additional preparation before sowing the seed. Perhaps it is a location where you have previously stored a recreational vehicle or trailer, or maybe you are dealing with a new construction site

Spring Bloomers
Perennials

Flat-top Buckwheat
(*Eriogonum fasciculatum* var. *poliofolium*)
pale pink

Globe Mallow
(*Sphaeralcea ambigua*)
assorted colors

Goodding's Verbena
(*Glandularia gooddingii*, syn.
Verbena gooddingii)
lavender

Palmer Penstemon
(*Penstemon palmeri*)
pale pink

Parry's Penstemon
(*Penstemon parryi*)
rose-magenta

Summer Bloomers
Annuals

Arizona Poppy
(Kallstroemia grandiflora)
orange

Blanketflower or Indian Blanket
(Gaillardia pulchella)
yellow tips, red at the base

Cosmos
(Cosmos bipinnatus)
rose-pink

Orange Cosmos
(Cosmos sulphureus)
orange and yellow

Spreading Fleabane
(Erigeron divergens)
white to lavender

Sunflower
(Helianthus spp.)
yellow

where heavy equipment has compacted the soil. Whatever the cause, it is important to remember that soil is a seed bank, most likely filled with weed seed. The more the soil is tilled or disturbed, the more seeds will be lifted to the surface, where they will find the sun and moisture they need to sprout. Keep this in mind as you cultivate the soil.

Loosening the soil to a maximum depth of an inch or so is all that is needed for wildflower seedlings. Shallow soil preparation will limit the disturbance of dormant weed seed. Once you have loosened the soil, lightly rake it to provide a smooth surface void of any pockets or swells where water and seed will collect. This will create a more uniform display.

Choosing Seeds

Read the label! Often you will find that there are grasses included in wildflower mixes. Grasses are far more aggressive and can outperform wildflowers. Grasses are recommended for the more experienced wildflower grower who wants to achieve a meadow-type look and can invest the time to weed and thin to achieve a balanced display.

It is important to plant species that are appropriate for your area. Be selective when purchasing regional or theme garden mixes. Many times they are filled with seed that may not be suited to your particular area. This can result in poor germination, or plants that are not well acclimated to your garden conditions. They will ultimately develop into unattractive plants that don't perform well. A very common problem when purchasing seed mixes is that the filler or bulk of the seed can be what the seed companies have an excess of, usually because it is an aggressive plant. If that is the case, it will most likely be aggressive in your landscape as well, ultimately choking out all the desirables and leaving you with a monoculture—just one tough species.

When you are first starting out, it is best to sow several species together. If you create elaborate plans with specific places for each flower, you could be greatly disappointed. Each year is different, and if the factors needed for germination for a particular species are not present, you will end up with poor results and possibly empty patches. To ensure success, mix several species together. A good combination is to incorporate some easy-to-grow annuals with some well-adapted perennials. The annuals will provide big impact for the first year and will continue to reseed each year. Many perennials will not bloom the first year from seed but will continue to bloom each year after. Well-adapted perennials will also reseed in the landscape. If you are an impatient gardener, you might want to make an investment in potted perennials to be transplanted throughout the bed. Don't waste money on annual transplants, which are easily grown from seed.

Sowing Seeds

When you have made your selections, mix all the seed together with filler such as sand, old potting soil, or soil borrowed directly from your planting site. Use four parts filler to one part seed. A filler will help with even distribution of the seed, as many wildflower species have tiny seeds. For a jump start on summer and fall color, don't forget to mix in summer blooming flowers as well.

Broadcast half of the seed as evenly as possible, going north to south; then sow the remaining half east to west. This will ensure even coverage. Press the seed into the soil by walking on the soil or using the backside of a rake. Do not cover the seed any deeper than one-sixteenth of an inch. The idea is to make soil-to-seed contact. Some of the seeds will remain visible, which is all right. Remember, the goal is to duplicate what happens in nature.

Avoid sowing too deep! Many wildflower seeds are very small and contain only enough stored food for a limited growth period. If seeds are buried too deeply, the seedling will either exhaust its food reserve before ever reaching the surface or may not germinate altogether due to lack of oxygen or light.

Summer Bloomers
Perennials

California Fuchsia
(*Epilobium canum*, syn.
Zauschneria californica)
red

Chocolate Flower
(*Berlandiera lyrata*)
yellow

Desert Senna
(*Senna covesii*)
rusty-yellow flowers

Mealy Cup Sage
(*Salvia farinacea*)
violet-blue

Rock Penstemon
(*Penstemon baccharifolius*)
red

Sacred Datura
(*Datura wrightii*)
white

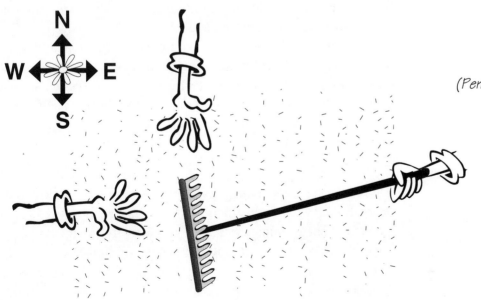

Broadcast seeds in two directions for even coverage.

Save a few seeds of each species to sow in a pot of sterile potting soil. As the seedlings emerge, press them on index cards or in your gardening journal as a reference to identify wildflower seedlings. This helps you start the weeding process early—anything that doesn't match these samples is most likely a weed. The earlier you begin to weed, the less disturbing it will be to the flowers' developing root systems.

Watering

A good rainy season occurs about once every seven to ten years. To ensure a flower display on the "off" years, you will need to supplement the rains to germinate seeds and establish seedlings. Plant wildflower displays in areas that have irrigation already installed or have easy access to a water source. Pop-up type sprayers work very well for germination of seeds, but they should have risers that extend a minimum of two feet high when activated. Shorter sprayers will eventually be blocked as flowers start to develop, leaving dry areas throughout the display.

Taking advantage of wetting patterns from drip irrigation will create colorful bouquets dotted throughout the landscape. However, if you will be handwatering displays with a hose, use a "water wand" or some similar type of hose-end sprayer to disperse the water softly to avoid washing the seed away.

The soil should be kept moist for four to six weeks. The frequency of watering will depend upon rainfall, soil type, and your yard's microclimate. A heavy clay soil will hold moisture for several days; a sandy, well-drained soil may require watering every day until germination occurs.

You will begin to see your seedlings emerge typically in 14 to 21 days. After seedlings are established—at a height of about one or two inches—watering can be cut back to a good soaking when plants show signs of stress. Stress will display itself in the form of wilt or yellowing.

The most common cause of poor wildflower germination is sowing seeds too deeply.

Thinning

When seedlings emerge, you will need to evaluate whether or not the bed will require thinning. Many gardeners are so thrilled with excellent germination that they hesitate to give up any seedlings. Understand that it is to the benefit of your flowers to do some thinning if the bed is overcrowded. Left alone, closely spaced flowers will not thrive, due to competition for water, nutrients, and light. Eventually you will be left with spindly, yellowing flowers; at that stage, it is too late to do anything about it.

Start thinning soon after germination. On average, most wildflowers spread at least one foot. Thinning to one plant every eight inches will create a densely planted bed. Know your flowers and their ultimate size and base your thinning on that information.

Fertilizing

In most cases, wildflowers do not need fertilizer. Remember that these plants are adapted to our poor soils and do not require heavy feeding. Only in a situation where the beds are planted heavily and the flowers are competing for the few nutrients that exist in the soil will you need to apply supplements. In such a situation, use a complete fertilizer that is low in nitrogen (the first number on the package) and high in phosphorus (the second number on the package) to promote blooms, such as 15-30-15. High nitrogen fertilizer promotes excessive foliage growth at the expense of blooms.

You should only apply a small amount of fertilizer. If you are tempted to cultivate your bed prior to planting—adding organic matter or granular fertilizers—remember that the more the soil is disturbed, the more weed seeds are brought to the surface. The glory of desert wildflowers is that they are highly specialized and adept at getting what they need from our soils. That's what makes them so easy and inexpensive to grow.

Weed Control

Weeds are an inevitable part of gardening. It may take three to five years of maintenance to establish a bed that is weed-free. As your wildflowers grow, be diligent about periodically handpulling any weeds before they go to seed. Weeds will be greatly reduced if the area has been prepared properly with as little disturbance as possible.

End of Season Clean Up

It is possible to have color year around. Perennials are key to carrying you through the seasonal transitions. You can prolong bloom time on both annuals and perennials by continuing a watering routine. Also, by "deadheading" or removing the spent flowers, plants will continue to produce blooms.

At the end of the season you will need to remove annuals and cut back perennials. An annual will have completed its life cycle leaving behind a dead plant. You can either remove it by pulling the entire plant out, or simply cut the plant down to the

Spring and Fall Bloomers
Perennials

Blackfoot Daisy
(*Melampodium leucanthum*)
white

Desert Marigold
(*Baileya multiradiata*)
lemon yellow

Eaton's Firecracker
(*Penstemon eatonii*)
red

Golden Dyssodia
(*Dyssodia pentachaeta*)
yellow

Paperflower
(*Psilostrophe cooperi*)
yellow

Cherry Sage
(*Salvia coccinea*)
red

Tufted Evening Primrose
(*Oenothera caespitosa*)
white

ground with a pair of clippers. Avoid leaving stubs, which look unattractive. If you take the extra time to cut, rather than pull, you will reap two benefits. The first is minimal disturbance to the surrounding soil, thereby reducing weed seeds that might be stirred up. The second benefit is that the root system will remain in the soil to decompose, adding nutrients and aeration to the soil. Perennials should be cut back to the new growth.

For large areas, you can also mow the flowers. Be sure to set the mower on high—six inches if possible—to avoid harming the perennials. This is a fast method but will not give you manicured results. Eventually the stubs of the annuals will break down and decompose. This is not a good method for someone who lives in a community with a stringent homeowner's association.

Save Seed

Both deadheading and cutting back are great opportunities to collect seed. This will allow you to share with a neighbor or friend, or to sow the seeds in another location in your landscape. A paper bag works great for collecting. Simply slip the bag over the seed heads and clip. This will help keep the spillage to a minimum. Store the bags in a cool, dark, dry place until the seed has dried out. Then clean the seed to discard the chaff and litter. Store in a jar or other sealed container to keep bugs and rodents out.

The plant lists throughout this chapter will help you decide what to plant in your wildflower garden. These are the author's choices for easy-to-grow, native and desert-adapted wildflowers that are least likely to spread aggressively and take over a planting site. Enjoy!❀

Michelle Rauscher is the Wildflower Horticulturist at the Desert Botanical Garden in Phoenix. She is also a landscape consultant and horticulture instructor, an International Society of Arboriculture Certified Arborist, a Certified Arizona Nursery Professional, and a University of Arizona Cooperative Extension Master Gardener.

Chapter 10

Landscaping for Wildlife

By Catherine Rymer

The presence of wildlife in our yards may bring us endless hours of joy. Listening to songbirds and cooing doves and watching colorful butterflies waft among flowers provide simple pleasure while reminding us of our bond with nature. As more and more desert land is transformed into housing tracts and commercial developments, natural habitats for urban wildlife are vanishing. With careful planning, the landscapes we create can be exciting, vibrant, and colorful havens for our desert neighbors. Inviting wildlife to the backyard can be enjoyable for the whole family. These habitats can serve as outdoor classrooms for environmental education. But most of all, a backyard with wildlife is a fun place to observe and enjoy.

Habitat is where wildlife lives. "Urban wildlife" includes birds, butterflies (and other insects), small native mammals, and even lizards, toads, and snakes. These creatures prefer areas where they can find the right combination of native food sources, dense vegetation, rocky crevices, open space, and available water to suit their needs.

Creating a Wildlife Habitat

The three ingredients necessary to create a habitat for wildlife are food, water, and shelter—for both nesting sites and protection from predators. Most of these animals will become accustomed to the presence of people, as long as these elements are provided. If you are willing to observe closely, your backyard can be a place of adventure for watching and enjoying a diverse range of creatures. You and your family will become stewards of

"There are some who can live without wild things, and some who cannot...Like winds and sunsets, wild things were taken for granted until progress began to do away with them. Now we face the question whether a still higher 'standard of living' is worth its cost in things natural, wild, and free."

— Aldo Leopold
A Sand County Almanac

the habitat you have created.

The most effective way to create a habitat in the Southwest is to include the wildlife's favorite food and shelter plants in your landscape. Studies have shown that native plants attract native birds, such as quail, cactus wrens, and hummingbirds, as well as other wildlife. Non-native landscape plants attract the more common non-native birds such as starlings, grackles, English sparrows, and pigeons. By selecting desert-adapted and native plants suited to our climate and soils, less maintenance, fertilizer, pesticide, or additional watering will be necessary for the plants to thrive. This results in time and cost savings as well as healthier surroundings for you, your family, and the wildlife that inhabit your yard.

Well-planned backyard habitats provide year-round food sources for wildlife. Choices of desert-adapted plant materials are numerous. You can easily have different plants blooming or providing seed sources throughout the year.

Habitats can save energy, protect soil, and improve water and air quality. Placed strategically, plants help regulate your home's interior temperature. For example, large trees placed on the west side of the house will offer shade from the intense summer sun. In winter, sunlight should be allowed to warm your home's southern exposure. Deciduous trees would be a good choice for this location, as they will drop their leaves and allow the sunlight to shine through. Plants can also enhance privacy and reduce dust and noise from road traffic.

Riparian Zones

The most endangered areas of native habitat in the low desert are those located in rare, fragile regions next to natural bodies of water. These are called riparian zones and include streams, rivers, natural springs, and ponds. Many broadleaf trees like Fremont cottonwood, willow, sycamore, ash, and walnut grow in these areas where they have unlimited access to water. Native riparian tree species provide additional layers of vegetation that attract some of the more unusual birds such as Say's phoebe, black phoebe, sharp-shinned hawk, killdeer, nighthawks, cardinals, lesser goldfinch, blue grosbeak, indigo bunting, lark sparrow, white-crowned sparrow, blackthroated sparrow, Bewick's wren, and phyrrhuloxia.

Only on flood irrigated lots can you create an environment that mimics riparian. This is where water from the canal systems is delivered through a series of ditches, flooding the property with 4–6 inches of water. The watering interval is set by the supplier, typically once per month in the winter and every two weeks in the summer. There are only limited numbers of these types of lots available in low desert urban areas. If you are lucky enough to have flood irrigation, you may want to consider the tree choices mentioned above.

Prepare to invite wildlife into your landscape. Be patient; give your landscape a chance to be discovered, and learn what to do once these visitors arrive.

Birds

Attracting birds has become a national pastime in backyards across the country. Many sources cite backyard bird watching as a favorite activity for the entire family. Birds eat a variety of foods. Some are nectar feeders like hummingbirds and are attracted to flowers. Those that prefer fruits and berries include mockingbirds and thrashers. Many are seed eaters like quail, dove, sparrows, and finches. Birds that prefer insects can be considered a method of natural pest control. These would include curve-billed thrasher, northern mockingbird, hooded oriole, and a winter visitor—yellow-rumped warbler.

Hummingbirds

Hummingbirds are especially intriguing for birdwatchers as they dart among flowers for nectar. They can sample thousands of flowers every day. In fact, flying consumes a great deal of energy, requiring them to "refuel" every 10 minutes. Wingbeats have been measured at 20–200 beats per second. Besides hovering, "hummers" can fly backward, forward, and upside down. They defend their territories fiercely, chasing intruders relentlessly.

Hummingbirds shimmer with iridescent colors produced by light bouncing off the prism-like surfaces of their feathers, rather than from actual pigments. There are 340 species of hummingbirds in the world and all are found only in the Western Hemisphere. Southeastern Arizona is the hummingbird capital of the United States. Fifteen different kinds have been sighted at the height of bird-watching season in the summer. Most of these tiny flyers migrate to Mexico for the winter, except the Anna's and Costa's, which remain in the Southwest deserts year round.

Did you know that hummingbirds not only sip nectar but also eat tiny insects and spiders? Nearly half of their diet consists of small insects. Hummingbird nestlings can consume up to 2000 insects per day. Instead of using feeders that require regular maintenance several times per week to keep the sugar-water fresh and the feeders clean, your well-planned garden can provide a low-maintenance source for both nectar and insects. You will

Hummingbirds provide insect control, consuming pests such as aphids, whiteflies, and thrips.

also help ensure their future by replacing food plants and habitat lost to agriculture and urbanization. Spread your hummingbird food sources throughout the entire garden to discourage dominance by any one bird. Hummingbirds are attracted to flowers growing either in the sun or shade.

At nesting time, female hummingbirds collect plant fibers and spider webs to craft their nests. Spider webs left intact in the outside corners of windows and patio doors allow excellent close-up views of the hovering birds. Placing small pinches of clothes drier lint in tree branches will also provide material for the hummers to use.

Hummingbirds are especially attracted to the tubular flowers of chuparosa, hummingbird trumpet, desert honeysuckle, and penstemon (all varieties). Although they love the color red, these tiny birds will visit other nectar-containing blossoms as well.

A Caution About Pesticide Use

Pesticides, especially sprays, can be lethal to hummingbirds. Pesticides also reduce the number of small insects available in your garden, forcing the birds to go elsewhere to feed. Be patient; it may take a few months to achieve a balance of insect populations after you cease to use chemicals. Over time, the tiny predators that feed on insects will keep their numbers within tolerable limits.

Attracting Other Birds

There are many other bird species that will visit your habitat. Traditional ways of attracting other birds, such as putting out birdseed, may actually be harmful. If numerous birds congregate at a large seed feeder, diseases can be transmitted. Offering seed for native birds like quail or dove may also attract pigeons, mice, or javelina. Small feeders that are accessible to only one or two birds at a time are an alternative. Place them where you can see them from your house to give you enjoyment.

For something different, try crafting a bird feeder from a dried gourd and hanging it from the branch of a tree. Remember to place feeders in an open space, where ambush from neighborhood cats can be avoided. Keep in mind that if you also have a flower or vegetable garden nearby, the birds you attract may feast on tender seedlings. These beds can be covered with netting until the seedlings are established and less attractive to birds.

A very effective way of attracting a diverse array of seed-eating birds is to plant an area of annual wildflowers that produce lots of seeds. These seeds will attract doves, white-crowned sparrow, lark sparrow, lesser goldfinch, and many birds that a bird feeder will not attract. Small-seeded native sunflowers will always bring lesser goldfinches into your garden.

By providing dense trees and shrubs, you will give birds places for nesting, escape from predators, and shelter from the weather. Seed-eating birds explore the ground under native trees and shrubs looking for food. Gambel's quail spends most of its time on the ground and so prefers shrubs with low-hanging branches and dense foliage. Abert's and green-tailed towhees will be attracted to dense low shrubs. A mature tree may offer seeds, flowers, insects, or fruit as well as song perches and roosting sites. Even dead and dying trees may provide nesting sites for many species, such as owls. Shrub choices for cover and seed sources include four-wing saltbush, desert ruellia, and brittlebush. Try trees like blue palo verde, desert willow, or velvet mesquite.

Fruit-eating birds are attracted to shrubs like desert hackberry, red barberry, gray thorn, or wolfberry. For an added treat, cut oranges or apples in half and poke onto nails hammered through wood strips. Simply hang the strip in your favorite tree or on a fence to provide a tasty feast.

Provide Water

Water can be supplied in a birdbath, a small pond, a recirculating waterfall, or a shallow dish. The water source can range from a faucet dripping into a saucer to a tiered fountain cascading over several levels. A container with standing water will need daily scrubbing to prevent the spread of disease. If predators are a threat, provide water in raised basins where wildlife can have warning of an attack. However you decide to provide water, make sure it remains clean.

Animals such as baby quail, lizards, and small mammals may fall into standing water and drown unless you ensure a means of escape. Many water ponds or basins may have sides that are too steep or slippery for animals to be able to climb out. Any water source should allow a way to escape: create rough, gently sloping sides at the edge of the water, or lay a log in the water for animals to use to climb out to dry ground.

More than 250 species of butterflies are native to the Southwest.

Butterflies

Butterfly families commonly seen in the Southwest include swallowtails, whites and sulphurs, blues, snouts, brushfoots, and skippers. Most adult butterflies feed on flowers that have large, exposed sites to easily obtain nectar. Butterflies carry their long "tongues," or proboscises, coiled like a spring. They use them with a straw-like siphoning action to sip the sugar-laden fluids.

Butterflies prefer brightly colored members of the sunflower or zinnia family that are shallow and wide enough to provide a perching platform. Choose a protected, sunny, and quiet area for your butterfly garden. If you place boulders or large stones in this area, butterflies will perch there to absorb heat. You will see the most butterfly activity on warm, sunny days when temperatures are between 65 and 95 degrees Fahrenheit.

Adult butterflies and moths, as well as their larval stage caterpillars, are often highly colored. Sometimes the colors are bright and are intended to warn away potential predators. This often indicates that they taste bad to a predator. Other times the bright colors are meant to attract mates. Some are camouflaged to look very much like a food plant in order to help the insect hide. Eggs often have very elaborate shells and may be either brightly colored or very hard to prevent predators from eating them.

Butterflies Seek Host Plants

When selecting a location to lay their eggs, butterflies are very specific about favorite host plants. To propagate the next generation of butterflies, provide food plants for caterpillars to eat as soon as they emerge from the eggs. The caterpillars do a lot of munching, so be prepared for damage to some leaves and stems. You may want to plant enough to share with the caterpillars so you can watch their development and metamorphosis into butterflies.

Caterpillars of queen and monarch butterflies feed on milkweeds. Black dalea is a host for the southern dogface. Plant dill and parsley for the black swallowtail. Most citrus varieties will serve as a food source for the giant swallowtail, and passion vines are favored by the gulf fritillary. By planting evergreen shrubs nearby, you will provide the adults with protection from heat, cold, and wind.

You may get a bonus when the flowers used to attract butterflies are also visited by some of our other native pollinators. Some gardeners plant these flowers among their vegetables to help ensure pollination.

A simple water source can be supplied by filling a shallow

Butterfly Plants

Butterflies are attracted to mass plantings of their favorite flowers rather than single plants. Purple, white, or yellow flowers seem to catch their attention. Try desert lavender, golden dyssodia, red bird of paradise, Goodding's verbena, and desert milkweed or pineleaf milkweed.

dish with sand. Top it off with pebbles for the butterflies to land on and fill it with water just to the bottom of the pebbles. Butterflies don't like to get their feet wet, so don't overfill.

Avoid using pesticides in your butterfly garden. Both adults and caterpillars will be adversely affected.

Beneficial Insects

If you conduct a little detective work in your garden, no doubt you will discover a myriad of beneficial insects. Besides the well-known ladybeetles, lacewings, praying mantises, assassin bugs, big-eyed bugs, and antlions will migrate to your landscape in search of food. The benefit is natural pest control, as these insects and their larvae feed on aphids, whiteflies, and other garden pests.

A surprise to some gardeners, the larval forms of beneficial insects are not as familiar looking as the adults. However, the larvae are often the most voracious predators of insect pests. The ladybird beetle larvae looks somewhat like a miniature black and red striped alligator as it climbs among foliage searching for its favorite food, aphids.

Antlion larvae, or "doodlebugs," trap ants by digging inverted cones or funnels in the soft dusty soil near the base of a house or wall where they are somewhat protected from direct rainfall. The cones are usually one or two inches across and one inch deep. The antlion larvae, about a half-inch long and the same color as the soil, wait just below the soil surface in the bottom of the cone. Wandering ants or insects that fall in can't climb out, and land in the jaws of the doodlebug. The doodlebug usually captures the ant but often flips soil helter-skelter in the process. Antlion larvae eventually pupate in the soil, becoming adult insects that look somewhat like drab-colored damselflies.

Take your children on an antlion safari. By dropping an ant into the edge of a sand cone, they can witness nature in action as the antlion grabs the ant and pulls it down below the soil.

Other Pollinators

The Southwest is sometimes called the pollinator capitol of the world. Besides birds and butterflies, moths, beetles, and some flies help distribute the pollen of flowers. Instead of depending on wind, more than 90 percent of all our native flowering plants and 70 percent of crop plants rely on insects and animals to disperse pollen for the next generation. Honey bees are only one of 1000 species of bees in the Southwest. These various bees pollinate one-third of the food crops we eat. Some species you might

Bees and other beneficial insects pollinate most of the food crops we eat.

discover in your yard range from gentle giant carpenter bees to tiny ground-nesting cactus bees, as well as bumblebees, digger bees, mason bees, leafcutter bees, and others.

Nighttime Pollinators

As evening falls, another group of visitors will find your habitat. Moths, beetles, and bats are attracted to pale, fragrant blossoms such as tufted evening primrose, night-blooming cereus, desert four o'clocks, or tall flowering stalks of agave. Sphinx moths hover over flowers as they feed. They can be mistaken for hummingbirds, as they are almost the same size.

A Note About Bug Zappers

Bug zapper lights are marketed as a way to rid your surroundings of mosquitos and biting flies. The insects are attracted to the light, fly into it, and are "zapped." Entomologists have discovered that these lights don't do the job they were intended for and may actually create more problems.

In reality, mosquitoes are attracted to the carbon dioxide produced by animals and people, not to the purple light of these zappers. Researchers examined six electric traps for 10 weeks and of the total 13,789 bugs killed during that time, only 18 were mosquitoes. Most of the dead turned out to be beneficial insects, including green lacewings, that eat insect pests in your garden. Thus, if you have a bug zapper in your yard, there may actually be more problem pests because there are fewer beneficial predators to keep them under control.

Another negative the researchers discovered: as insects are zapped, bacteria and other particulates on their bodies become airborne, which could spread disease-causing organisms.

Small Native Mammals

Small native mammals are attracted to areas with plants that produce numerous seeds. Round-tailed ground squirrels, which look like miniature prairie dogs, are active during the day and also eat fruit and green foliage. Woodrats resemble large gerbils and are seldom seen because of their nocturnal habits. They eat insects, fruit, mesquite beans, and cacti, and are prone to collecting bright shiny objects for their debris-pile nests. Rabbits may feast on gardens, shrubs, and young woody plants.

Javelina

If you live on the fringes of metropolitan areas, you may have seen the medium-sized, piglike mammal known as javelina. They eat cacti, agave, bulbs, tubers, mesquite beans, pet food, and bird and grass seed and have been known to raid flower and vegetable beds. Usually wild javelina avoid encounters with people; however, if food sources are easily available, they will take advantage of "easy pickins." The crawl spaces under mobile homes sometimes attract them by creating a "burrow substitute." They can be dangerous if cornered or frightened, but the rare attacks on people are usually associated with deliberate feeding by humans. If you know javelina are present in the area, don't leave dogs tied up where they would be vulnerable to injury by an aggressive individual.

A single small brown bat can catch 1,200 mosquito-sized insects in just one hour.

Bats

We are fortunate to live in an area frequented by nectar-feeding bats. The Mexican long-nosed bat and the lesser long-nosed bat (an endangered species) travel thousands of miles each year as they migrate north from Mexico. Bats are strongly attracted to night-scented flowers. In the desert they love saguaro flowers and the fragrant flowers of yuccas and are seen most frequently between April and October. Some agave species have evolved with bats as their primary pollinator and cannot set seed without the support of the bats. There are also several annuals and wildflowers that attract them. Wildflowers like the desert four o'clocks, verbena, tufted evening primrose, sacred datura, desert tobacco, and gilias give added fragrance for these evening visitors. Herbs like spearmint offer additional enticement.

Worldwide, insect-eating bats are an important natural enemy of night-flying insects. Bats are more likely to "hang around" if they have shelter during the day. Bat houses can be made or purchased, but they must be located in a shady place. Small bat houses are not very effective in hot areas of the Southwest, but large bat houses may be very helpful.

All bats are protected by law from being killed or collected (trapped) unless you have a permit. To discourage bats from visiting your home, remove water sources and turn lights that attract insects off at night. If bats take up residence in your attic, seal off their means of entrance while they are out foraging for food at night. Do this in early spring before they have young, which could be left behind in the attic.

Lizards

Most species of lizards, frogs, toads, and snakes found in the desert are beneficial. They consume volumes of insects that would otherwise be harmful to gardens and landscapes. They patrol urban yards looking for spiders, crickets, ants, and flying insects. While lizards are usually active during the day sunning themselves on rocks or walls, you will see geckos, frogs, and toads at night, usually congregating near the lights that attract their food sources.

Geckos are small lizards that have smooth soft skin and are able to utter sounds. They have vertical eye pupils and excellent vision. Climbing walls is easy for the Mediterranean gecko but much more difficult for banded geckos. Often geckos are mistaken for baby gila monsters; however, gila monsters have distinctly beaded skin and very large heads.

Frogs and Toads

There are several species of frogs and toads seen in urban areas. Both are amphibians and must return to water to breed. Toads have rough, dry skin with bumps and are basically land dwellers. Frogs are smooth-skinned and can be found in or near water. Toads burrow into soft soil during the day to reduce moisture loss; frogs seek the shelter of aquatic habitats. With heavy rain, toads come to the surface and sit in puddles as water is absorbed through a spot on their abdomens. Toads reproduce quickly in temporary bodies of water; eggs become tadpoles in 13 hours and develop into toads in seven to ten days.

These creatures are not a threat to people and are important in controlling insects. Piles of rocks will give lizards hiding places from predators, as will the cover of vines on walls or fences. You may find toads burrowing in the soft soil of garden beds. They actually help aerate the soil, an added bonus.

Snakes

All species of snakes are beneficial but some of Arizona's snakes are venomous. Some of these are not dangerous to people, such as the night snake. Rattlesnakes pose a threat to people and pets, but they are also considered beneficial because they eat ro-

Toads can lie dormant deep in the soil for up to two years during droughts, cloaking themselves with a dry hard covering to help prevent loss of body moisture.

dents. If you want to have rattlesnakes removed from your yard, call a professional.

Coral snakes are the only other Arizona native snake that may be a threat to humans. On the positive side, they are found only in remote mountain areas, and their mouth is so small that it is almost impossible for them to bite a person. Many other snakes resemble coral snakes, but their pattern of bands is different. Coral snakes display the red and yellow bands next to each other; other snakes do not. (This old rhyme may help you remember the difference: "Red and yellow, kill a fellow; red and black, venom lack.") Other than rattlesnakes and the unlikely coral snake visitor, you can welcome snakes to your garden.

Be Prepared for Wildlife

If you invite wildlife into your yard, you must be prepared for their impact. While critters like these may be fun to watch, some can cause damage to landscapes and gardens or create other problems. If you want to discourage them from coming into your yard, follow the same principles—remove sources of water, food, and shelter.

Exclusion may be your best option for reducing damage and can be accomplished with fencing. Individual plants may need a barrier of hardware cloth for protection. It is also wise to contain garbage, pick up fallen fruit, keep bird seed off the ground and remove pet food. (If bird seed attracts unwanted rodents, add pepper powder to the seed. Although mammals such as mice are affected by the burn of pepper, birds are not. A product created for this purpose can be found at bird seed specialty stores.) It may be necessary to ask your neighbors to join you in control measures that encourage unwanted wildlife to relocate.

Where to Start

Many residents consider watching wildlife to be a part of their recreation and enjoyment. Sometimes this can even inspire us to learn more about the creatures around us. Why wait for weekends or a vacation to connect with nature? With a bit of attention, we can create a healthy habitat for ourselves and for wildlife. Our yards, neighborhoods, towns, and cities will become a part of the ecosystem and much more enjoyable places to live. As an added incentive, the National Wildlife Federation has found that attractive landscaping installed with wildlife in mind substantially increases the value of a house and lot: a $200 investment in plants can yield a three to ten percent increase in real estate value.

If you are starting with a vacant lot or are planning major renovations, draw inspiration from the surrounding natural environment, including indigenous colors, forms, and textures. Your goal should be to recreate an atmosphere or mood that harmonizes with the desert. Even a small yard can be landscaped to attract birds, butterflies, beneficial insects, and small animals.

Step One

Try to frame your property with a backdrop of native trees. This will help screen the property from neighbors while providing the maximum benefits for wildlife. Choose a variety of species—a few evergreen and a few deciduous. This will mimic nature and provide food and cover for small mammals and birds as well as nesting sites for birds. Plan for the mature size of your trees: a tree with a 30-foot canopy should not be crowded into a 15-foot space. Deciduous trees should be planted on the west and south side of your house to provide shade in the summer, while allowing light to penetrate in the winter when leaves have dropped. Be careful not to block special views.

Step Two

Add shrubs and flowering perennials, keeping their mature size in mind. Mix color and texture of both leaves and flowers for an interesting visual effect. Keep low-water-use plants together. Instead of planting in rows, try staggering and grouping for a more natural-looking landscape. Choose plants that bloom at various times of the year. This will give the wildlife year-round nectar and seed sources.

Step Three

By mingling, rather than equally spacing, masses of smaller shrubs, groundcovers, and native grasses, you will provide protective cover areas for ground-feeding birds. Various birds tend to occupy various "layers" in your yard's landscape. Some are comfortable perching on the tips of the upper canopy of trees. Others prefer lower branches of the same tree. The inner branches may provide special nesting locations. Large shrubs provide the next layer, small shrubs the next and so on down to the ground. Consider the density of vegetation and open areas as layers as well. By providing a diversity of layers as well as a diversity of plant species, you will be more successful in attracting birds and other wildlife.

Changing an Existing Landscape

To create a successful wildlife habitat, it is not necessary to pull out your existing plants and start over. Until new plants become established, some of the trees and shrubs in your yard may provide cover. Develop a plan and work steadily toward that goal until the habitat you envision becomes reality.

Step One

Add small desert-adapted shrubs and ground covers near existing trees. It's never too late to add a tree or replace one that blocks a view with one that attracts wildlife.

Step Two

Use mulch around trees and shrubs to conserve moisture and help insulate the soil against intense summer heat. Birds like to take dustbaths in open areas of loose soil or mulch. Small reptiles can find shelter in wood chips.

Step Three

Design irregular borders around your lawn areas to create interest. Meandering lines or curves slow movement and make things appear natural and undisturbed, mimicking a native habitat.

Group plants and layer heights for a natural appearance and to create multiple habitats.

Step Four

You may want to consider replacing water-intensive trees, like cottonwood, ash, and mulberry, with more desert-adapted ones. They thrive in our soils and climate, usually require less maintenance, are more resistant to pests and disease, and offer a more natural habitat for desert dwellers.

You can restore a small part of the desert ecosystem by incorporating a variety of desert-adapted and native plants into your landscape. The following pages contain a plant list and landscape design to help you start creating your own wildlife habitat. The design contains plant suggestions to create a unique natural landscape combined with a few urban elements.❦

Catherine Rymer is a second-generation native Arizonan. She was born and raised in Phoenix and earned her bachelor's degree from Arizona State University in Education, specializing in biological sciences. Her love of horticulture developed at an early age while exploring the family citrus farm and spending time at her mother's crop-dusting business. She works as an Instructional Specialist in urban horticulture with the University of Arizona Maricopa County Cooperative Extension office where she helps administer the Master Gardener volunteer program. Cathy is a Certified Arborist and member of the Arizona Community Tree Council.

The habitat design in this chapter was adapted from *Planting a Refuge for Wildlife* with permission from the Florida Fish and Wildlife Conservation Commission.

Plants to Attract Wildlife

Trees

Blue Palo Verde, *Cercidium floridum*
Cascalote, *Caesalpinia cacalaco*
Desert Willow, *Chilopsis linearis*
Foothill Palo Verde, *Cercidium microphyllum*
Ironwood, *Olneya tesota*
Lysiloma, *Lysiloma watsonii thornberi*
Mexican Elderberry, *Sambucus mexicana*
Netleaf Hackberry, *Celtis reticulata*
Sweet Acacia, *Acacia farnesiana*
Velvet Mesquite, *Prosopis velutina*

Tall Shrubs

Baja Red Fairy Duster, *Calliandra californica*
Desert Hackberry, *Celtis pallida*
Desert Lavender, *Hyptis emoryi*
Firebush, *Hamelia patens*
Gray Thorn, *Zizyphus obtusifolia*
Hopbush, *Dodonaea viscosa*
Littleleaf Cordia, *Cordia parvifolia*
Quailbush, *Atriplex lentiformis*
Red Barberry, *Berberis haematocarpa*
Wolfberry, *Lycium* spp.
Yellow Bells, *Tecoma stans* spp.

Small Shrubs

Autumn Sage, *Salvia greggii*
Bee Brush, *Aloysia gratissima*
Black Dalea, *Dalea frutescens*
Brittlebush, *Encelia farinosa*
Bush Dalea, *Dalea pulchra*
Chaparral Sage, *Salvia clevelandii*
Cherry Sage, *Salvia coccinea*
Chuparosa, *Justicia californica*
Desert Honeysuckle, *Anisacanthus quadrifidus*
Desert Milkweed, *Asclepias subulata*
Desert Ruellia, *Ruellia peninsularis*
Fairy Duster, *Calliandra eriophylla*
Feather Plume, *Dalea formosa*
Four-wing Saltbush, *Atriplex canescens*
Hummingbird Trumpet, *Zauschneria californica*
Mexican Bush Sage, *Salvia leucantha*
Mexican Honeysuckle, *Justicia spicigera*
Pineleaf Milkweed, *Asclepias linaria*
Red Bird of Paradise, *Caesalpinia pulcherrima*
Red Justicia, *Justicia candicans*
Wooly Butterfly Bush, *Buddleia marrubifolia*

Cacti and Succulents

Agave, *Agave* spp.
Aloe, *Aloe* spp.
Arizona Queen of the Night, *Peniocereus greggii*
Cholla, *Opuntia* spp.
Harrisia, *Harrisia bonplandii*
Hesperaloe, *Hesperaloe* spp.
Night-blooming Cereus, *Cereus hildmannianus*
Ocotillo, *Fouquieria splendens*
Prickly Pear, *Opuntia* spp.
Saguaro, *Carnegiea gigantea*
Yucca, *Yucca* spp.

Flowers, Herbs, and Grasses

Blackfoot Daisy, *Melampodium leucanthum*
Blue Grama Grass, *Bouteloua gracilis*
Butterfly Mist, *Ageratum corymbosum*
Buffalograss, *Buchloe dactyloides*
Desert Bluebell, *Phacelia campanularia*
Desert Four O'Clock, *Mirabilis multiflora*
Desert Marigold, *Baileya multiradiata*
Desert Tobacco, *Nicotiana trigonophylla*
Dill, *Anethum graveolens*
Gaillardia, *Gaillardia pulchella*
Gilia, *Gilia* spp.
Globe Mallow, *Sphaeralcea ambigua*
Golden Dyssodia, *Dyssodia pentachaeta*
Goodding's Verbena, *Glandularia gooddingii*, syn. *Verbena gooddingii*
Lupine, *Lupinus* spp.
Mexican Gold Poppy, *Eschscholzia mexicana*
Sandpaper Verbena, *Verbena rigida*
Sideoats Grama Grass, *Bouteloua curtipendula*
Spearmint, *Mentha spicata*
Spreading Fleabane, *Erigeron divergens*
Sunflower, *Helianthus* spp.
Trailing Dalea, *Dalea greggii*
Tufted Evening Primrose, *Oenothera caespitosa*

Vines

Pink Trumpet Vine, *Podranea ricasoliana*
Hardenbergia/Purple Coral Pea, *Hardenbergia violacea*
Passion Vine, *Passiflora* spp.
Queen's Wreath, *Antigonon leptopus*

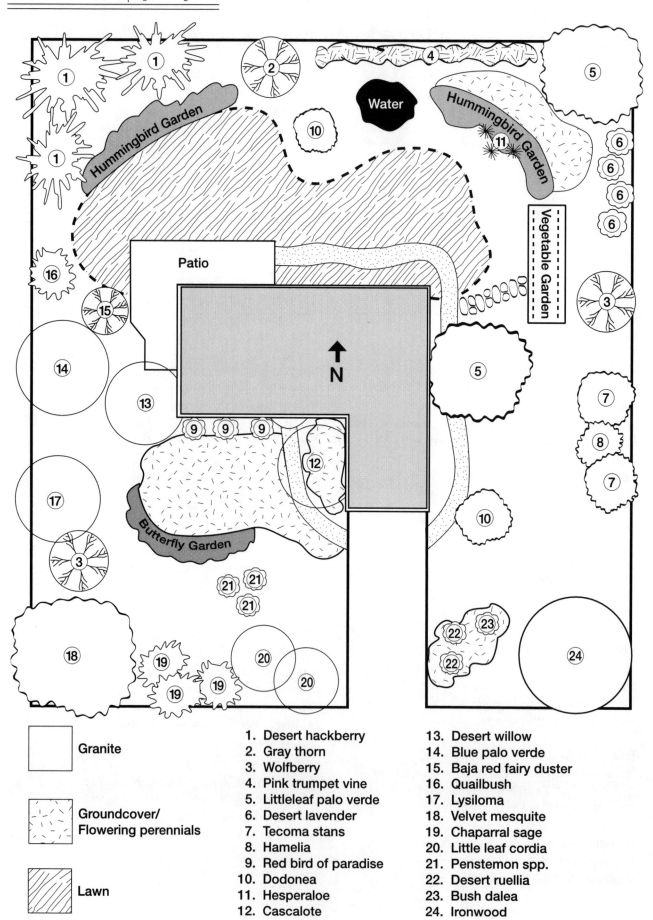

Granite

Groundcover/
Flowering perennials

Lawn

1. Desert hackberry
2. Gray thorn
3. Wolfberry
4. Pink trumpet vine
5. Littleleaf palo verde
6. Desert lavender
7. Tecoma stans
8. Hamelia
9. Red bird of paradise
10. Dodonea
11. Hesperaloe
12. Cascalote

13. Desert willow
14. Blue palo verde
15. Baja red fairy duster
16. Quailbush
17. Lysiloma
18. Velvet mesquite
19. Chaparral sage
20. Little leaf cordia
21. Penstemon spp.
22. Desert ruellia
23. Bush dalea
24. Ironwood

Chapter 11

Citrus Trees

By George Chott

C itrus trees are favored plants for desert landscaping. Fresh citrus, ready to be handpicked, is an easy-to-grow treat. As another positive feature, the trees can have a long life. One of the three original Washington navel orange trees that launched the citrus industry in the United States is still producing fruit! It was planted in 1873 in Riverside, California. Although citrus probably won't live that long in your backyard, it can thrive for many years with proper care.

Selecting Varieties

There are many types of citrus that grow in the low desert, including oranges, grapefruits, lemons, limes, mandarins (also called tangerines), tangelos, kumquats, limequats, and even hybrid crosses between grapefruit and pummelo. For each type of citrus, there are many varieties with different characteristics from which to choose. Do spend some time selecting varieties that suit your needs.

An important characteristic is the taste of the fruit. However, flavor can vary depending on weather conditions, the tree's health, and when the fruit is harvested. The Citrus Harvesting Calendar at the end of the chapter shows the range of dates when fruit is most likely ready to be eaten. You may use this as a guideline to choose varieties to extend your harvest season or to be available for harvest when convenient to your schedule. The varieties listed grow well in the low desert environment.

Important considerations when selecting trees include location in the landscape and overall size at maturity. Many factors influence how well a citrus tree will grow, including the summer's intense afternoon sun, distance from buildings, overhead wires, and other plants, as well as cold spots in the winter.

Tree Size

It is essential to plant trees in a place that will allow them to reach full size without obstruction or excessive pruning. Mature adult citrus trees average 20–25 feet tall and 16–18 feet wide. Dwarf varieties usually grow to 10–12 feet tall and 9–11 feet wide. If you do not want tall trees or if space is at a premium, consider planting dwarf citrus trees. Dwarf varieties produce the same size and quality of fruit but yield about 50–60 percent less. This is still sufficient fruit and it is easier to harvest from a shorter tree.

When determining where to plant the tree, choose locations that are:

✔ Away from all power lines and overhead wires. Do not plant under wires!

✔ Far enough away from buildings, fences, other trees, and property lines to allow the tree to reach its mature size.

✔ Protected from late afternoon sun or western exposures. During summer, the sun's intense rays can burn the skin of the fruit, especially if it is not shaded by the tree's leaves. Even with protection, some fruit loss is to be expected on healthy trees, especially during extremely strong winds or spring months, when trees drop excess fruit.

✔ Protected from cold spots during winter months (November through February). Citrus trees are frost tender. Cold air flows to lower elevations. If you live at the base of hills or mountains, or have low areas in the landscape, you will likely have cold spots where the temperatures drop lower than the official weather report.

Rootstock

Citrus varieties with fruit that is good to eat are grafted onto a second citrus variety, which is called the rootstock. The bud union—where the graft took place— is usually visible as a slight bump or raised area towards the base of the trunk. The rootstock variety offers cold hardiness, resistance to soil-borne diseases, vigor, and/or the ability to thrive in different soil types. Usually, the fruit variety doesn't offer these characteristics and the root-stock variety doesn't bear high-quality fruit. However, together they can produce a long-lived tree with tasty citrus.

For many years Sour Orange rootstock has been the recommended choice for citrus in the low desert. It is adaptable to harsh climates and heavy clay soils, pest and disease resistant, frost tolerant, and it positively influences fruit quality. However, a threat to citrus on Sour Orange rootstock is the Citrus Tristeza Virus (CTV). Once the rootstock is infected with CTV, the tree will die. This virus has effectively eliminated Sour Orange rootstock trees in South America and is active in Florida. CTV has been identified in Arizona, although the citrus brown aphid that carries this virus from tree to tree has not yet been detected. Alternate rootstocks that are resistant to CTV are available. In the low desert, Carrizo or Troyer rootstocks are good choices for full-sized trees and Flying Dragon for dwarf citrus.

When buying citrus, it is recommended that trees be properly tagged with the fruit variety, the rootstock, and the original grower's name so that you know exactly what you are getting. For example, a tag might read: Variety: Lane Late navel orange; Rootstock: Troyer; Grower: "Mighty Sweet Citrus Company."

Citrus Characteristics

Navel Oranges

Navel oranges are favorites for eating fresh, because they are seedless and easy to peel. They can be juiced, but the juice cannot be stored because navel oranges contain a compound called limonin, which produces a bitter taste. A drawback of navels is their sensitivity to heat. The plant will drop many, if not all, of the fruits in early summer. People are sometimes disappointed in the quantity, not quality, of fruits.

Parent Washington is one of the most popular navels grown in the low desert. This mid-season navel variety produces a large fruit of good quality. It is ready for harvest beginning around Thanksgiving or the first of December. Other mid-season navels include Atwood, Fisher, Newhall, Robertson, Spring, and Thompson Improved.

Fukumoto is an early-season, medium-sized navel that can be harvested starting in late October or early November. Currently being evaluated for Arizona, this variety has performed well in California trials. Due to its early maturity it may not have full orange peel color at harvest, although it is ready to eat.

Beck Early should be harvested about the same time as the Fukumoto. Depending on climatic conditions, this navel tends to be more oblong in shape. Beck Early is also being evaluated for Arizona.

Lane Late is one of many new Australian late-season navels. Although these are often called summer navels, they can be harvested beginning in January in the low desert. There are over 13 different varieties of late navels with the Lane Late being one of the most promising. It is currently being evaluated for Arizona conditions. Other varieties include Autumn Gold, Barnsfield, Chislett, Powell, and Summer Gold.

Cara Cara shows off crimson flesh similar to red grapefruit. The flavor and peel color of the Cara Cara is similar to other navel orange varieties. Fruit segments are attractive in salads due to the crimson color.

Sweet Oranges

"Sweets" is a term commonly used to refer to a group of sweet orange varieties that are good for both juice and eating fresh.

Diller originated in Arizona and is a small to medium fruit with comparatively few seeds. This variety is popular due to its productivity and is excellent for juicing.

Hamlin is an early-season sweet orange that performs well in the low desert. The fruit is medium in size with 0–6 seeds per fruit. (Note: 0–6 seeds per fruit is considered "seedless.")

Marrs is another early-season, sweet orange that is a semi-dwarf tree. The fruit is medium to large in size and has 7–10 seeds per fruit. It reaches maturity early in the season and is best when it fully ripens in November.

Pineapple produces medium-sized oranges with 15–25 seeds per fruit. It is very productive; although, it tends to bear in alternate years. The variety was named Pineapple because of its fragrance.

Trovita is an excellent sweet orange and produces well in Arizona's low desert. The fruit is medium to large with 6–10 seeds per fruit.

Valencia Oranges

Valencia oranges are known for their excellent juice, which has a deep orange color and high sugar content. The fruit does not reach maturity until about March, after the earlier-maturing navel oranges have been harvested. Thus, the valencia is a welcome orange when others are no longer available. The fruit is medium in size with few seeds (0–6). Two popular varieties that have performed well in Arizona's low desert are the Campbell and Olinda. Two newer seedless varieties are the Delta and Midknight.

Pigmented or Burgundy Oranges

In cool climates, pigmented oranges are characterized by the dark red color they develop, both internally and on the peel, hence the common name "blood oranges." However, in the warm climate of the low desert many of the blood oranges fail to achieve this typical color. It develops best after a hot dry summer followed by a cold winter. The Salustiana variety produces the most consistent dark red internal color. Other varieties of blood oranges that may or may not develop this coloring, depending on the climate, are Moro, Ruby, Sanguinelli, and Tarroco.

Many mandarin varieties bear fruit in alternate years.

Mandarins (Tangerines)

Mandarins are popular because most of the varieties are easy to peel and section well. The peel is thin and, when ripe, may "plug" (a section of the peel where the stem was attached is removed if the fruit is pulled from the tree). If you are going to store mandarins it is advisable to cut the stem of the fruit from the tree to prevent plugging that otherwise may lead to desiccation or decay.

Algerian (also called Clementine) is an early-season mandarin ripening in November. Fruit size is small to medium. Cross-pollination will increase fruit production and the number of seeds per fruit. If the tree is self-pollinated it produces less fruit with fewer seeds.

Daisy is an excellent early season, very sweet, red/orange mandarin. Fruit size is medium to large, with 0–5 seeds.

Dancy is harvested beginning in December. Fruit is medium in size with 6–20 seeds. Like many mandarins, Dancy tends to bear fruit in alternate years.

Fairchild is a popular early-season mandarin in Arizona's low desert. The fruit is medium in size and ripens in November about the same time as the Algerian. The trees tend to produce more fruit with cross-pollination, but also more seeds. They are alternate bearing.

Kinnow is a popular late-season mandarin maturing in January in the low desert. The fruit is medium in size and has numerous seeds if cross-pollinated. Kinnow is very likely to be alternate bearing. This variety is very sweet when ripe.

Tangelos

Tangelos are hybrids resulting from the cross of mandarin and grapefruit or mandarin and pummelo.

Minneola is a hybrid of Duncan grapefruit and Dancy mandarin. Fruit matures beginning in January. The bright, orange-red fruit is large and pear-shaped and usually has a fairly prominent neck. The fruit has 7–12 seeds. Cross-pollination with Dancy, Algerian, and Kinnow mandarins is recommended for better fruit production.

Pummelo fruit resembles a very large grapefruit but has sweeter, firmer flesh and a thicker peel.

Orlando is the result of the same cross as the Minneola but is distinctly different. The fruit is medium in size without the neck. Harvest begins in November. There can be anywhere from 0–35 seeds. Cross-pollination is recommended with Algerian, Dancy, or Kinnow. This is one of the best juicing fruits available.

Grapefruit

Grapefruit varieties can be divided into two natural categories: white and pink (also called blush or red). Although there is greater demand for pink grapefruit due to a misconception that it is sweeter, white grapefruit is just as sweet if allowed to fully ripen.

Duncan is one of the oldest white grapefruit varieties and, according to some, the best-tasting grapefruit. However, it is seedy (30–70) and lost favor after the Marsh was introduced.

Marsh is the most common and widely planted white grapefruit in the low desert. Although the fruit is ready to harvest in December, it will continue to mature and become sweeter with time if left on the tree. Fruit is typically best from March through

May after acid levels in the fruit have declined. Grapefruits are large with only 0–6 seeds.

Redblush (Ruby Red) was one of the first pigmented grapefruit varieties. It has large fruit with few seeds (0–6). The internal color is a light pink. Fruit is usually picked beginning in December, but becomes better the longer it remains on the tree. Interior fruit color becomes golden in spring.

Flame is a new release from Florida producing large pink fruit with few seeds (0–6). The fruit is mature beginning in December. Flame is being evaluated for the low desert.

Rio Red produces a large fruit with few seeds (0–6). The flesh is one the darkest pinks and the peel may develop a red tint. Fruit is picked beginning in December; however, it can still be harvested as late as July.

Texas Star Ruby produces the darkest flesh color of any variety. However, it is not recommended for Arizona's low desert. The trees are sensitive to hot summers and leaves will sunburn more readily than other citrus trees. Temperatures above 115 degrees Fahrenheit may prove fatal to these trees.

Grapefruit x Pummelo Hybrids

These hybrids are vigorous growers, producing large fruits that can weigh several pounds.

Melogold hybrid has retained more of the pummelo characteristics. The fruit is large, has a thick peel, and a distinctive taste with a high sugar content. It is less acidic than grapefruit.

Oro Blanco fruit is about the size of a grapefruit with a slightly thicker peel. The fruit is lower in acid and higher in sugar than grapefruit and has a pummelo flavor. The flesh provides an excellent sweet taste, but the membranes between the segments are somewhat bitter.

Lemons

Lemons are typically treated with ethylene gas by commercial growers to develop the yellow color early in the season. Fruit can be harvested when green and used well before the rind turns yellow at maturity. Lemon trees are more frost sensitive than most other citrus.

White grapefruit is just as sweet as pink if allowed to fully ripen on the tree.

Eureka is ridged, with a rough rind surface and a small or less pronounced nipple. The tree is thornless.

Lisbon fruit is medium in size and characterized by a prominent nipple. The rind is smoother than the Eureka.

Meyer is illegal (and therefore not available) in the State of Arizona. This variety is known to harbor the Citrus Tristeza Virus (CTV), which is a fatal disease of citrus. (Meyer is not a true lemon, but likely a hybrid of a sweet orange and lemon.)

Ponderosa is most likely the hybrid of a lemon and a citron, which has thick-skinned fruit similar to lemons. The Ponderosa is more characteristic of the citron than a lemon and although edible, is often grown as a garden ornamental. The acidic fruit is the size of grapefruit and has a thick peel.

Limes

Note that limes are extremely frost sensitive and need to be planted in warm areas or protected from frost.

Mexican lime (also called Key Lime) ripens in September. The fruit is small and prized because it is flavorful and juicy.

Tahiti (also called Bearss or Persian) is believed to be a hybrid between the small acid lime and possibly the citron. The fruit ripens in June and is larger than the Mexican lime.

Kumquats

Fukushu has small, bright orange fruit that can be entirely consumed, peel and all. It is a small, symmetrical tree with attractive dark green leaves and is a beautiful landscape or container plant.

Meiwa has round fruit with a spicy-sweet peel and pulp. The fruit is used for preserves and candied fruit.

Nagami is more oblong than the Meiwa, more acidic, and has a brighter orange color. The Nagami and the Meiwa trees are used in home and commercial landscaping and are cold hardy to about 18–20 degrees F.

Limequats

Tavares is a hybrid (East Indian lime x oblong kumquat).

The fruit is characteristic of the kumquat but has a small neck. The trees are popular in home landscaping, and the fruit may substitute for lime as a condiment. The limequat is not quite as cold tolerant as the kumquat, perhaps hardy at 21–23 degrees F.

Planting

Citrus trees are purchased in a container with an intact root ball, as opposed to deciduous fruit trees, which are sold as bare-root plants. Citrus trees are cold-tender, so plant them in the low desert after danger of frost has passed. Spring is their most vigorous growing time and the root structures can expand rapidly as the temperature warms. However, citrus can also be planted from October through February but will need protection against frost.

Young two- to five-year-old trees transplant most successfully. Larger, older trees are more costly, harder to transplant without injury (to yourself and the tree), and suffer more from transplant shock. It will generally be two to three years after transplant before a tree starts bearing significant quantities of fruit. That is the same whether you plant a two- or ten-year old tree, so save work and money by purchasing a young tree.

To plant citrus, follow the tree-planting instructions in Chapter 2. The bud union should be planted above ground, not buried. Citrus trees require regular irrigation, so it is important to build a water-holding basin, or berm, around the trunk, as described in that chapter. The goal is to allow water to seep slowly and deeply

March and April are the best months to plant citrus in the low desert.

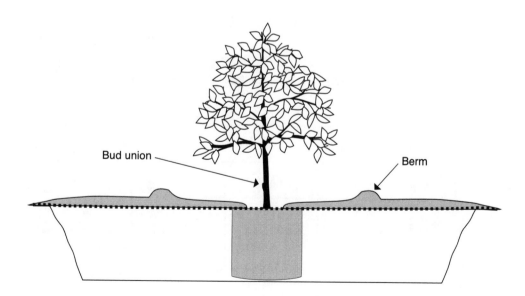

Bud union

Berm

The bud union should be planted above ground to keep it free from moisture.

down past the citrus tree's roots, and to keep water away from the trunk. There should be an inner berm around the trunk of citrus trees one foot out from the base of the tree to keep standing water from touching the bark during irrigation. An outer berm holds the water in the root zone. Keeping the bark dry is especially important as citrus is susceptible to *Phytophthora*, a water-borne fungus. Enlarge the watering berms about once a year for six to eight years to ensure that the outermost roots are being irrigated at least one to two feet beyond the tree's drip line.

It is best not to allow grass to grow under young citrus trees because turf will compete vigorously for water and nutrients.

Watering

The most important thing you can do to maintain the health of your citrus is to water it correctly. The best way to irrigate is slow, deep applications of water that help leach—or push—the salt build-up below the root zone to the bottom of the wet soil.

Table 1 provides information on watering depths for newly planted citrus. Mature citrus should be watered to a depth of about 36 inches.

Clay soils hold moisture extremely well, so watering intervals may need to be extended to allow clay soil to dry out. Sandy or rocky soils drain quickly, so watering will need to be more frequent.

To determine how far water has penetrated into the soil, use a soil probe. A thin pointed piece of wood or metal rod that is at least three feet long will suffice. Push it into the soil. It will move easily through moist soil but stops at dry soil. Repeat in case your probe is blocked by a rock.

TABLE 1 Depth to Water Newly Planted Citrus (In Inches)			
Years after planting	Size of original container		
	5 gallon	15 gallon	24" box
0-1	18	20	26
1-2	24	28	30
3-4	30	33	36
4 +	36	36	36

Irrigation water should also reach past the tree's drip line or canopy. This is where the roots' growing tips are found. The tree needs a strong, expanding root system that allows it to absorb water and nutrients and provides good structural support.

How Often to Water

The following information and Table 2 provide guidelines on watering frequency but adjust as necessary for the condition of your citrus trees. Consider specific features at your site, such as soil type, elevation, and sun and wind exposure. Long-time gardeners realize that each year must be treated individually. Temperatures can be cooler one year than the last, or rainfall can be more plentiful than in past years. It is important to examine your site to determine what is best for your trees.

Newly Planted And Young Citrus Trees

The age of citrus trees begins with the first day you transplant them into your landscape. Newly planted and young citrus—up to three years old—require more frequent watering than mature, established citrus.

Let's assume that you planted your citrus trees during the optimum planting months of March–April. Water deeply every two to three days during the month after planting to help establish a strong root system. Water should penetrate below the root ball. During the second month, water deeply at intervals of three to five days. Thereafter, water every five to seven days through

TABLE 2 Intervals Between Watering Citrus											
Tree Age[1]	Nov	Dec	Jan	Feb	Mar	Apr	May	Jun	Jul	Aug	Sep	Oct
0-1[2]	14 days			10 days			5 to 7 days					
1-2	14 to 21 days				10 days		7 to 10 days			10 days		
3-4	30 days			21 days		14 days		10 to 14 days			14 to 21 days	
4+	30 days			21 days				10 to 14 days			14 to 21 days	

[1]In years, after transplanting.
[2]Water first month after planting at 2-3 day intervals. Water second month after planting at 3-5 day intervals.

the summer until temperatures start cooling off in November. During the cool months of November, December and January, water every 14 days. As spring rolls around and your tree has reached the one-year-mark, continue following the guidelines in Table 2.

Increase the depth of watering on newly planted trees each year until the tree has been in the ground for three years. Thereafter, mature trees should be watered to a depth of three feet.

Mature Citrus

Trees that were transplanted four or more years ago are considered to be mature trees. In the cool days of November, December, and January, water mature trees every 30 days. As temperatures start to warm in late February, March, April, and May, deep water at least every 21 days, depending on the average daily temperatures and the amount of rain received. As the thermometer rises in summer, increase the frequency to every ten to 14 days. With the approach of cooler temperatures in late September and October, reduce watering intervals to 14–21 days.

Usually, how *often* you apply water remains the same for mature citrus trees as they age. However, it may be necessary to increase the *amount* of water used to satisfy the large root zone as a tree grows and the water well is enlarged to encompass its larger dripline.

Do not forget your citrus when you leave on vacation, especially if you are gone during the summer. Water is essential during the hot summer months when fruit is expanding. Set timers properly and check that all emitters, bubblers, and sprinklers are functioning. A reliable neighbor, friend, or gardener who will check your trees for proper care is an invaluable asset. Usually a weekly or biweekly check is adequate. If you do not have an automatic system, leave detailed instructions on handwatering. Do a trial-run with your plant sitter before you leave. You have spent a lot of time and money on your citrus: don't let it disappear while you're away!

Fertilizing

Recent research demonstrated that fertilizing newly planted citrus is unnecessary. Fertilizer is not required until the tree has been in the ground for two years. Once established, citrus trees are heavy nitrogen "feeders" and supplemental fertilizer is required to assure a good fruit crop and a healthy tree. It is important not to overfertilize, which may burn the tree roots. The amount of fertilizer to apply varies depending on the age and size of the tree, as well as the type of fruit. Established grapefruit trees requires less nitrogen than other citrus. Table 3 at the end of this chapter provides a simple way to determine the optimum amount of fertilizer to apply.

Citrus is fertilized three times a year with one-third of the tree's total annual nitrogen requirements applied each time. Trees are best fertilized in January or February, April or May, and August or September. A simple method is to put the fertilizer into a bucket of water and pour the solution into the tree's water well. Water the day before and immediately after applying to prevent burn.

Maintenance

Mulching

Layer several inches of mulch around the base of the tree after planting. Mulch will help maintain soil moisture, reduce soil temperature, and inhibit weed germination. Do not let the mulch build up against the tree's trunk, as that promotes an environment conducive to disease and pests. Apply additional mulch each year. As it slowly decomposes, it adds nutrients to the soil.

Sunburn Protection

Sunburn can seriously damage a citrus tree, leading to a weakened resistance against diseases. The bark on the south or west sides of the trunk becomes discolored or black and may split, crack, or peel off, exposing the wood beneath to diseases and insects. Protect tree trunks or any branches that are exposed to late morning through late afternoon sun from April through September. An effective method is to paint the trunk or exposed branches with a white latex paint specifically designed for tree trunks. It is okay to paint over the bud union. Another method is to shade the exposed bark with a loose wrapping of cloth or newspaper (never plastic), but to remove it at the end of summer.

Frost Protection

Citrus are susceptible to frost and require protection if temperatures will dip below the freezing point of 32 degrees F. Young trees in particular will need protection. Wrap the trunks with cloth, cardboard, or several layers of newspaper (never plastic) to protect them from the winter freeze. Leave the wrap on until the danger of frost is over, usually around mid-March in the low desert. See Chapter 7 for details on covering trees and planting the trees in protected locations.

Different types of citrus can survive different levels of cold weather. The trees can tolerate a few degrees colder than the ripening fruit can withstand. Kumquats are the hardiest citrus, withstanding temperatures around 18–20 degrees F; limes are the most cold sensitive, with leaf damage occurring around 30 degrees. Other citrus varieties fall somewhere in between. As a guideline, ripe navel oranges may be damaged when temperatures are below 27–28 degrees for more than three hours. Fruit on the outside of the tree is more likely to suffer damage than inner fruit protected by the canopy.

Pruning

Note that commercial citrus growers do not prune their orchards, so little pruning is required for a healthy, productive tree. Prune only to remove dead branches or to remove suckers on the lower trunk. Suckers are usually long, fast-growing shoots heading straight up. Prune suckers that are below the bud union, which will be the rootstock's variety, not the variety of fruit that you chose. Pruning should take place in spring (in the low desert from late-February to early March) after all chance of freeze has passed, but before new growth starts. Avoid cutting off excess amounts of new growth and buds. This could significantly reduce the amount of fruit that the tree can bear.

Do not prune citrus trees during the summer, from April through September. When leaves are removed, this opens up the possibility of sunburn on the bark of the tree trunk or branches, as well as sunburning the fruit. Also, it is a good idea to leave the "skirt" branches that grow from the lower portion of the trunk. The fruit they produce can be easily harvested, and their foliage will shade the lower trunk.

Conditions Caused By Weather

The following conditions are fairly common with citrus and need not be a cause for alarm. If you follow the guidelines for effective irrigating and fertilizing, you will have healthy citrus trees that should survive most demanding weather conditions.

Citrus Fruit Drop

Fruit from pea-size to golf-ball-size will drop from citrus during May and June. Citrus trees set many times more fruit than the tree is capable of supporting, therefore natural thinning occurs. Nothing needs to be done, other than disposing of the fallen fruit. Despite what seems like a large amount dropping off, a normal amount of fruit will remain. Fruit drop can be worsened by hot weather and high winds.

Citrus Leaf Drop

Leaves may turn yellow and fall off. Some leaf drop is normal for citrus, particularly in the late winter and early spring as new growth begins. Unusually heavy leaf drop may be caused by overfertilizing or improper watering.

Citrus Fruit Split

Fruit may start splitting in September or October, due to either a sunburned rind or a tough rind that can not expand as the fruit becomes larger. The latter is caused by insufficient water during the summer when fruit is developing. There is no treatment. Remember to irrigate carefully next summer.

Citrus Mesophyll Collapse

This condition will show itself by leaves and fruit drying up and dropping off, whereas stems and branches will remain vital. Rarely is the entire tree afflicted. Grapefruit is particularly susceptible, and it is not uncommon for grapefruit trees to be affected and other citrus in the same landscape to be free of problems.

Mesophyll collapse occurs when there are sudden, unseasonable weather changes. For example, temperatures might become abnormally cold in October for a few days or a week and then warm up to above-average temperatures in November. This extreme fluctuation stresses the trees, as they plunge in and out of dormancy. It is especially stressful if the summer was dry, with little relief from summer rainstorms.

If mesophyll collapse happens, clean up fallen fruit to prevent fungal and bacterial diseases. Maintain a consistent irrigation schedule and your citrus should produce leaves again in the spring. Do not prune out any defoliated branches until spring, and then only after the tree has completely leafed out. You may inadvertently cut out living branches.

Pest And Disease Problems

Citrus Thrips

Insects called citrus thrips may feed on the foliage and rinds of tiny fruit, usually starting in February and continuing into March and April. Thrips are difficult to see with the naked eye. A telltale sign of thrips is the curling and deforming of leaves as they grow larger. Shake citrus blossoms over a piece of white paper and look for tiny yellow insects (about one-sixteenth-inch long) that resemble wood splinters. The wings of adult thrips have a fringe of hairs when viewed under a magnifying lens.

As long as leaves stay green, they are still viable. Do not remove these leaves. Thrips may also scar new fruit as it forms, but this damage is cosmetic only and will not affect the fruit's edibility. Do not use insecticides, as spraying at this time can kill the pollinating insects, thus decreasing the tree's fruit production. Often the thrips are gone before their damage is noticed, so no control is necessary.

Damage from thrips will become more evident as leaves and fruit grow larger as the year progresses. Mandarins and tangelos are preferred hosts, so more fruit and leaves may be affected on these trees than on other citrus.

Phytophthora

Phytophthora fungi live everywhere in the soil. It is a water-borne fungus, requiring moisture to move. It can enter a tree when water is allowed to stand against the trunk, as in a water-filled berm that has no inner circle to keep the trunk dry.

Phytophthora is most likely to affect older established citrus on Sweet Orange or Rough Lemon rootstocks. It kills the bark. Bark peeling off below the bud union is a common sign of this disease. It also shows up as a brown, oozing gum (like dark, thick honey) on the trunk and branches, or the roots may have brown or black lesions. These symptoms account for the disease's common names of "brown rot" or "foot rot gummosis."

Because this disease can quickly kill citrus within a year, your best course of action is to prevent it from taking hold. Start by using resistant rootstock. Sour Orange rootstock is highly resistant to *phytophthora*; however, it is vulnerable to CTV disease carried by the brown citrus aphid which is projected to become a problem in the future. (In practice, Sour Orange is not always available for purchase; Carrizo is becoming a more popular rootstock for the low desert.)

The bud union is a slightly weaker, therefore easier, spot for disease to enter, so choose trees that are grafted at least six inches above the soil line. This makes the graft less likely to come into contact with water.

Build a berm around the trunk of citrus trees one foot out from the base of the tree to keep standing water from touching the trunk during irrigation.

If your citrus tree is infected with *phytophthora*, remove any infected bark, as well as a half-inch buffer zone of healthy tissue. Treat the wound with a Bordeaux fungicide paste. Apply metalaxyl or tris-Aluminum as a drench. These are systemic fungicides that will enter the roots and kill *phytophthora* in the soil

Do not let lawn sprinklers overspray onto the tree. This will help keep bark tissue dry and prevent the spread of fungal disease.

and roots. Follow product instructions exactly when using any fungicide.

Alternaria (Navel End Rot)

This fungal disease may show up on oranges and also on Minneola and Orlando tangelos. It's primarily a problem when storing fruit, but it sometimes occurs on the tree where it can cause premature fruit drop. The decay may appear as a dark spot on the navel end (blossom end) of the fruit while it is still on the tree, but it can be difficult to see. The rot may be restricted to the end of the fruit, or the brown to blackish discoloration may eventually spread and even extend deep into the central cavity. The tips of several fruit segments may display a dark rot, and the juice of the entire fruit will have an unpleasant taste. The fruit may dry and become black and mummy-like in appearance.

This disease is spread by airborne fungal spores. The best control method is to eliminate overhead sprinklers which can spread spores, prune out dead wood that can host the fungi, and dispose of fruit that has fallen to the ground. There is no effective fungicide spray. Refrigerating the fruit will stop the progression of the disease.

Citrus trees do not produce large crops until they have been in the ground at least three years.

Harvesting Fruit

Do not expect much fruit for the first two or more years after planting. Sometimes, it may take five or six years to develop a reasonable crop. It is a good idea to remove fruit on trees that have been in the ground less than two years. This will promote stronger and faster root growth and a healthier tree.

The ultimate test of when fruit is ready to be picked is when it suits your palate! Generally, the longer citrus fruit stays on the tree, the sweeter it will become. As the fruit ripens over time, its acid content goes down and its sugar content goes up. The degree of sweetness is dependent on several factors, including the fruit variety, when it is harvested, and past weather conditions.

The trick is to test the fruit to determine when it is sweet for your tastes and then continue harvesting while it remains viable on the tree. Once picked, the fruit will not become sweeter. Some fruit needs to be harvested over as little as a two-month period, while other varieties may provide edible fruit for as long as seven to eight months, or longer, if the weather is favorable. Varieties such as the Ponderosa lemon or the Mexican Key lime can produce edible fruit year round.

Another factor is the fruit's variety. Different tree varieties will ripen at different times. For example, Marrs sweet orange and the Fukumoto navel orange can begin ripening as early as mid-October. However, Valencia oranges will seldom start to ripen before February. To expand your harvest, plant varieties that ripen through an extended period.

The color of the fruit's rind is not a reliable guide for harvesting because the color is affected by the weather. When it becomes cold enough, the rind will turn from green to yellow for grapefruit and lemons, and from green to orange for oranges. If the weather does not turn cold, some fruit is still perfectly ripe and edible even if the rind is green.❀

George Chott has been growing plants for almost 60 years, including 20 years of citrus growing in California and eight years in Arizona. He completed the University of Arizona Cooperative Extension Master Gardener course in 1995 and has continued to study the care and maintenance of citrus. This includes learning about the citrus problems that residents have and helping to solve them as a Master Gardener volunteer. He has helped to develop simplified documentation on citrus care for the general public. In addition, he has written articles and made presentations to many garden clubs and schools over the years.

Before retirement, George was an Aeronautical Engineer developing aircraft systems, jet engines, rocket engines, and support equipment for several large companies in these fields. He has extensive background in research and development and in test, design, and building of manufacturing machinery and equipment for use in manufacturing.

Information in this chapter on citrus variety characteristics and the citrus harvesting calendar was adapted from The University of Arizona Cooperative Extension Publication AZ 1001, *Low Desert Citrus Varieties*, co-authored by Michael Maurer and Lucy K. Bradley. The fertilizing chart was adapted from The University of Arizona Cooperative Extension Publication MC91, *Fertilizing Citrus Chart*, co-authored by George Chott, Carolyn Chard, and Lucy K. Bradley.

How To Use the Fertilizer Table

1. In the left column of Table 3 on the next page, find a description of the tree you plan to fertilize. The total pounds of actual nitrogen recommended for this tree *for one year* is indicated in a column to the right. Since no fertilizer is 100 percent nitrogen, use the chart to determine the amount of a specific type of fertilizer to use.

2. Look at the top edge of the table for the percent nitrogen that your fertilizer contains. By regulation, every container of fertilizer must have 3 numbers written on it. The first number indicates the percent nitrogen, the second the percent phosphorus, and the third the percent potassium. (For example: 21-0-0 has 21 percent nitrogen, no phosphorus and no potassium.)

3. The intersection of the row describing your tree and the column indicating percent nitrogen in your fertilizer is the number of pounds of that product to use during the entire *year* for that tree.

4. Give one-third of the yearly total of fertilizer during January-February, one-third during April-May, and one-third during August-September. (This is to prevent loss of nitrogen from the root zone and environmental concerns regarding the leaching of nitrates into groundwater.)

EXAMPLE 1: You have a young tree, planted one year ago and a bag of ammonium sulfate (21-0-0) that has 21 percent nitrogen. Find the row for a young tree. Find the column for 21 percent nitrogen. They meet at the number 1.25 lbs. Therefore, apply 1.25 lbs. ammonium sulfate during the year. Apply one-third of that amount (about 0.4 lbs.) during January-February, one-third in April-May, and one-third in August-September.

EXAMPLE 2: You have a mid-sized adult grapefruit tree, planted 5 years ago and "citrus food" fertilizer with 10 percent nitrogen. (10 is the first of the three numbers on the bag.) *Note that mature grapefruit trees require only half of the amounts listed.* The row for this tree and the column for 10 percent nitrogen intersect at 12.5 lbs. Therefore, the year's total for this tree will be about 6.25 lbs. of your "citrus food." Weigh the fertilizer to obtain 2 lbs. Apply one-third (about 2 lbs.) during January-February, one-third in April-May, and one-third in August-September.

All citus trees except grapefruit[1]	Years after planting	Pounds of actual nitrogen each year[2]	Percentage nitrogen contained in various fertilizers[3]						
			5	10	15	21	25	33	46
Newly planted[4]	0-1	0-0.12	0-2.5	0-1.25	0-.75	0-.5	0-.5	0-.33	0-.25
Young	1-2	0.25	5.0	2.5	1.75	1.25	1.0	0.75	0.5
Small, young	2-3	0.50	10.0	5.0	3.33	2.5	2.0	1.5	1.0
Mid-size, young	3-4	0.75	15.0	7.5	5.0	3.75	3.0	2.25	1.5
Small adult or adult dwarf	4-5	1.0	20.0	10.0	6.75	5.0	4.0	3.0	2.0
Mid-size adult or fully grown adult, trimmed	5-6	1.25	25.0	12.5	8.33	6.25	5.0	3.75	2.5
Large, fully grown adult, untrimmed	6 +	1.5	30.0	15.0	10.0	7.5	6.0	4.5	3.0

TABLE 3
Annual Fertilizer Requirements in Pounds for Citrus Trees

[1]Grapefruit trees five or more years after planting: use half of amounts shown.
[2]Pounds of fertilizer are rounded to the nearest quarter- or third-pound for ease of calculation.
[3]Fertilizer products have three numbers on the package, e.g., 15-30-15. The first number is nitrogen content.
[4]Newly planted trees usually require no fertilizing; however, you may apply small amounts of nitrogen after tree is established and new growth has emerged.

How to Use the Table At a Glance

→ Select the row which most closely describes your tree.

→ Select the column that matches the first number on your fertilizer product (nitrogen).

→ Find the box where the row and column intersect.

→ Apply one-third that amount in Jan-Feb, one-third in Apr-May, and one-third in Aug-Sept.

Citrus Harvesting Calendar for the Low Desert

Citrus Variety	Jan 1	Jan 15	Feb 1	Feb 15	Mar 1	Mar 15	Apr 1	Apr 15	May 1	May 15	Jun 1	Jun 15	Jul 1	Jul 15	Aug 1	Aug 15	Sep 1	Sep 15	Oct 1	Oct 15	Nov 1	Nov 15	Dec 1	Dec 15
Navel																								
Cara Cara	■	■																					■	■
Fukumoto																				■	■	■	■	■
Lane Late	■	■	■	■	■	■																		
Parent Washington	■	■																				■	■	■
Sweet																								
Diller	■	■	■	■																			■	■
Hamlin	■	■																				■	■	■
Marrs	■	■	■																	■	■	■	■	■
Pineapple	■	■	■	■																			■	■
Trovita	■	■	■	■																			■	■
Valencia																								
Campbell			■	■	■	■	■	■	■	■														
Delta			■	■	■	■	■	■	■	■														
Midknight			■	■	■	■	■	■	■	■														
Olinda			■	■	■	■	■	■	■	■														
Pigmented																								
Moro	■	■	■	■																		■	■	■
Ruby	■	■	■	■																				
Salustiana	■	■	■	■																				
Sanguinelli	■	■	■	■	■	■																		
Tarroco	■	■	■	■																				
Mandarin																								
Algerian																					■	■	■	■
Daisy	■	■																					■	■
Dancy	■	■																					■	■
Fairchild																					■	■	■	■
Kinnow	■	■	■	■																				■

Citrus Harvesting Calendar for the Low Desert

Citrus Variety	Jan 1	Jan 15	Feb 1	Feb 15	Mar 1	Mar 15	Apr 1	Apr 15	May 1	May 15	Jun 1	Jun 15	Jul 1	Jul 15	Aug 1	Aug 15	Sep 1	Sep 15	Oct 1	Oct 15	Nov 1	Nov 15	Dec 1	Dec 15
Tangelo																								
Minneola	■	■	■	■																				■
Orlando	■																				■	■	■	■
Grapefruit																								
Duncan	■	■	■	■	■	■	■	■	■	■													■	■
Marsh	■	■	■	■	■	■	■	■	■	■												■	■	■
Flame	■	■	■	■	■	■	■	■	■	■												■	■	■
Redblush	■	■	■	■	■	■	■	■	■	■												■	■	■
Texas Star Ruby	■	■	■	■	■	■	■	■																
Grapefruit x Pummelo																								
Melogold	■	■																					■	■
Oro Blanco	■	■																			■	■	■	■
Lemon																								
Eureka	■	■	■	■											■	■	■	■	■	■	■	■	■	■
Lisbon	■	■	■	■											■	■	■	■	■	■	■	■	■	■
Ponderosa	■	■	■	■	■	■	■	■	■	■	■	■	■	■	■	■	■	■	■	■	■	■	■	■
Lime																								
Mexican	■	■	■	■	■	■	■	■	■	■	■	■	■	■	■	■	■	■	■	■	■	■	■	■
Tahiti	■	■													■	■	■	■	■	■	■	■	■	■
Kumquat																								
Fukushu	■	■	■	■	■	■													■	■	■	■	■	■
Meiwa	■	■	■	■	■	■													■	■	■	■	■	■
Nagami	■	■	■	■	■	■													■	■	■	■	■	■
Limequat																								
Tavares	■	■	■	■	■	■															■	■	■	■

Chapter 12

Roses in the Landscape

By Marylou Coffman & Rod McKusick

The culture of roses in the low desert is much easier than in other more temperate climates and we have the added bonus of fewer insect and disease problems. Roses provide splendid color during the cooler months of March to June and October to February. The hot summer weather between these two blooming seasons only limits the size and quality of flowers produced. Once established, roses will live and bloom for many years in the low desert with moderate care.

There are many different types of roses. Two broad groups are Modern Roses and Old Garden Roses, sometimes referred to as antique roses. Modern Roses are those that were developed after the introduction of the first hybrid tea rose in 1867. Old Garden Roses are those classes of roses that existed before this event. Generally, Old Garden Roses can be divided into roses of European origin, which are cold hardy and once blooming (one bloom period per year), and roses that originated in Asia and their many resulting crosses, which are repeat bloomers. Rosarians who grow both types often find that Old Garden Roses require less maintenance than Modern Roses, especially during the hot summer months.

Modern Roses
Hybrid Tea

The hybrid tea is usually considered the most popular of all the rose classes. They are crosses between hybrid perpetuals, bourbons, and teas. They are usually grafted onto other rootstock. Dr. Huey is the preferred rootstock for the low desert area.

The blooms are borne on strong stems with usually one rose per stem. The blooms range in shape from single to very doubles. Hybrid teas are continuous bloomers and many are disease resistant. They make excellent cut flowers.

Floribunda and Polyantha

Floribundas and polyanthas have gained in popularity recently. The floribunda is a cross between the hybrid tea and the polyantha. The floribundas are known for their vigorous growth and profusion of medium to large blooms, which are borne in clusters. There are single blooms as well as double and very double. The canes are strong and shorter than the hybrid tea. These plants are very hardy and most of the varieties bloom continuously.

The polyantha rose is a cross between *Rosa multiflora*, tea, and dwarf china roses. They are small, low-growing bushes (one to four feet) with small flowers usually borne in clusters. Some are quite fragrant. They are very hardy and disease resistant. Polyanthas make excellent borders and small hedges and do well in containers.

Rose Bloom Descriptions

single	5-12 petals
semi double	13-24 petals
double	25-50 petals
very double	50-200 petals

Grandiflora

Grandifloras were developed in 1954 as a cross between hybrid teas and floribundas. They have the flower form and long stems of the hybrid tea, and the hardiness and continuous bloom cycle of the floribunda. The blooms are borne singly or in clusters. The plants are usually tall and bushy. Grandifloras are disease resistant and some are fragrant.

Miniature

The popularity of miniature roses has increased in the past several years. They are descendants of the miniature China roses and hybrid teas, floribundas and grandifloras, with various characteristics of these larger roses. Some have hybrid tea form and others the floribunda. Some are shrubby and there are several climbing miniatures, as well. Sizes range from ten inches to three to four feet. The flowers can be one to a stem or borne in clusters, with single or very double blooms. Very few miniatures have a fragrance. Limited space allocations make them ideal for patios, townhouse gardens, and containers.

Shrub Rose and David Austin English Shrub

Shrub roses descended from many different groups of roses, including rugosa, moss, damask, and species. They vary in shape, color, and flower form. They are very hardy and disease resistant. The flowers are usually borne in clusters and they can be single, double, or very double. Some of the more modern ones are repeat bloomers. The shrub rose makes an excellent hedge.

The David Austin English shrubs are becoming the most popular of the modern roses. Many gardeners consider them to be the most beautiful, fragrant roses available. They were developed over the past forty years by the English breeder, David Austin. He wanted to create a rose that would be a repeat bloomer, disease resistant, with an Old Garden Rose form. Austin used the old shrub roses for their hardiness and fragrance and floribundas for the clusters of flowers, modern colors, and repeat blooming qualities.

Climber and Rambler

Climbers and ramblers are vigorous growers. They have long canes and need sturdy support. There are large-flowered natural climbers and many are climbing sports of hybrid teas and floribundas.

Old Garden Roses (Once Blooming)

As a general rule, the majority of the rose varieties in the following classes are once blooming; however, a few varieties can be found that are exceptions to the rule and can be repeat bloomers.

Once blooming: one major flowering period per year.

Repeat blooming: a flowering period in spring/early summer and another in the fall.

Gallica

Plants are low (three to four feet) and spreading, with small, soft thorns. The foliage is rough, dark green, and oval. Blooms tend to be pink or shades of red and there are lots of stripes and variegated blooms in this class of rose. They bloom once in the spring with small flowers borne on strong stems. Gallicas have been grown from ancient times. They are the roses of medieval monastery gardens.

Damask

These spreading roses are larger than gallicas, reaching five feet or more. Damasks are very thorny, with large, grayish leaves that show noticeable "down" on the surface. The blooms are mostly pink and white and are usually clustered. Some have a "button eye," a round center surrounded by stamens. They are extremely fragrant once bloomers and the source for Attar of Roses perfume oil. Damask roses have been hybridized from ancient times.

Alba

These plants feature an upright and dense growth pattern, reaching six feet or more. They have strong stems and few thorns. Alba blooms are mostly white or light to medium pink, clustered, and semi double. The foliage is bluish-gray, with a powdery appearance. They bloom once in the spring. Albas have been hybridized from the 1600s.

Centifolia

These bushes are five to six feet tall with some dwarf varieties. Thorns can be small or large. The foliage is large, light green, rounded, and some varieties have hair "tuffs" at the base. Blooms are large, very double, and tend to droop. The petals are large on the outside and smaller toward the center. Centifolias are once bloomers, usually light to dark pink and very fragrant. Centifolias have been hybridized from the early 1500s.

Hybridize: crossing two different plants to create another distinct plant. Can occur naturally or by deliberate intervention.

Old Garden Roses (Repeat Blooming)

China

Although considered to be small plants elsewhere, chinas are an excellent choice for the low desert and attain average sizes of four feet by four feet. They form twiggy bushes; the foliage is medium green and pointed and new leaves may be tinted red. The lightly fragrant blooms are small and cupped with thin petals. Chinas are in nearly constant bloom in the low desert, even through the heat of the summer. China roses have been hybridized from the early 1700s.

Tea

The canes on teas are weaker than the hybrid tea canes. Their medium-size blooms may have weak necks and tend to nod. The foliage is dark green and shiny. Teas have a slight fragrance and are repeat bloomers. They have been hybridized since the early 1800s.

Bourbon

These roses range from low-growing bushes to large climbers. New canes tend to be purplish and have some thorns. Leaves are large and dull green. Blooms also vary from medium to large, and can be double, cupped, and quartered. (Cupped blooms have a profile resembling a cup; quartered blooms have petals arranged so that the center appears to be in four sections.) Bourbons are mostly white to dark pink with thin petals. Most bourbons are fragrant repeat bloomers and have been hybridized from the early 1800s.

Hybrid Perpetual

The bushes are usually tall, narrow, and vigorous with large, dark green leaves. Large blooms come in shades of pink and red. Many have the classic modern hybrid tea form. Most hybrid perpetuals are repeat bloomers. They have been hybridized since the early 1800s.

Noisette

These roses are related to the chinas and were first bred in South Carolina about 1802. They vary widely in size and can be small and compact or large and rambling. Foliage is light green and shiny. Blooms have thin delicate petals and come either in clusters or one bloom per stem. They are fragrant and are usually repeat bloomers.

Other Roses

Species

These are the original wild roses. Plants are large and bushy, growing up to 20 feet or more. They are once bloomers in small clusters. Flowers in shades of white and pink are mostly singles (five petals) and have a long blooming cycle. They usually have leaves with seven or more leaflets. They have been grown from ancient times.

There are several other fairly new groups of roses. There are patio or tree roses, landscaping roses, groundcover roses, and cascading roses. They come in all of the above types, including miniatures.

Choosing Roses To Plant

When you consider purchasing a rose, you'll find a variety, color, shape, or size to fit any space. (See Appendix B for help in choosing varieties.) Roses can be purchased through a catalog or from a nursery or discount store. Old Garden Roses are not as easily found at nurseries, so are frequently purchased through mail-order companies that specialize in these roses.

Choose only #1 grade rose bushes, as they have the best chance of surviving our summer heat. Most Modern Roses are bought as bare-root plants, meaning they're not in containers with soil. The plant should have at least three to four plump, green healthy canes. Do not buy them if the canes are spindly or if they have started to leaf out. Examine the roots, which should be soft and pliable, not dried out. Don't buy the rose if it has been dipped in wax, as our hot sun will burn it.

Most Old Garden Roses and miniatures are propagated from cuttings and thus are living on their own roots, as opposed to being grafted onto a different variety of rootstock. For novice growers, it is sometimes easier to get started with container-grown plants. Also, if you won't have time to plant the roses immediately, it may be better to buy container roses so that bare roots aren't left exposed.

Determine the mature size of the rose and the space where you want to plant it. Roses need plenty of sunshine and air circulation to help prevent powdery mildew, so don't crowd the bushes. See the Spacing Between Plants chart for help in determining how much overall room you will require.

*Old Garden Roses can often grow considerably larger in the low desert than most catalog descriptions indicate. Add two feet to the width and three feet to the height given in catalogs. For plant descriptions that do not include width dimensions, a general guideline is that the width of the plant will equal the height.

Planting Bare-Root Modern Roses

Locate your rose garden in an area where it will receive at least six hours of sunlight a day. Roses can be grown in beds, borders, and pots, as hedges or fences, along a walkway, or just about anywhere as long as they have good soil and drainage.

An eastern exposure is best as they will receive morning sun and protection from the hot afternoon rays. Avoid locations close to light-colored walls with southern or western exposures, which will have a lot of reflected heat. Place roses where they do not compete with roots of trees or shrubs for nutrients.

Climbers do well on eastern walls. Modern Roses should be planted about 12–18 inches away from the wall to allow for air circulation. Old Garden Climbers are often larger and should be planted about 18–24 inches away from the wall. Spread the canes to produce large masses of flowers. Carefully evaluate northern walls before deciding to plant there. Even if the climber receives enought light to live, it may have spindly growth on the bottom of the plant, with the majority of the leaves and blooms high on the top, where the sun hits.

The best time to plant bare-root roses in the low desert is mid-December through February. Soak the entire rose bush in water for eight to 24 hours prior to planting. Dig the hole at least

Spacing Between Plants	
Rose type	Distance (feet)
Hybrid teas	3-5
Grandifloras	3-5
Floribundas	3
Shrubs	2-4
Polyanthas	1-1.5
Miniatures	1-2
Climbers	6-10
Tree roses	3-5
Old garden*	3-5

*See text for explanation.

18–30 inches deep and 18–30 inches wide, depending on the size of the rose. In the bottom of the hole, add one cup soil sulfur or gypsum and one cup triple superphosphate or bone meal for phosphorus. Phosphorus promotes vigorous blooming.

Create a soil mix to fill in the hole. You can simply mix half native soil and half forest mulch. Another recommended soil mixture is one-third each native soil, compost or forest mulch, and sand, perlite, or pumice. The most important feature is good drainage and these "recipes" will promote that.

Add two or three shovels of the soil mix to the planting hole and make a cone shape of it. Spread the roots of the rose bush over the cone. The bud union should be about two inches above the soil level to prevent possible disease. The bud union is where the rose was grafted onto the rootstock. It is usually noticeable as a slight bump or raised area.

Cover the roots with the rest of the soil mixture, firming the soil around the bush. Mounding with moist soil or mulch protects the canes from drying out while the root system is becoming established. Leave this on for 14–21 days. Water slowly and deeply to eliminate air pockets and prevent the rose from drying out. Water every day for the first week.

Immediately after planting, trim the canes back to eight to

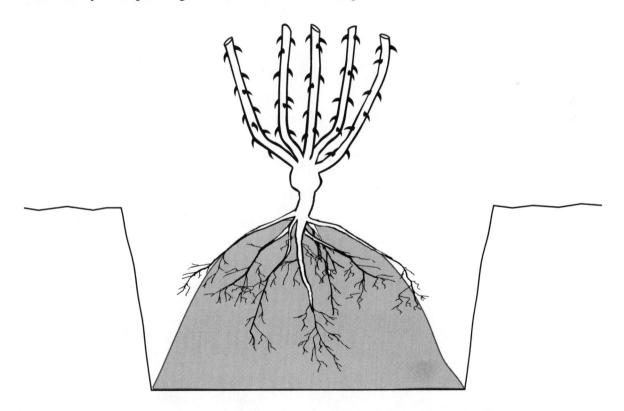

To plant a bareroot rose, spread the roots over a cone of soil.
The bud union should be above the soil line.

ten inches. Cut to an outward facing bud eye. (A bud eye is found at the end of each leaf axil, where the leaf joins the stem. When canes are bare, it can usually be seen as a slight swelling or bump.) An outward facing bud eye can face in any direction, except towards the center of the bush, which would interfere with air circulation and cause branches to cross or rub against each other. Seal the cuts with a wood glue to help prevent cane borer insects from entering.

Transplanting Container-Grown Modern Roses and Old Garden Roses

Container-grown roses can be planted any time of the year, but spring or fall is best. Soil preparation is the same as for bare-root roses. There is no need for a cone, but dig the hole as wide and as deep as for the bare-root roses. The plants should be carefully removed from the containers, disturbing the root ball as little as possible. If the roots are coiled, carefully straighten them out. Place the plant in the ground at the same level as it was in the pot and firm the soil around the root ball to eliminate any air pockets.

Old Garden Roses are sold in containers that range from three-inch tubes to one- or two-gallon pots. If desired, the smaller ones can be "potted up" into larger containers to establish more vigorous root systems before transplanting into the landscape. The one- and two-gallon Old Garden Roses are ready to be planted directly into the ground. Recall that they are usually not grafted onto other rootstock, so you don't have to be concerned about planting the bud union above ground. Nor is it necessary to mound soil around the base of the canes on Old Garden Roses.

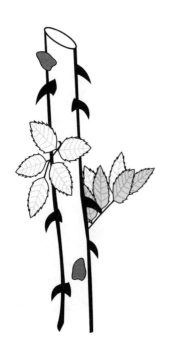

When trimming canes, cut back to an outward facing bud eye so the new growth won't head towards the center of the bush. Make cuts at a 45-degree angle.

Transplanting Existing Roses

Roses that are healthy and have grown well can be transplanted to another location, if necessary. However, if they are three years or older, consider buying new plants. Most varieties are inexpensive and available all year.

Before transplanting, cut the top back one-third to one-half. Save as much of the root system as possible when digging. Small bushes can be moved as bare-root plants. Larger specimens should be transplanted by taking a ball of soil with the roots. Plant in the same manner as described for new roses. The best time for transplanting is December through March.

Growing Roses in Containers

Almost any rose can be grown in a container. They require more frequent watering and fertilizing, as well as protection during hot summer afternoons. Container-grown roses need to be repotted at least every three years or sooner if they become root bound. Just move them to a larger pot. Miniature roses can easily be divided when they outgrow their pots.

Basic Rose Care

Watering

Soil moisture should be maintained to a depth of two to three feet. The amount of water required depends on your soil's characteristics, weather conditions, and the particular microclimate in which you live. Irrigate slowly to ensure water penetrates through the entire root zone. This is important not only to supply moisture to the root system, but also to leach—or push—salts beyond the root zone.

Roses require more frequent watering than most other landscape plants. During the cool winter months, water roses once a week or when needed. In spring and fall, loam soils are usually irrigated two to three times per week. During the summer heat you will probably need to water three or four times per week. You may have to water every day, depending on your soil and weather conditions. (Clay soil retains more moisture than sandy soil. Loam soil is in the middle.)

Container roses need to be watered two or three times per week during cool weather and as much as once a day in warm temperatures. Watch them carefully in the summer for signs of stress, such as wilting or yellow leaves.

Cultivating

The principal reason for cultivation is to keep grasses and weeds from invading the rose beds. If your rose bed is not too large, you can pull weeds by hand. Or cut weeds by shallow scraping of the soil so as not to disturb the rose's feeder roots developing and functioning near the surface. Shallower feeder roots are especially abundant if a mulch has been used. Avoid spading the bed as it will cut large numbers of feeding roots.

Mulching materials such as compost, forest mulch, straw, or wood chips should be applied throughout the year. Layer three to four inches around each bush but away from the stem. Mulch helps reduce weeds, retains soil moisture, and keeps roots cool. It also builds a healthy soil structure as it decomposes over time.

Fertilizing

Roses are heavy "feeders" that need to be supplied with nitrogen and phosphorus. It is better to apply small amounts of a slow-release fertilizer every six weeks during the growing season, rather than a heavy application once a year. The first application of slow-release fertilizer should be applied after the roses have been pruned in January and February and repeated every six weeks until June. For Old Garden Roses that aren't pruned until after blooming, start fertilizing in January or February anyway to promote flowers. This is usually sufficient for most roses in a home landscape situation.

However, gardeners who compete in rose shows often supplement the above regimen with a liquid fertilizer every week or two during the same months. Liquid rose fertilizers, which are readily available to the plant, can be applied to the soil or sprayed directly on the foliage. A note of caution is in order: foliar feedings are practiced only during the relatively cooler weather of March–April and late September–October when the roses are in peak bloom periods. Apply early in the day before the sun heats up. Test a few leaves before spraying the entire bush. Using spray fertilizers during the hot summer will likely burn the foliage and is not recommended.

Some rosarians recommend that roses be given a break during the hot summer months with no fertilizer applications. Then start the slow-release fertilizer again in September, with the last application around mid-October. Other rosarians prefer to continue using slow-release fertilizer at half-strength throughout the summer. Determine what works best for your conditions.

Miniature roses usually require less fertilizer than other types. Container roses require less total fertilizer than those grown in the ground; however, they need more frequent applications as their roots can't seek further nutrients beyond the confines of their pot. Always water thoroughly before and after fertilizing to help prevent burn. Follow directions on the container when using any fertilizer.

Hose off roses periodically with water. This will keep the roses clean, increase the surrounding humidity, and help to control insects. Spray early in the morning before the sun gets hot to decrease chances of leaf burn. Be sure to spray the undersides of leaves.

Tips for Summer Care

Roses slow down during our hot months and produce smaller and fewer blooms. Remove spent blooms by cutting back to the first five-leaflet set. Leave as much foliage as possible, which will help to shade the bush.

Shade the trunks of tree roses during hot summers to prevent sunburn. Painting the trunk with white tree paint or covering the trunk with cardboard or shade cloth will also help.

Pruning

Why Do We Prune Roses?

The reason for pruning is to cut back the size and number of canes to produce the highest quality of blooms. A rose bush will come out of dormancy with a certain amount of stored energy. If the energy is directed to a few bud eyes, then the resulting stems will be longer and the blooms larger. The bush will also direct some of the energy toward producing highly prized basal canes. These are new canes that grow from the bud union and will produce blooms. If the top growth is allowed to become too thick, there will be very little, if any, basal growth.

Light pruning removes about one-third of the plant. This will result in a larger bush with more blooms on shorter, smaller stems. This is sufficient pruning for floribundas, shrubs, and hedge roses.

Moderate pruning will leave six to ten canes. Canes are pruned back to remove about one-half the bush. This will produce a larger bush and ample blooms and is the best method for the average garden.

Heavy pruning will leave three or four canes. The canes will produce a few large long-stemmed blooms of show quality.

Pruning Modern Roses

The correct balance of pruning is to keep the bush producing an adequate number of long healthy canes for an abundance of flowers every year. These are the canes growing directly from the bud union thereby supplying new wood on an annual basis. For Modern Roses, new wood produces the best blooms. Even bushes fifty years old can remain productive with annual pruning. A rose left unpruned will still continue to grow and bloom, though its stems will be short and the flowers small. It will produce fewer canes to supply the best blooms for the next three or four years.

When pruning, cut out dead and diseased wood, thin out weak and crossing canes, and shape the bush. If you have two canes that grow right next to each other and they can't be spread apart, remove the older or smaller of the two, leaving the most vigorous on the bush. Prune to achieve plant balance.

Winter pruning also provides the best opportunity for you to practice your artistic talents in shaping your bushes for better appearance and performance. The most desirable Modern Rose bush form is an urn or vase, where canes grow from the bud union like spokes of a wheel, outward and upward around an open cen-

Clean up all debris around your rose bush after pruning. Plant debris can harbor disease and pest problems.

ter. The perfect shape is sometimes hard to achieve, but you can work toward that end by removing canes that grow straight up through the center of the bush and those that grow into the center.

Pruning Old Garden Roses

There are a few differences to note when pruning Old Garden Roses. The once-blooming antique roses bloom on old wood (not new wood) and should be pruned *after* their bloom cycle in spring. The preferred shape is round, as opposed to urn-like. Leaves are not stripped from the canes on evergreen Old Garden Roses, such as the chinas, teas, and noisettes.

When to Prune

Roses don't truly go dormant in our climate, but they do need a break from the effects of long hot summers. They need to rest to store up sugars and starches to produce new spring growth.

The ideal time for pruning Modern Roses is January or February. If you prune earlier you run the risk of frost damage, later the risk of sunburn. When you cut back roses and strip off the leaves, this is the signal for the bush to start growing again. It takes approximately 70–85 days for the bush to turn around.

Once-blooming Old Garden Roses are pruned after their bloom cycle finishes in spring, usually April and May. Repeat-flowering Old Garden Roses are pruned in winter (January) as are Modern Roses.

Rose Pruning Equipment

✔ Leather gloves and protection for the arms.

✔ Pruning shears with by-pass blades. Other types will crush the canes.

✔ Lopping shears are great for older, woodier canes.

✔ Pruning saw with a narrow blade to reach into smaller areas.

✔ Wire brush to gently remove debris from the bud union, which encourages new basal canes to grow.

✔ Elmer's wood glue to seal any pruned canes one-quarter inch or larger. This will prevent cane borers.

✔ A container of alcohol or bleach (one part bleach to nine parts water) to dip shears in when cutting diseased canes.

How to Prune Different Types Of Roses

Hybrid Teas, Hybrid Perpetuals, and Grandifloras. Prune in January or February, usually after all danger of frost. Make pruning cuts one-quarter-inch above a bud eye that is pointing in the direction you want it to grow. Cut at a 45-degree angle, sloping down. This will allow excess sap to run down the opposite side of the cut.

Prune out deadwood and remove any twiggy growth. Next, prune any canes growing into the center of the bush or crossing other canes. This opens up the center of the bush, allowing the sunshine and air to circulate, which helps prevent diseases such as powdery mildew. It also reduces damage caused by canes rubbing against each other.

Remove one-third to one-half of the bush. Leave four to eight good healthy canes. Remove all foliage. When older canes fail to produce good blooms, cut them back to the crown. If old canes are left on the bush too long, it may be difficult for new replacement canes to start at the base of the bush, so the plant becomes leggy and unattractive. Remove suckers (stems coming from below the bud union) at any time during the season as they are noticed. The sucker growth canes are tall, slender, light green in color with smaller leaves than those of the budded variety.

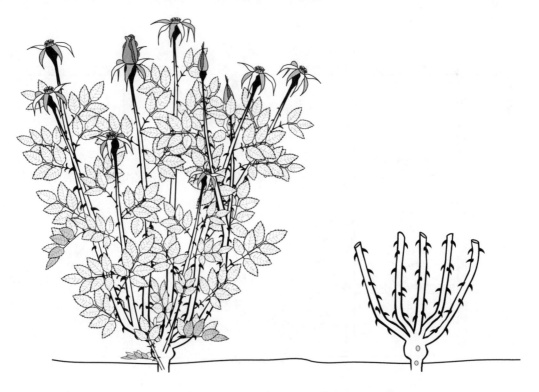

The pruning of hybrid tea roses may seem drastic, but it promotes the growth of healthy new canes that will produce blooms.

Floribundas, Shrubs, and Miniatures. Floribundas are pruned differently from hybrid teas. The bushes are more compact and usually are grown for the mass effect of the flowers. The canes are smaller and will have more twiggy growth. Leave eight to 12 healthy canes. Cut out all crossing canes and any dead or diseased wood. Prune about one-third of the bush. Cut to an outward facing bud eye. Clean up all debris around the bush.

Climbers and Ramblers. These roses usually do not need to be pruned for the first or second year, other than deadheading of the flowering shoots. Then they should be pruned to make them fit trellises, walls, or fences. Train canes to grow up and then out, with the long arching canes trained horizontally. (A vertical stem will only flower at the end of the cane.) The best blooms are on the laterals growing from two- to three-year-old canes. Laterals are the stems that grow from the leaf axils of the canes. Continuous-blooming climbers are pruned in January or February. To prune, cut out all dead or diseased wood and remove all crossing canes. Trim laterals back to three or four bud eyes. Do not prune the tips of canes except to keep the climbers in bounds. Always retain the newest canes.

Train canes on climbing roses to grow up and then horizontally for maximum flowering.

Gallicas, Damasks, Albas, and Centifolias. Prune in the spring after the plant has bloomed. Cut the wood back to the level of the flowers. Cut out any dead or diseased wood.

Chinas, Teas, Bourbons, and Noisettes. Cut out any dead or diseased wood. Prune lightly only to shape the bush.

Container Grown Roses. These roses should be pruned just like those grown in the ground.

Insect And Disease Problems

Desert Southwest gardeners are fortunate to have fewer insect and disease problems on roses than most rose growers in other parts of the country. Some advance knowledge about problems that might occur will help you recognize and manage them before they get out of control.

Cane Borers

The first problem that might crop up in January is the cane borer, an insect that tunnels into the cane soon after roses are pruned in winter. The borer larva eats the pith and the infested cane grows poorly or dies. Cane borers can be stopped by sealing all newly cut canes with wood glue or one of the commercial preparations available. Their presence can be detected by a hole in the end of the cane. Cut the cane back an inch or two at a time until the hole is no longer visible. Seal the cane with wood glue. (Note that pruning cuts on roses are the only cuts that should be sealed. Pruning cuts on trees and shrubs should be left alone.)

Aphids

When tender new growth appears on roses in February, aphids are not far behind. The rose aphid is a soft-bodied pink or light green insect that sucks the juice out of new growth and buds. Aphids are best controlled with a forceful spray of water from the hose. A second line of defense is to use a soapy water spray. (See Chapter 5 for a "recipe.") Spraying with water or soapy water can be repeated daily, if necessary, to control aphid populations. If you monitor the rose bushes regularly and take action as soon as aphids start appearing, it should not be necessary to use a chemical insecticide. Beneficial insects such as lady beetles and green lacewings will soon appear to feast on the juicy aphids.

Thrips

As the buds start to form on roses, look for thrips. Thrips are slender, brownish-yellow winged insects, barely visible to the naked eye. They hide inside newly opened buds and lunch on the flower petal edges, causing them to turn brown. The damage is cosmetic and won't harm the bush. Some gardeners don't experience problems from thrips and report that they are eaten by the same beneficial insects that consume aphids.

On the other hand, gardeners who plan to exhibit in rose shows often control for thrips. If you must have perfect blooms for competition, you may want to spray the buds before opening with an insecticide such as orthene. Spray only the unopened bud, not the entire bush. Otherwise, you will destroy beneficial insects that will consume these pests.

Spider Mites

When the weather becomes hot and dry (May, June, July, and August), be on the lookout for spider mites. The lower leaves will become fuzzy yellow with red specks (mites), with webbing on the underside of foliage. Shake the leaves over a white sheet of paper, look closely, and the rascals can be seen scurrying around. Spider mites can be controlled by washing off the plants with a strong stream of water every two or three days, or more frequently if necessary.

Leafcutter Bees

Circular or half-moon-shaped leaf cuts are caused by leafcutter bees. This is only aesthetic damage and is not detrimental except for roses that will be entered in competitions. Since the bees use the leaves to make a nest and do not ingest the plant tissue, it is impossible to control them with chemicals. Try covering show roses with floating row cover to keep leafcutters at bay.

Powdery Mildew

Powdery mildew will show itself about the same time as the aphids appear. It is a seasonal problem that thrives with cool, damp nights, warm daytime temperatures in the 70s or above, moderate to high humidity, and poor air circulation. Powdery mildew may first appear as small blisters on the upper surface of leaves, followed by white or gray powdery spots. The spots merge and eventually cover entire surfaces. Leaves may become twisted and distorted. Powdery mildew can attack stems, leaves, petals and buds. The growing tips and buds may die if the condition is severe. Powdery mildew is unsightly, but it seldom results in the plant's death.

The incidence of powdery mildew can be lessened considerably by simply using good gardening practices. When plant-

Leafcutter bees take a bite of plant tissue in the shape of a half-moon. This does not harm the plant and no control is needed.

ing, provide sufficient space among bushes to allow air circulation and sunlight. Always clean up old leaves from the roses after pruning and discard them. Periodically wash down the leaves of the roses with water from the hose. This is important to do on a regular basis, as this particular fungus is not able to establish a foothold on wet leaves.

A home remedy for battling powdery mildew is a spray composed of one tablespoon of baking soda to one gallon of water, plus a few drops of liquid dish soap. Products that contain neem or horticultural oil may be used but exercise caution. These should not be sprayed during hot temperatures or sunny conditions, or the foliage will burn. Spray just when the sun is going down or coming up. Before purchasing, read the label carefully to determine in which temperature range the product is effective.

Another control method is to apply dusting sulfur to the foliage every two weeks as soon as symptoms appear. Note that dusting sulfur is not effective after temperatures climb above 90 degrees Fahrenheit.

Rosarians who exhibit in shows usually begin their managment program before powdery mildew appears because it is difficult, if not impossible, to eradicate once it becomes established. They spray with a fungicide immediately after pruning in January or February. Fungicide works better as a preventive measure early in the season before the mildew takes hold.

With any product, follow the instructions exactly. It's also a good idea to test a few leaves first before spraying the entire plant.

Other Problems

Salt burn appears as brown edges on leaves. It is a common problem caused by a buildup of salts in the soil. Salts can accumulate from ineffective watering practices or if an excessive amount of fertilizer is used. Avoid this problem by periodically watering slowly and deeply to leach salts past the root zone. Also, carefully follow the instructions on fertilizer containers and don't overapply. (If a little bit is good, then a lot must be better, does not hold true for fertilizer!) Water thoroughly before and after fertilizing to help prevent burn.

Nutrient deficiency can sometimes be a problem. In the Southwest, the soils are typically high pH (8.0 to 8.5), or alkaline. Ideal pH for growing roses is from 6.0 to 6.5. If the pH of the soil is either too high or too low, some nutrients may become unavailable for uptake by the plant roots. A nutrient imbalance can cause symptoms of nutrient deficiency.

Nitrogen deficiency is signaled by older leaves that turn light green or completely yellow. Reduced growth and leaf size, weak and spindly stems, and small flowers are other symptoms. Preclude a nitrogen deficiency by fertilizing regularly. However, don't apply too much nitrogen, which will show up as abundant foliar growth and very few blooms.

Iron deficiency, often called iron chlorosis, shows up with young leaves becoming yellow, while the veins remain green. If this problem occurs, supply iron in a chelated form, which is more readily available for uptake by the plant roots.

Magnesium deficiency is manifested by older leaves becoming chlorotic (yellow) and reduced in size with dead white tissue areas that are symmetrically distributed on both sides of the leaflet. Edges of older leaves cup down. Some varieties may develop dark brown or purplish blotches scattered randomly across the leaf. To prevent this condition, apply one-quarter cup of magnesium sulfate (epsom salts) to the rose bush two or three times per year. Don't overapply.❀

Marylou Coffman is a University of Arizona Cooperative Extension Master Gardener and certified Consulting Rosarian. She has been a member of the Mesa-East Valley Rose Society for over 10 years. Marylou has grown roses for 21 years and exhibits in shows. Over 200 roses thrive in her landscape. She has published articles on growing roses and is currently co-authoring a book on growing roses in the desert.

Rod McKusick has been growing roses for 47 years and 23 of those have been in the Phoenix area. His favorites are hybrid teas and floribundas. Rod has been an active member of the Mesa-East Valley Rose Society for over 10 years and has exhibited in rose shows during that period. As a retired engineer, Rod fell in love with the landscape industry and has been working as a landscape designer and landscape maintenance supervisor for 13 years. He is celebrating 11 years as a University of Arizona Cooperative Extension Master Gardener.

Chapter 13

Growing a Healthy Lawn

By Sharon Dewey

Landscaping can turn your home environment into a retreat from the everyday stresses of the outside world. A practical turf area as part of an overall landscape design can help achieve this feeling of serenity at home. But can you really have a lush landscape and still participate in water conservation?

The answer is a definite yes! The principles of Xeriscape include low-water-use, desert-adapted plants that can be creatively balanced to achieve a colorful, oasis-like effect. It is surprising to many people that a turf area is included in the principles of Xeriscape. Many low-water-use landscape designs include a practical turf area, usually close to the house, that is a play area for children and pets, a relaxing place for lawn chairs and family gatherings, and an area that traps dust and cools the house, reducing energy needs.

Turfgrass helps break down air pollutants. Since a single grass plant has multiple shoots, a thick lawn can have several thousand grass shoots in a square foot. One square foot of grass can generate 387 miles of roots. This translates into an above ground and underground system that is able to trap dust, smoke, and pollutants such as sulfur dioxide, ozone, and hydrogen fluoride. Turf's root mass and the accompanying microorganisms act as filters to capture and break down pollutants into chemicals that can be used by the grass. Grass, like every plant, releases oxygen, and university studies have shown that a 50 by 50 foot area generates enough oxygen to meet the needs of a family of four. The turfgrass and trees that line our country's interstate highways produce enough oxygen to support 22 million people.

Turfgrasses are efficient groundcovers that lower the air temperature around your home because each blade of grass acts as an evaporative cooler. When the temperature of the sidewalk or street is well above 100 degrees Fahrenheit, the temperature at the surface of the lawn will remain around 75 degrees. Materials such as cement and stone create heat islands, with surfaces that are much hotter than turf in the sun. Turfgrasses are able to trap rainfall better than most surfaces and prevent erosion. In addition to these benefits, a lawn adds a pleasant green that contrasts and blends with surrounding trees, shrubs, flowers, and vegetable gardens.

Turfgrass Choices

Which turfgrass is right for you? Each species and variety differs in maintenance requirements, as well as sun, shade, temperature, and traffic tolerance. Your choice should be based on these criteria. Turfgrasses are divided into two groups based on temperature requirements. Warm season grasses grow in low desert climates from about April to October, and cool season grasses grow well from about mid-October to June.

Warm Season Grasses

Most warm season grasses spread by stolons and/or rhizomes. Stolons are above ground runners—pieces of stem that grow along the ground, capable of rooting themselves. Rhizomes are similar stems, usually growing and rooting underground. Rhizomes can be slender as in grasses, or thick and tuberous as in iris "bulbs." Both stolons and rhizomes produce plants that become established and fill in quickly. Warm season grasses are dominant in low desert lawns, and several choices are available.

Bermudagrass spreads by stolons that grow above ground and rhizomes that grow below ground and send out new roots.

Bermudagrass is the most widely used, but zoysiagrass, St. Augustine grass, and buffalograss are also available. Warm season grasses fade and turn brown in cool weather. Dormancy sets in when day temperatures are below 60 degrees Fahrenheit.

Cool Season Grasses

Cool season grasses that do well in the low desert have a non-spreading, bunch-type growth pattern. They grow by producing shoots (stems) in bunches or "tillers." Perennial ryegrass is the primary cool season grass used for overseeding bermuda. Overseeding with ryegrass provides winter color and protects the dormant bermudagrass. Annual ryegrass is sometimes used but perennial is preferred because its blade is darker green, hardier, finer, and easier to mow. Annual ryegrass is more likely to stain walkways and clothing. When temperatures reach 90 degrees F and above, cool season grasses struggle or die.

Turfgrass Features

Bermudagrass may be common, improved, or hybrid. Common and improved turf types are available as seed. If grass is planted by seed, it produces pollen. Sterile vegetative hybrid bermuda varieties have no pollen production, which makes them non-allergenic. Sterile hybrids can either be low growing types or have a more upright growing habit. Tables 1 and 2 provide information on the main features of different types of bermuda and other turfgrass options.

Planting Method: Sod, Seed, or Stolons

After choosing a grass, you will need to decide on the method of planting—whether to use sod, seed, or stolons. There are sev-

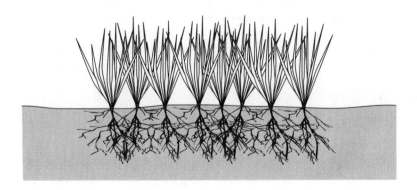

Ryegrass grows in bunches called tillers.

TABLE 1 Vegetative Bermudagrass Hybrids[1] (Warm season, full sun, non-allergenic grasses)					
Features	Tifgreen 328	Pee Dee 102 (Siesta™)	Santa Ana	Midiron (E-Z Turf™)	Tifway 419	Bull's-eye (Bob Sod™)
Color	Bright green	Bright green	Dark green	Dark green	Bright green	Deep blue-green
Texture	Fine	Fine	Medium fine	Medium	Medium fine	Medium to coarse
Shoot density	High. Forms dense turf.	High. Forms dense turf.	Very high. Forms very dense turf.	Low. Forms open turf.	Very high. Forms very dense turf.	High. Forms dense turf.
Use	Lawn. Play area. Putting green.	Lawn. Low traffic. Oasis area in Xeriscape.	Lawn. Average traffic.	Lawn. Play area. High traffic.	Lawn. Sports field. Golf fairway.	Lawn. Sports field. High traffic.
Maintenance	Low to high. Depends on desired appearance.	Low. Needs less mowing.	High. Needs more mowing and dethatching due to fast growth.	Low. Easy to mow with rotary mower.	Average. Stays green longest in fall.	Low. Needs less nitrogen and mowing. Resists scalping. Better shade tolerance.
Drought tolerance	Excellent	Very good	Good	Excellent	Very good	Very good
Recovery from damage	Excellent	Slow	Slow	Excellent	Excellent	Excellent
Available forms	Sod or stolons	Sod is best. Stolons slow to fill in.	Sod is best. Stolons slow to fill in.	Sod or stolons	Sod or stolons	Sod

[1]There are numerous bermudagrass hybrid varieties available as sod or stolons (vegetative). This table lists a few commonly found in the low desert. Different companies may offer the same variety under different product or trade names, as shown in parentheses. When choosing any variety for your lawn, consider the features described here.

Features	Common Bermuda	Improved Bermuda	St. Augustine	Zoysia	Buffalo-grass	Perennial & Annual Ryegrass
TABLE 2 — Other Turfgrass Choices						
Color	Medium green	Medium to dark green	Dark green	Dark green	Blue-green	Perennial is darker green
Texture	Medium to course	Medium to fine	Coarse	Medium	Medium	Medium. Perennial has finer blade
Shoot density	Low. Forms open turf.	Medium. Forms open to dense turf.	High. Forms dense turf.	Medium. Forms open turf.	Medium. Forms open turf.	Low. Forms open turf. Perennial is higher.
Season	Warm	Warm	Warm	Warm	Warm	Cool
Use	Large areas. Not shaded.	Large areas. Not shaded.	Low traffic. Shaded areas. Needs 30% filtered sunlight.	Hardy. Some shade tolerance.	Low traffic	Overseeding dormant bermuda
Maintenance	Average	Average. Fewer blooms than Common.	Average to high. If needed, leach salts and apply iron occasionally. Don't overseed.	Low to average. Do not overseed.	Low. Not shade or salt tolerant. Do not overseed.	Average. Annual needs more than perennial. Quick growth. Annual costs less, but more seed is needed to cover.
Drought tolerance	Very good	Excellent	Good	Very good	Good	Poor
Recovery from damage	Very good	Excellent	Good, but slower than bermuda	Good, but much slower than bermuda	Slow after drought and wear	Poor
Available forms	Seed	Seed	Sod	Sod or seed	Sod or seed	Seed, but don't mix the two species

eral factors to consider when selecting the grass form to be planted, including time of year, water requirements, weed control, runoff, intended use and traffic, and cost.

Bermudagrass sod can be installed year round. Fall is best for cool season grass seed and spring is best for warm season grass seed. Stolons can be planted from late spring to mid-summer.

Sod provides an "instant lawn," although full rooting may take six to ten weeks. A seeded lawn or stolons takes six to 12 weeks to cover the area, but may take up to one year to withstand normal traffic. Seeds and stolons require more initial watering than sod. Some factors to consider when using seed include seed quality, ensuring that seed uniformly covers the lawn area, heavy rains washing seeds away, birds or other animals eating the seeds, and higher initial maintenance. If choosing sod or stolons, check their health and quality closely. Although seed and stolons will get a lawn started at a lower cost, the easier initial maintenance associated with sod may offset its higher initial cost.

> The pH scale measures acidity or alkalinity. Desert soils are usually alkaline, in a range of 8.0 to 8.5 on the pH scale.

Planting a New Lawn

It is essential to properly prepare the soil and install an irrigation system before planting. Other regions of the country may

Which Planting Method to Use?		
Planting Method	Season	Influencing Factors
Sod	Year round	Do not winter overseed unless the sod has been down at least three months, but one year is preferable for rhizome development.
Seed	Fall: ryegrass	Overseed when night temperatures are under 65 F or it is less than 78-83 F during the day (usually October 10th - November 10th).
Seed	Late spring to late summer: common or improved bermuda	Seed when night temperatures are 60 F and higher, usually May to August. Preferable to not winter overseed the first season for a healthier bermuda base.
Stolons	Late spring to mid-summer	Plant when night temperatures are higher than 60 F, usually after May 15 in Phoenix and June 15 in Tucson. It is not recommended to plant after August 31. Bermuda can be planted with stolons.
Plugs	Early spring	Starting a lawn from plugs is not recommended in Arizona. Plugs are not commercially available and if ordered from another state they will not be adapted to local conditions. You can cut plugs from existing sod, but it is labor intensive and not cost effective. Plugs are very slow to fill in.

water lawns by hand or hose, but that does not promote healthy turf in the low desert. See the Resources for information on installing irrigation systems or consider having a professional do it for you.

Soil preparation follows the same steps whether you use seeds, stolons, or sod. It is the most important part of your investment to give the lawn the kick-start it needs to maintain long-term vigorous growth. You may want to have a soil test done if you are unsure about your soil's characteristics.

Basic Steps to Prepare Soil

✔ Remove debris, large rocks, construction material, old turf, and weeds.

✔ Establish rough grade at one inch below the sprinkler heads by filling in low spots and leveling high spots.

✔ Wet the soil to a depth of at least six to nine inches, but ten to 12 inches is even better. Let it dry for two days.

✔ Add soil amendments per the recommendations of the soil test. Without a test, incorporate at least two inches of nitrified wood mulch or other organic matter. Nitrified wood mulch has nitrogen added, which helps boost the organic matter's decomposition process in the soil. If you can't find it at your local nursery, use plain wood mulch. Gypsum applied at a rate of 100 pounds per 1,000 square feet improves drainage. Soil sulfur applied at a rate of five pounds per 1,000 square feet assists in soil pH reduction on a limited and temporary basis. Ammonium phosphate fertilizer (16-20-0) can be added.

✔ Always till in amendments, preferably to a depth of six to eight inches, but at least four to six inches. Never leave in layers on top of the soil.

✔ Install sprinklers. An automated system is best for the lawn's long-term health and for water conservation.

✔ Water to settle sprinkler trenches and soil and to build water reserves in the soil. Allow the soil to dry for one to three days so that it is workable. If soil is too wet, its structure can be permanently damaged. It should crumble easily. When workable, rake and level the soil surface for the finished grade.

✔ Roll the area with a lawn roller half filled with water.

✔ Follow planting instructions for seed, sod, or stolons.

A soil test analyzes the soil type, nutrient content, pH, and salt levels. It takes the guesswork out of fertilizer and amendment applications. Refer to 'Soil Services' in the Yellow Pages or check with your local nursery.

Installing Sod

Sod should be installed as soon as possible after delivery. First, install the long edge of the sod along the longest straight edge of the lawn area. Push edges and ends tightly against each other, then stagger, or alternate, the joints in each row in a brick-like pattern. Sod can be cut to conform to curved boundaries, trees wells, or other landscape features.

Do not let sod that you are installing sit longer than 30 minutes without light watering. Sections installed first may need several waterings before the entire area is completed. After installation, water lightly and roll in two directions with a sod roller. Water four times daily in the summer and two times daily in the winter for newly planted sod. Soak the sod enough to keep the top three inches of soil along with the layer of sod constantly wet, but do not allow water to stand for long periods. When rooting has sufficiently developed to prevent sod from being lifted from the soil (about 14 days), cut watering to once a day in the summer, and every other day in the winter. After 21 days, water two to three times a week in the summer and every five to ten days in the winter. Tables 3 and 4 detail watering frequency and duration for new sod in summer or winter.

How much sod to buy?

1. Measure your planned lawn area to determine the overall square footage.

2. Add 5% for easy-to-measure areas. Add 10% for more difficult areas, such as curved edges.

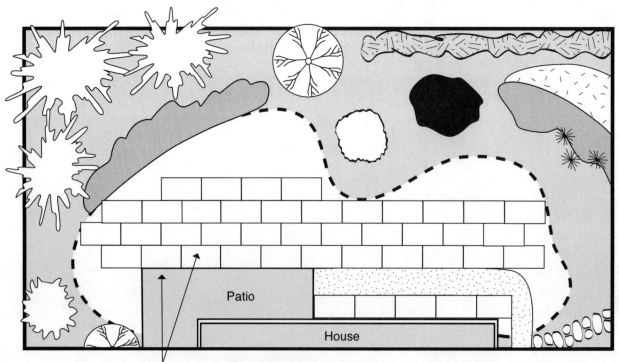

SOD   Begin sod installation along the longest straight edge of the lawn area, staggering the joints in a brick-like pattern.

Sowing Seed

First, measure the lawn and determine the square footage. Calculate how much seed is needed. A general guideline for each 1,000 square feet of lawn area is to use 1 to 1.5 pounds of seed for bermuda, 1 to 1.5 pounds for buffalograss, 10 to 20 pounds for annual ryegrass, and 10 to 15 pounds for perennial ryegrass. Before sowing, divide the seed into two equal lots. Spread the first lot across the lawn area in rows, then spread the second lot at right angles to create a crisscross pattern. Spread seed with a broadcast spreader or a drop spreader. Small hand-held spreaders are available for bermudagrass, which has very small seeds.

After spreading the seed, lightly rake the entire area. Then go over it with a roller half filled with water. Bermuda must be planted very shallow. Apply no more than a quarter-inch layer of mulch to help retain moisture and speed germination. Seed germination varies from five to ten days depending on the variety and weather. Water thoroughly enough to soak the soil six inches deep, then lightly water as often as three to four times a day (five to ten minutes each time) until the grass is established. After three weeks, cut back to once a day until the lawn is filled in.

Sow equal amounts of seed at right angles to ensure even coverage.

Planting Stolons

Certain grass choices, such as hybrid bermuda, St. Augustine, and zoysia, can be started from stolons (sometimes called sprigs) obtained from sod. Stolons have several growing points (nodes) that can regenerate roots and shoots. Common or improved bermudagrass can also be started from stolons. They are planted at intervals of several inches, eventually growing together to cover the desired area. They can be slow to fill in.

Start by digging or hoeing furrows two to three inches deep

TABLE 3 Watering New Bermudagrass Sod Summer Schedule: Temperatures Above 90 Degrees F.			
Time since planting	Watering frequency	Suggested schedule	Duration
First 14 days	4 times daily	8 & 11 a.m. 2 & 5 p.m.	5 to 10 minutes
15 to 21 days	1 time daily	Between 10 a.m. & 3 p.m.	15 to 20 minutes
Roots usually established after 21 days	2 to 3 times per week	Between 3 & 6 a.m.	Water should penetrate 8 to 10 inches deep

Store bagged stolons out of direct sunlight while planting.

and four to 12 inches apart. Next, place the stolons in each furrow and firm the soil around each stem. Alternatively, it may be faster to lay them out over the surface by hand, then cover lightly with soil and roll lightly with a water-filled roller. Bagged stolons should be kept moist at all times before planting. Add water to the bags if you cannot plant fast enough. When planting by hand, plant small sections and water immediately.

Stolons have no root system and must be kept constantly moist for the first two to three weeks or they will die. Root formation normally occurs within seven to ten days. Stolons can be lightly covered with 50 pounds of straw per 1,000 square feet or with topdressing materials, such as nitrified wood mulch, not more than one-quarter inch thick. This will help retain soil moisture and still let the sunlight reach the stolons.

Since stolons are highly perishable, water six to eight times a day (five to ten minutes each time) for the first two to three weeks. Use small amounts of water. Do not allow water to run off or stand for long periods. After 14 to 21 days, reduce watering to three times a day as the grass starts to establish or the weather cools. Once the lawn is established, water according to the guidelines in Tables 6 or 7. It may take up to one year for the lawn to completely fill in, so a regular maintenance schedule is a must to prevent weed invasion.

TABLE 4 Watering New Bermudagrass Sod Winter Schedule: Temperatures Below 90 Degrees F.			
Time since planting	Watering frequency	Suggested schedule	Duration
Dormant Bermuda Sod Overseeded with Winter Ryegrass			
First 14 days	2 times daily	9 a.m. & 2 p.m.	10 to 15 minutes
15 to 21 days	1 time, every other day	10 a.m.	15 to 20 minutes
Roots usually established after 21 days	5 to 10 days, depending on weather	Between 3 & 6 a.m.	Water should penetrate 4 to 6 inches deep
Dormant Bermuda Sod NOT Overseeded with Winter Ryegrass			
Planted in current summer	20 to 30 days in winter	Between 3 & 6 a.m.	Water should penetrate 8 to 10 inches deep

Maintenance for New Plantings

Watering

Watering the lawn is always important, but it is critical in the first ten to 14 days no matter which grass or planting method. Newly planted lawns must be kept moist and may require watering up to four times per day (five to ten minutes each time) until a deep root system is established. A lawn planted from stolons will require more frequent watering.

Mowing

The first mowing depends on the planting method. Mow sodded lawns within two weeks of installation. Seed and stolon lawns must become established and reach their recommended height before the first mowing, usually three to four weeks. Thereafter, the rule is to cut only the top one-third of the grass blade at any mowing, using sharp mower blades and the type of mower recommended for the specific grass planted. Mow when the grass is dry, not after watering or rainfall. Mowing wet grass may damage the plant and spread disease. Table 5 contains recommended mowing heights.

Mowing height refers to the height of the grass just after mowing.

Fertilizing

For seeded lawns, two weeks after seedlings emerge apply two pounds of 16-20-0 (ammonium phosphate) per 1,000 square feet every week until the lawn has filled in. Ammonium phosphate promotes root growth. For lawns established from stolons, apply five pounds of 16-20-0 every week, starting two weeks after initial stolon placement. For newly sodded lawns, apply five pounds of 16-20-0 per 1,000 square feet every two weeks for the first month.

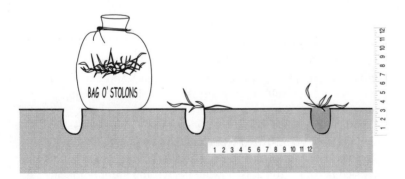

Plant stolons two to three inches deep and four to 12 inches apart. The closer they are planted, the faster they will fill in. Don't let them dry out while planting!

Advantages of mowing at the higher recommended height

✔ Encourages deeper rooting

✔ Uses water efficiently

✔ Shades the soil, reducing evaporation

✔ Insulates the growing crown

✔ Increases ability to produce food through photosynthesis

✔ Grass grows slower

TABLE 5 Mowing Heights[1]		
Turf	Mower type	Height (inches)
Common Bermuda	Rotary or Reel	1 1/2 – 2
Improved Bermuda	Rotary or Reel	1/2 – 2
Hybrid Bermuda Varieties[2]		
Tifgreen 328	Reel	1/3 – 3/4
Pee Dee 102	Reel	1/3 – 3/4
Santa Ana	Rotary or Reel	3/4 – 1
Midiron	Rotary or Reel	3/4 – 1 1/2
Tifway 419	Rotary or Reel	1/2 – 1 1/2
Bull's-eye	Rotary or Reel	1/2 – 1 1/2
Other Turf Species		
St. Augustine	Rotary	2 – 3
Zoysiagrass	Rotary or Reel	3/4 – 2
Buffalograss	Rotary	2 – 3
Annual Ryegrass	Rotary	1 – 2 1/2
Perennial Ryegrass	Rotary or Reel	3/4 – 2 1/2

[1]Mowing heights refer to height of grass just after mowing.

[2]For hybrid bermuda, higher mowing heights of 1.5 to 2 inches with a rotary mower can result in puffy turf that is subject to scalping. Midiron is an exception.

NOTE: These mowing heights will vary during spring and fall transitions from bermuda to ryegrass and ryegrass to bermuda. During September and October, the mowing height for bermuda may be lower than listed because growth is slowing in preparation for dormancy. If overseeded with ryegrass, bermuda can be mowed at a lower height to reduce competition. During April through May, overseeded ryegrass can be cut to one-half inch with a reel mower or three-quarters inch with a rotary mower to reduce competition and shade for the emerging bermuda.

Maintenance for Established Lawns

A healthy lawn is a happy lawn. If you choose the right grass for your needs and follow proper soil preparation and lawn maintenance practices, you will save water, time, and money. You will also give your lawn its best protection against weeds, insects, and diseases. The following sections provide information on watering, fertilizing, mowing, dethatching, aerating, overseeding, and troubleshooting.

Watering

The basic guidelines are to water no more than necessary and to water deeply. The soil surface should dry out between waterings. Do not water daily because it encourages the grass to maintain a shallow root system and to be susceptible to disease. The best time to water is early morning when evaporation is at its lowest, and surface winds have not yet developed. How often and how deep to water will vary depending on the grass type, weather, and soil conditions. Most cities and the weather sections of newspapers have information on watering for local climate and soil conditions.

How Often to Water

Only water often enough to avoid wilt between irrigations. Symptoms of wilt include a bluish tinge and noticeable footprints of crushed grass after walking across a lawn. If wilt occurs five days after the last watering, water every four days. If wilt occurs after four days, water every three days.

Your lawn's specific water needs depend on the weather and soil conditions, but usually two to three deep waterings a week are sufficient for *warm-season grasses* when the temperatures are 90 degrees F and above. Water every five to ten days after the temperature drops below 90 degrees; water once a month during the winter for dormant bermudagrass; and water every five to ten days for bermudagrass overseeded with ryegrass.

Cool-season grasses have different watering needs. See Tables 6 and 7 for watering schedules for other grasses.

How Deep to Water

For each irrigation, water should penetrate the soil to a depth of eight to ten inches for bermudagrass, because 80 percent of the lawn's roots are in the top eight inches of soil. (In winter months, bermuda overseeded with ryegrass can be watered to a depth of four to six inches.) To test if you are watering deeply

Keys to a Happy Lawn

✔ Prepare and maintain soil correctly.

✔ Choose the right turf for your needs.

✔ Water only enough to avoid wilt, but water should penetrate 8 to 10 inches.

✔ Fertilize monthly with a 3-1-2 ratio fertilizer.

✔ Take off no more than one-third of the grass blade at each mowing, using sharp mower blades.

✔ Remove thatch if it is more than one-half inch thick.

TABLE 6 Basic Maintenance for Bermudagrass Overseeded with Winter Ryegrass (OSR)						
	Fertilizing	Watering: Soil depth[1]	Mowing[2]	Dethatch & aerify	Seeding	Sod	Pre- emergent weed control
JAN	Monthly	Every 5-10 days: 4-6 inches	Suggested height			OSR on hybrid bermuda	
FEB	Monthly	Every 5-10 days: 4-6 inches	Suggested height			OSR on hybrid bermuda	
MAR	Monthly	Every 3-5 days: 8-10 inches	Above 60 F for 5 nights in a row, mow gradually lower to .5 inch			OSR on hybrid bermuda	Apply once in March or April, *only* if needed[3]
APR	Monthly	Every 3-5 days: 8-10 inches	.5 inch height for transition to bermuda			Non-OSR hybrid bermuda	See March
MAY	Monthly	Every 3-5 days: 8-10 inches	.5 inch height until OSR dies	Aerify after May 15			
JUNE JULY AUG	Spring transition back to bermudagrass should be completed by the end of June. Refer to Table 7 on non-overseeded bermuda for maintenance recommendations for June, July, and August. If you have followed the mowing recommendations and still have areas growing with ryegrass, they are probably shaded or wet areas, which favor ryegrass over bermuda. Reduce shade and improve drainage to reintroduce bermuda.						
SEPT	Don't fertilize 4-6 weeks before OSR	90 F and up: every 2-3 days. Below 90, every 3-5 days	Below 100 F: start to lower to .5 inch to prepare for overseed				
OCT	Don't fertilize OSR before 1st mowing	New OSR, 3-4 times daily: 5-10 minutes each	When OSR is 2 inches, mow at 1 inch	Lightly dethatch if needed before OSR	Night less than 65. Day less than 78-83.		
NOV	Don't fertilize OSR before 1st mowing	Established OSR, 3-7 days: 4-6 inches	When OSR is 2 inches, mow at 1 inch		Same as Oct. OSR by Nov. 15	OSR on hybrid bermuda	After 3rd OSR mowing, use by Nov. 30 *only* if needed
DEC	Monthly	Established OSR, 4-10 days, 4-6 inches	When OSR is established, lower height			OSR on hybrid bermuda	

[1]Watering frequency depends on weather and soil conditions. Sandy soil requires more frequent watering than clay.
[2]See Table 5 for suggested mowing heights.
[3]Do not apply pre-emergent weed control if reseeding bermuda.

	Fertilizing	Watering[1] to a depth 8-10 inches	Mowing[2]	Dethatch & aerify	Seeding	Sod	Stolons (nights above 60 F)	Pre-emergent weed control
JAN		Monthly	Dormant					
FEB		Monthly	Dormant					
MAR		Monthly	Dormant					Apply once in March or April, *only* if needed[3]
APR	Monthly	Every 5-7 days	Minimum suggested height			Hybrid bermuda		See March
MAY	Monthly	Every 3-5 days	Gradually raise to suggested height	Aerify after May 15	Common or Improved	Hybrid bermuda	After May 15, Phoenix	
JUNE	Monthly	90 F and up: every 2-3 days	Suggested height	Dethatch if over half inch. Aerify as needed	Common or Improved	Hybrid bermuda	After June 15, Tucson	
JULY	Monthly	90 F and up: every 2-3 days	Maximum suggested height	Dethatch if over half inch. Aerify as needed	Common or Improved	Hybrid bermuda	Phoenix & Tucson	
AUG	Monthly	90 F and up: every 2-3 days	Maximum suggested height	Aerify no later than August 15	Common or Improved	Hybrid bermuda	Phoenix & Tucson	Apply once in late Aug or Sept *only* if needed
SEPT	Only if not overseeded	90 F and up: every 2-3 days; below 90, every 3-5	Maximum suggested height			Hybrid bermuda		See August
OCT	Only if not overseeded	Every 3-7 days	Maximum suggested height			Hybrid bermuda		
NOV		If dormant, monthly	Dormant					
DEC		Monthly	Dormant					

TABLE 7
Basic Lawn Maintenance for Non-Overseeded Bermudagrass

[1]Watering frequency depends on weather and soil conditions. Sandy soil requires more frequent watering than clay.
[2]See Table 5 for suggested mowing heights.
[3]Do not apply pre-emergent weed control if reseeding bermuda.

enough, push a probe (such as a long screwdriver) into the ground 30 minutes after watering, allowing time for the water to move down into the soil. The probe should easily penetrate the proper depth. Watering efficiency is significantly increased when the lawn has a deep, strong root system. Proper soil preparation and maintenance will help hold water longer. Also, root depth is directly related to grass plant height. When you mow at the maximum recommended height, the roots will be deeper; thus the plant is more drought tolerant, and should be able to last longer between waterings.

Water Coverage with Sprinkler Systems

Sprinkler systems should have even, head-to-head coverage, enabling water to spray to the center of each sprinkler head next to it and to the heads across from it. Check for uniform coverage and proper operation, at least seasonally, or more often if you see uneven growth, dry patches, or puddles. Gradually change your automatic timer or watering with seasonal weather and temperature changes. After a power outage, check the settings on timers and reset if necessary. Also, reduce watering after heavy rains to avoid soil that stays wet for seven to ten days. To avoid water runoff on slopes, or if water does not penetrate eight to ten inches without runoff, use the "water-and-wait" cycle. Program your sprinkler system to run for a few minutes, shut down long enough for the water to soak in, then water a few more minutes. Keep this water-and-wait cycle going until water penetrates eight to ten inches without runoff.

Fertilizing

Turfgrass plants, like all other plants, require 16 nutrients for healthy growth and maintenance. Most nutrients are naturally present in the soil, air, or water in adequate quantities with the exceptions of nitrogen, phosphorus, and potassium. There are a few other exceptions, but they are not very common in desert soils.

The purpose of fertilizing is to supplement nutrients that are not supplied by the soil in adequate amounts. Overfertilization can cause disease, increased water use, and excessive thatching. Also, the grass grows extremely fast, requiring more frequent mowing, which increases the risk of scalping the lawn. (Thatching and scalping will be described below.) Underfertilizing can result in yellowing, greater susceptibility to disease, weeds, insects, and lower tolerance of active use. It is a good idea to fertilize immediately before a regularly scheduled watering, since the fertilizer needs to be washed off the foliage to avoid burning. It also helps carry fertilizer into the soil to be available for the roots.

Different experts have varying recommendations concerning lawn fertilization. To keep the process as simple as possible, fertilize once a month during the growing season. Use a product that contains a complete NPK blend with a 3-1-2 ratio, such as 21-7-14. This means 3 parts nitrogen, 1 part phosphorus, and 2 parts potassium.

It is sometimes recommended to use ammonium nitrate in cooler months and ammonium sulfate in the warmer months because they provide a faster response in cold or warm soils, respectively. Another suggestion is to use fertilizer high in phosphorus such as 16-20-0 before lawn establishment, after overseeding with ryegrass, or during renovation of an old lawn because phosphorus helps get the grass off to a fast start with a strong root system. However, once the lawn is established, if you use a 3-1-2 ratio fertilizer that contains both ammonium nitrate and ammonium sulfate plus traces of sulfur, iron, zinc, and magnesium, your lawn will receive good nutrition and you will only need to purchase one type of fertilizer for turf. As an added bonus, you won't have to keep track of when to apply which type.

If you choose to use another type of fertilizer, it is important to apply a complete blend fertilizer that contains sulfur, iron, magnesium, and zinc at least once a year. Regardless of the product you choose, apply nitrogen once a month during the growing season in the low desert. This regular schedule is different from other parts of the country where lawns may be fertilized heavily just two or three times per year.

If the uppermost grass leaves are yellow, apply iron three to four times per season. Iron may be present in the soil, but it is not available for root uptake when the soil is cold and wet or the soil is alkaline. A chelated source of iron is readily available for roots to uptake and lasts longer, but is more expensive than the shorter-lived ferrous sulfate. For an even quicker response, use a foliar application, which is a liquid or water soluble fertilizer usually applied through a sprayer. Be careful when using iron supplements as they can stain hardscape features such as pools, decks, walkways, and patios. It is best to apply iron in the morning and let it dry on the leaves all day before watering. Because iron uptake is more efficient when the temperature is higher, apply it after 10 a.m. (especially in the winter).

You may want to do an occasional soil or tissue test to establish guidelines for fertility and soil amendment applications.

All fertilizers list three numbers on the container, such as 21-7-14. This is the NPK ratio, referring to the percentage of nitrogen (N), phosphorus (P), and potassium (K) contained in the product.

A soil test will tell you the nutrient levels in your soil. A tissue test will tell you if the plant is absorbing available nutrients. If you don't have a soil test, you might want to apply gypsum two times per year before the summer and winter rains. Not all soils need gypsum.

Mowing

It is very important that you know how to properly mow your lawn. Improper mowing, along with uneven watering, causes more problems than all other lawn maintenance procedures. Proper mowing will maintain density, texture, color, uniformity, smoothness, vigor, and durability of your lawn. Water use, weeds, disease, tolerance to high and low temperature stress, and the ability to withstand traffic are all influenced by mowing. Mowing also encourages branching and spreading for a thicker lawn. Mowing helps prevent grasses from developing flowers and setting seed. (Hybrid vegetative bermudagrasses do bloom but are pollen-free and do not produce viable seeds.)

Grass Growth and Structure

Before mowing, it is helpful to have some knowledge of grass growth and structure. Turfgrasses grow differently than most other plants. Rather than developing buds and shoots from the top of the plant, grasses regenerate from growing points just above the soil. The growth point is called the crown. Since the growing point is not at the tip of each blade, lawn grasses survive mowing by "escape." Mowing removes just the tops of the blades, so the growing point near the soil surface escapes and grows.

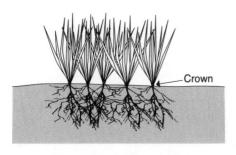
Crown

Roots and shoots originate from the crown. Below ground, the fibrous root system absorbs nutrients and water from the soil and anchors the plant. Deep, thick root systems are necessary for developing drought tolerance and producing a healthy, thick turf. Above ground, stems and leaves take in light and carbon dioxide. A leaf consists of a blade and a sheath; the blade is the broad upper portion, and the sheath is the lower portion that encircles the stem. As the plant grows, older leaves wither and die and new ones take their place. Tillers (upright stems) and stolons (creeping surface stems) also grow from the crown. As they expand, they help make a lawn thick and full. Grasses are either annuals that will last only one season or perennials that will continue to grow as long as conditions allow.

Special Maintenance Needs for Other Grasses

St. Augustine

Fertilizing. From March through October, fertilize once a month with five pounds of a 21-7-14 blend for 1,000 square feet. To prevent yellow leaves, apply iron once in October and once in March, or as needed. A chelated form of iron will last longer than the ferrous form.

Mowing. The denser the shade, the higher the mowing height.

Leaching Salts. Certain varieties have poor salt tolerance. Thus, it is necessary to leach the salts below the root zone about every three months. This can be done by leaving the sprinklers on long enough to flood the yard, but only if your yard is level enough to contain the extra water.

Dethatching. After well-established, lightly dethatch every year, early to mid-summer to reduce thatch build-up.

Overseeding. Not recommended.

Zoysia

Mowing. Although zoysia can be cut at heights of three-quarter to two inches, mowing at the higher heights can encourage thatch build-up. Zoysia usually needs less frequent mowing than bermudagrass. In shaded areas, mow at the higher suggested height of two inches.

Wear Tolerance. Zoysia has excellent wear tolerance when it is growing well during the summer, but it is slower to recover from injury than bermuda.

Overseeding. Can be overseeded lightly, at half the recommended seed rates.

Buffalograss

Planting. June is the best time to plant seed or sod. Sod loses color after transplanting, but greens up after two weeks. Seed germinates in ten days and establishes in six to eight weeks.

Fertilizing. Buffalograss needs less nitrogen than bermuda. Apply one-half pound of nitrogen in May or June and one-half pound in July or August.

Mowing. Requires less frequent mowing.

Leaching Salts. Buffalograss can be salt intolerant, so it is necessary to leach salts below the root zone every one to three months.

Overseeding. Not recommended.

Mowing frequency should be determined by turf growth, not by a set weekly schedule.

Before Mowing

It is essential to make sure the mower blades are sharp before mowing. Dull blades tear and shred the leaf tips, causing browning and an unsightly appearance as well as creating entry wounds for diseases. Continual mowing with a dull blade will drastically reduce the quality and health of your lawn.

The term "mowing height" refers to the height of the grass just *after* mowing. The grass height is measured from the soil surface to the tip of the grass blade. The turfgrass species, lawn use, and environmental conditions are the primary factors that determine the best mowing height. Table 5 provides the recommended mowing heights for several turfgrass species. *It is important not to mow lower than the lowest height in the table since it might expose or damage the crowns.* When the grass is one-third higher than the mowing height, it is time to mow.

When to Mow: The One-Third Rule

"The One-Third Rule" recommends removing only the top one-third of the grass blade at each mowing. Removing more than one-third can decrease root growth and deplete the plant's food reserves by removing the leaves that absorb sunlight and make food for the plant through photosynthesis. This reduces the turf's ability to recover from stresses such as extreme temperatures and drought.

A special consideration exists for the bermudagrass variety Santa Ana. Because Santa Ana has a smaller percentage of leaves to stem, mowing at one-third will result in scalping, which is an excessive removal of green leaves that causes browning. Mow it more frequently in smaller increments to avoid scalping.

Mowing Equipment

The type of mower you use is very important to maintain a healthy lawn. Using the wrong mower can result in scalping,

If you do not want to mow often, you must mow the grass "tall," which means using the higher numbers in the mowing chart.

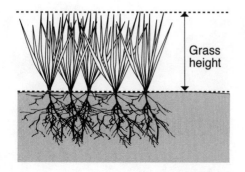

Grass height

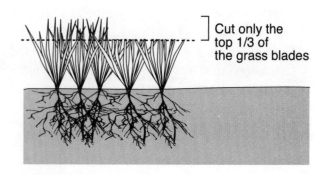

Cut only the top 1/3 of the grass blades

poor mowing quality, and damaged turf. Buy a mower that can be set low enough to mow at the recommended heights.

Reel mowers are the best choice for trimming hybrid bermuda lawns that need to be kept at one and one-half inch or lower. This will result in a fine, well-manicured lawn. Reel mowers are best suited to smooth surfaces and will not cut grass above the centerline of the height of the reel, or tough stalks and weeds.

Rotary mowers work well on turf and are recommended for grass species that must be maintained at heights of one and one-half inches and higher. These mowers can run over rough terrain and cut tougher, overgrown growth; they also are good for trimming around trees. For rotary mowers it is convenient to have an extra mower blade to replace a dull blade that has been removed for sharpening.

Mulching mowers reduce the size of the clippings, allowing for faster decomposition. However, if too many clippings are left on the lawn surface, it may shade and weaken the grass. Do not change proper mowing habits just because you are using a mulching mower. Scalped grass results in a weak turf, whether or not the clippings are mulched in place.

Mowing Tips

✔ Changing directions each time you mow helps distribute wear, reduces compaction, and discourages scalping in the same spots. It also can change the grain, or direction, of stem orientation. This is especially true for reel mowers.

✔ Remove clippings if excessive (more than one-third of the grass blade), if the lawn is diseased, or weeds are setting seeds.

> ### Tip
> A mulching mower allows you to leave clippings on the turf if it is mowed at the proper frequency and height. Clippings decompose quickly and return about 25 percent of the total fertilizer required. Thus, you can use 25 percent less fertilizer. Do NOT mow wet grass with a mulching mower or it will turn into a mass of green "peanut butter!"

Mulching Mower

Mowing at the recommended lowest height increases shoot density and finer leaf texture, but requires more frequent mowing to prevent scalping.

DO NOT!

Mow for the first time before the turf has grown 30 percent of its recommended height. This can decrease root growth and deplete the plant's food reserves.

Mow too frequently. This can compact soil, make plants more tender, and results in unnecessary labor, as well as increased expense and wear on mowing equipment.

Trim grass more than 40 percent. Root growth will stop. It can take several days to several weeks, depending on the severity of the scalping and the lawn's prior condition, before the roots resume growing. Also, scalping allows sunlight to penetrate and enhance germination of weed seeds hiding in the soil, which would otherwise be shaded by the turf.

Mow the lawn when the grass is wet or immediately after watering. It can cause uneven mowing, mat and suffocate the grass, and leave behind clippings that are messy and difficult to collect. However, during extended rainy weather, it is better to mow wet grass than to let it get too tall.

Bump trees with mowing equipment. Any damage to bark allows disease and insects to gain access and can reduce the tree's ability to uptake water.

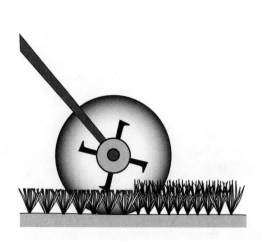

Reel Mower

Rotary Mower

Dethatching and Aerating

Dethatching and aerating compacted soil are an important part of lawn maintenance, but they are procedures that do not have to be done as frequently as mowing and fertilizing. Thatch can be your lawn's friend or its enemy. But compacted soil is never your lawn's friend. Proper lawn maintenance helps prevent unhealthy thatch build-up and soil compaction.

How to Dethatch

Thatch is a fibrous, straw-like layer of dead grass stems, leaves, roots, and stolons that builds up faster than it decays. The thatch is the layer between the green leaves and the surface of the soil. When this layer is less than one-half inch thick, it is beneficial. It acts as a mulch, insulating soil temperature, preserving moisture, protecting the crown, reducing soil compaction, cushioning the turf, and improving wear tolerance.

However, when thatch is over one-half inch thick, it can prevent water and fertilizer from reaching the roots. Thatch can harbor pests and disease organisms. Thatch can cause mowers to bounce, resulting in uneven mowing. An unhealthy thatch layer may be caused by poor or compacted soil, too much fast-acting nitrogen fertilizer, overwatering, and improper mowing.

Check the thickness of the thatch layer by using a hand trowel to dig into the lawn. Or use a knife or hand trowel to cut and lift out a two-inch deep, pie-shaped wedge of grass, and measure the straw-like material between the green grass blades and the soil. If it is more than one-half inch thick it is time to dethatch your lawn. Test several sections of your lawn since thatch is not always evenly distributed.

The best time for dethatching is early to mid-summer, when the bermudagrass is actively growing. This process causes some injury to the grass, so dethatching during its peak growing season enables the grass to recover faster and stronger. Allow at least 30 days of good growing conditions after dethatching.

Hire a professional lawn care service for dethatching or do it yourself with proper equipment. For small areas or moderate thatch, use a thatch rake (which you can buy at a nursery or gardening center) or dethatching blades available for some rotary mowers. For large areas or heavy thatch, rent a dethatching machine with vertical blades that slice through the thatch and lift it to the surface. *Make sure the blades are set at a level that prevents them from reaching the soil so you do not damage the grass crowns.* Dethatch in at least two directions, and fertilize the lawn after dethatching to help it recover faster.

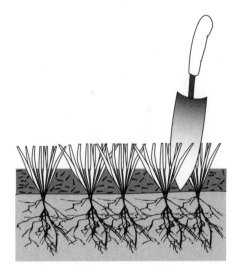

A thick layer of thatch prevents water and fertilizer from reaching roots.

How to Aerate

Aeration is necessary because compacted soil restricts movement of air, nutrients, and water, depriving roots of needed elements. Compaction prevents the deep root growth necessary for efficient water use and high temperature survival. Symptoms of compacted soil include poor drainage, yellowing of leaves, thatch, a thinning lawn, and lowered resistance to disease and pest organisms.

Aerating your lawn is a simple process performed every two to four years during the active growing season. It involves perforating the thatch and underlying soil with small holes that allow water, air, and fertilizer to reach the roots. Aeration is not a substitute for dethatching.

Use a foot press aerator for small lawns. This tool is pushed into the soil like a spade. For large lawns, you can rent an en-

How To Slow Down Thatch Build-Up

✔ Use a slow-release complete fertilizer (a 3-1-2 blend such as 21-7-14) only as directed, monthly.

✔ Water only enough to avoid wilt, but enough so the water penetrates the proper depth for that grass.

✔ Mow no more than one-third of the grass blade, using sharp mower blades. (Remember that Santa Ana is an exception to the One-Third Rule. It needs more mowing.)

✔ Encourage natural thatch-busters such as worms and soil microorganisms. These organisms prefer well-aerated, properly watered soil with organic matter and turf free of unnecessary chemicals.

✔ Aerate your lawn every two to four years. Hard clay or soils with heavy traffic may need to be aerated more often. Heavy foot traffic or temporary parking of heavy equipment on a lawn also can compact the soil.

✔ Topdressing is optional but usually beneficial, since desert soil is deficient in organic material. Every two to four years, layer no more than a one-eighth inch of organic material, such as compost or well-aged manure, on top of the turf.

gine-powered aerator. In either case, the soil should be moist, but not too wet, when using aeration equipment. The aerating machine will remove thin plugs of soil and deposit them on the lawn surface. Leave these plugs on the lawn for a day or more to dry, then break them up with a rake or use a rotary mower with a dethatching attachment. A dethatching machine with vertical blades will also work. This pulverizes the cores and redistributes the soil. Another type of aerification process is solid core aerification, in which holes are punched but no cores are removed. Both core aerating and solid core aeration are beneficial for better root growth. Although the grass will respond favorably to the aeration alone, it is an ideal time to also topdress with up to one-quarter inch of organic material and rake the surface smooth.

Fall Overseeding of Bermudagrass

Overseeding means to sow a cool-season grass on top of a dormant warm-season grass. If you have spent all spring and summer nurturing your lawn, start planning for overseeding established bermuda lawns with winter ryegrass so you can enjoy your little patch of green all year. You also will be protecting the dormant bermuda by insulating the growing crown, which produces new shoots. You may also decide not to overseed, allowing the bermuda to go dormant and rest through the winter.

Overseeding can be done from mid-October through mid-November. Temperatures should be in the mid-sixties at night on a consistent basis for good overseeding weather. Do not overseed a bermuda lawn until it has been established for at least three months; however, it is best not to overseed a lawn the first year that the bermuda is established to allow rhizomes to fully mature.

Tip
Remove thatch from the lawn surface, but do not use immediately for compost piles since it contains live stolons that may resprout. It must compost at temperatures up to 160 degrees F for several days to destroy any bermuda with growing potential. Spread the thatch on plastic or concrete for a week and stolons will dry out and die. Then add it to the compost pile.

Aeration: side view

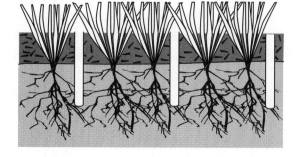

Aeration: overhead view

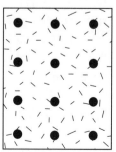

Preparing the Soil

Bermuda needs to be managed to slow growth and encourage food storage for dormancy. Do not fertilize four to six weeks before overseeding. Ten to 14 days before overseeding, cut the watering frequency in half. Stop mowing seven days before overseeding. This forces the leaves farther apart on the stem, so the winter grass seed can more easily fall to the soil surface.

The day of overseeding, mow the grass three times. The first cut should be at the regular height at which you have been mowing, then again at the next lower height setting on the mower. If you are using a rotary mower only, then decrease the height further and mow once more. Collect the clippings as part of each mowing. If you are using a reel mower, you can seed in between the second and third mowings, using the uncollected clippings of the third mowing as a mulch.

Hybid bermudagrass varieties will most likely need to be lightly dethatched for overseeding since they are so dense. (Midiron may be an exception.) Set the dethatching machine so the blades go to one-quarter inch above the thatch. Dethatch in two directions. Do not "dig" into the soil; this will only damage the bermuda for next year's spring transition.

Overseeding

Ryegrasses, both annual and perennial, make up the majority of the grass types used for overseeding in the low desert. Refer to Table 2 for a comparison of annual and perennial ryegrass before deciding which one to use. For each 1,000 square feet of lawn area use 10 to 20 pounds of seed for annual ryegrass and 10 to 15 pounds of seed for perennial ryegrass. To sow, follow the procedures for seeding warm-season lawns discussed earlier.

After spreading the grass seed and raking to ensure the seeds make contact with the soil, cover the seed with no more than one-quarter inch of weed-free organic material such as composted steer manure or forest mulch. Another option for a mulch is to cover the seed with the uncollected grass clippings of the third mowing (as mentioned above). Top dressing is an optional step that can help retain moisture and moderate temperature for improved seed germination. It is especially helpful if cool temperatures come early. However, some people have had success without top dressing during years with normal, moderate weather or autumn rains.

Maintenance

Follow the information on watering, mowing, and fertilizing in the section Maintenance for New Plantings. In addition, there are a few recommendations specific for fall overseeded lawns. If temperatures are below 100 degrees F, water two times a day (about 9 a.m. and 2 p.m. is ideal) for five to ten minutes. When the seedlings emerge to one inch, reduce watering to once a day, applying one-quarter inch of water. After the second mowing, reduce the water to an as-needed basis depending on weather and soil conditions, applying one-half to one inch per week. Once the lawn is established, depending on temperature, wind, and rain, watering may be reduced to every other week or as often as two to three times per week.

When the grass is about two inches high (about two weeks after overseeding), mow to a height of one and one-half inches. Perennial ryegrass can be mowed lower, but it is best to allow the grass to become established before closer mowing, or seedlings may be pulled out.

About two weeks after overseeding, fertilize with 16-20-0, or lawn starter fertilizer. Then water in the fertilizer. Do not fertilize too early or the bermuda may start to compete with the ryegrass; don't wait too long or the ryegrass seeds may die for lack of nutrition. After your winter lawn is established, fertilize monthly using a balanced fertilizer such as a blend of 21-7-14.

Spring Green-up Transition

When spring comes to the low desert it is time to wake your dormant bermuda lawn. You can have a beautiful, lush summer lawn by following these recommended procedures.

For Overseeded Lawns

Whether you installed new sod this winter (hybrid bermudagrass overseeded with perennial ryegrass) or overseeded an established bermuda lawn (one that has been through at least one growing season), the spring transition procedures are similar. The goal is to help the bermuda get its share of sunlight, nutrients, and water so it can successfully compete with the ryegrass until the rye is gone. Bermuda lawns need to be managed throughout the spring transition, which begins when the temperature is 60 degrees F or higher for five nights in a row.

Mowing

Beginning in late March, gradually lower the mowing height one setting every week until the mowing height is down to one-half inch for reel mowers and three-quarters inch for rotary mowers. Remember to remove no more than one-third of the grass

Watering Tip

Use this simple method to determine how much water has been applied to the lawn. Place several small cans (such as tuna fish or pet food) around different areas of the lawn before turning on the sprinklers. Measure the depth of water collected in the cans. Compare the depth to the time the sprinklers were on to establish how long to run the system. One inch of water will penetrate five inches in clay soils, seven to eight inches in loam, and 12 inches in sandy soils.

leaf per mowing as you work down to these heights. Keep the mower at this lowered setting until the transition is complete—the ryegrass is gone and only bermuda is growing.

Watering

Continue a normal watering schedule of deep watering (the water should penetrate 8 to 10 inches) every three to five days. Some people are under the misconception that if they withhold water for 10 to 14 days the ryegrass will be killed. Do not do this! Withholding water may only achieve a partial kill-off of the ryegrass while damaging the underlying bermuda as it is coming out of dormancy.

Fertilizing

Refer to the section on Fertilizing under Maintenance for Established Lawns for general information. Supplemental iron may be needed for good color during spring transition.

Maintaining a thick, dense lawn will reduce most weed problems.

Weed Control

Pre-emergent weed controls are applied early in the season before spring and summer weeds sprout; post-emergent weed controls are applied after they sprout. Apply a pre-emergent weed control once in March or April for control of grass weeds and spurge. Use a post-emergent weed control agent *only* if weeds become a problem that cannot be solved by hand-pulling.

Other Tips

Do not verticut or scalp the ryegrass to force it out during transition. Experience has shown that this not only results in partial kill-off, but your lawn will look terrible for about a month, and you still have to mow the ryegrass. It also is a good idea to avoid using herbicides during transition periods as the tender bermuda can be damaged. By following the green transition procedure described above, you will notice a minimum of browning from the dying overseed, which will start about the first of May and should be complete by mid-June. This process is based primarily on soil temperature. Areas of your lawn that show poor transition to bermuda by mid-summer are probably growing in shaded and/or wet areas, which favor the ryegrass.

For Non-Overseeded Lawns

If you did not overseed your bermuda lawn for the winter, you still need to nurture it out of dormancy. Bermudagrass growth resumes when night temperatures reach 60 degrees F. This may happen any time between March and May. Begin applying fertilizer when night temperatures are 60 degrees or higher for five nights in a row, and not just at the first sign of green leaves. For other spring tips follow the procedures for March, April, and May in Table 7 and refer to earlier sections on maintenance.

Turfgrass Problems and Solutions

Turfgrass problems occur when the grass becomes unhealthy to the point of losing its competitiveness and ability to survive. When lawns show signs of problems or damage there are two basic steps to follow: determine the problem and implement a solution.

Determine the Cause of the Problem

This is a process of elimination and includes two major categories: poor management by the homeowner or naturally occuring stresses in the environment.

Poor Management

Soil. Improper soil preparation or management. Thin or layered soils cause wet turf conditions, as water does not penetrate deeply.
Water. Too little, too much, poor timing, or uneven coverage.
Mowing. Improper height, frequency, or the wrong type of mower; dull blade.
Fertilization. Over- or underfertilizing or using the wrong type.
Thatch. Not dethatching when necessary.
Aeration. Not using core aeration when necessary.
Drainage. Poor or lack of drainage.
Traffic. Too much traffic without adequate aeration or soil amendment.
Soil Test. Lack of soil testing information may lead to soil that is inadequately prepared for turf growth.

Naturally Occurring Stresses and Other Disturbances

Environmental. High temperatures, high humidity, and other unfavorable weather conditions.
Animals. Fecal and urine burn from pets.
Pests and Diseases. Includes weeds, insects, and fungal diseases.
Shade. Most warm season turf does not do well in shaded areas.
Hardpan or Caliche. Causes problems with water penetration and root development.
Disruptive Use. Includes foot traffic, marks from sporting equipment and heavy equipment.

Implement a Solution

If you determine that your lawn's problems are a result of improper management, reread the corresponding section(s) in this chapter and correct the problem through proper management procedures. *Proper maintenance prevents the majority of turfgrass problems.* If you are still in doubt about the cause of the problem, consult a turfgrass professional.

Sometimes certain environmental conditions are beyond your control, while others have more easily implemented solutions. Here are a few potential problems that have not been discussed previously in this chapter.

Hardpan or Caliche

This soil condition is found in some desert areas. Hardpan can cause problems by restricting the downward movement of water and roots. If you do not have at least six inches of properly prepared soil, it is hard to grow turfgrasses. It is important to till or disturb the soil to a depth of six to eight inches. If necessary, break through the hardpan layer or add more soil to raise the surface.

Excessive Traffic

Physical injury to grass and soil compaction can result from excessive traffic. Different turfgrass species vary in their tolerance to wear. Excessive traffic compacts the soil, so you may need to core aerate the soil, rake up cores and mix with sand and organic matter, then top dress. It is a good idea to determine traffic patterns and choose the species appropriate for your intended use before planting a lawn. Turf is not the proper choice for high traffic dog runs: use bark or gravel. In high traffic areas raise the mowing height as well.

Animals

People who have dogs sometimes have conflicts with turf damage resulting from fecal or urine burn. Fecal material can be picked up or your dog can be trained to use a certain area of the yard. Dog urine is more of a problem because it is high in concentrated nitrogen, which turns the grass yellow, then brown and dead. The damaged spot is sometimes encircled by dark green turf because the "nitrogen effect" is diluted further out, and it acts as a fertilizer. Do not apply fertilizer to the area, because it only adds more nitrogen.

There are a few suggestions for this problem. Fences can be used to keep neighborhood dogs from lawns, dog runs can be used in a back yard, or dogs can be trained to use only certain areas. Dietary modifications or nutritional supplements for dogs have been tried, but with limited or no success, and there is potential harm for the dog. *Always consult your veterinarian before trying any dietary supplements. Keep plenty of fresh drinking water available, so your dog's urine will be less concentrated.*

Lightly watering the affected lawn area within eight hours after the dog has urinated will dilute the urine, and may also minimize the odor that attracts dogs since they tend to return to the same elimination areas (this may work for the front yard to discourage neighborhood dogs). Also, if you own dogs you may want to plan ahead before planting a lawn, and choose a turf variety that has a more open canopy. This may allow more urine to flow down to the soil rather than remain on the grass shoots. When lawn burn is mild, warm season turfgrasses that spread by stolons and rhizomes will often repair the damage through new growth. However, it is sometimes necessary to reseed or resod a patch of lawn, especially with winter ryegrass, which is more sensitive to urine damage and has no regrowth ability.

Shade

Bermuda does not grow well in shade. Shade blocks sunlight needed for proper plant growth. Plan well and plant St. Augustine or perennial ryegrass in October. If you mow higher and do not overfertilize, the ryegrass may last until August or later. St. Augustine needs at least 30 percent sunlight to thrive. Excessively shaded areas of bermudagrass lawns should be relandscaped to either hardscapes or mulches. There is no sense in trying to grow bermuda in the shade.

Weeds

Identify the weed and select the right control. If practical, hand pulling is the first choice for removing most weeds *before* they set seed. Use chemical herbicides only as a last resort on existing weeds and always follow label instructions.

Seedheads

These are a series of small flowers that can give the lawn an unfavorable appearance. All grasses produce seedheads; however, hybrid bermudagrass varieties produce no viable seeds. Expect bermuda to produce seedheads in late May to early June. Following a proper fertilizing and mowing program will usually reduce seedhead formation.

Insects

At any given time, insects can be found in a typical lawn, but *rarely* in large enough numbers to cause damage to a healthy lawn. Many insects are actually beneficial, part of the natural balance, and harmless to turfgrass. So don't get worried if you find a grub or two. If you find five to ten grubs in a square foot of soil, you might consider treatment. The goal is to keep damage at an aesthetically acceptable level that is not threatening the health of the grass. If your lawn is showing unacceptable levels of damage, look for insect pests above the soil, or dig into the soil and examine the top four to six inches. Determine how many insects are in a square foot area and identify the insect or have a professional identify it for you. Only large populations may require treatment. Apply pesticides only as a last resort since they can harm beneficial insects.

Pearl scales are pests that are occasionally found in bermudagrass and St. Augustine grass. They suck fluids from the plant and cause circular patches of weakened or dead grass. Examine the roots at the edge of the dying area and the healthy turf for miniature white "pearls" about the size of a pinhead and seldom larger than one-sixteenth inch. The best chance for control is early detection when the dead patches are small and manageable. Carefully remove and dispose of the affected roots and soil to a depth of one foot, as well as one foot beyond the affected area. It is a good idea to place the affected roots and soil on a disposable tarp or in a container and take the affected roots and soil to a landfill. Also remember to clean your equipment in a way that will not allow contaminated soil to reach unaffected areas.

There are no chemical control methods that completely rid the lawn of pearl scale. Applications of systemic insecticides followed by a contact insecticide in and around the affected areas works best. Adults have a protective coating, but the young do not. Therefore, only apply insecticides around May 1, when the young "crawlers" are active. Check with your garden center to find out which chemicals to use and whether they need to be professionally applied. Pearl scale prefers alkaline soil, so applications of soil acidifiers, such as soil sulfur, may slow down its spread. Apply in May through July and plan to treat again in most cases for years, as the problem persists.

Disease

Disease organisms are always present in the soil and thatch but only become a problem when the grass is weak or environmental conditions favor the spread of the pest. The good news is that the varieties of grass recommended for the low desert are resistant to diseases or are relatively free of disease. We just do not have very many problems in this area with turfgrass diseases. *A healthy, well maintained lawn, along with proper soil preparation and planning, is your lawn's best protection against weeds, insects, and diseases.* But if you do suspect a fungus or other problem you cannot diagnose, contact your County Cooperative Extension office or a turfgrass professional.

Enjoy Your Lawn

Your lawn is there for you to enjoy and to enhance your home environment. Remember to choose the right grass variety for your needs, to properly prepare the soil, and to install the correct irrigation system before planting. Then select the planting method that best suits your needs and preferences and follow the maintenance guidelines in this chapter. Through careful planning and proper maintenance your lawn will remain green, lush, and healthy.❀

Sharon Dewey is currently the Director of Marketing and Client Service Representative for Western Sod. Previously, she was a partner in a landscape management business in Scottsdale. Sharon has a MA from Texas Woman's University and received her Turfgrass Professional Certification from the University of Georgia.

Sharon was the first woman elected as President of the Arizona Landscape Contractor's Association and Arizona Certified Landscape Professional Program. She speaks and writes extensively on turf in the low desert and is dedicated to helping people understand the basics of good lawn management. Sharon is a Certified Master Gardener with the University of Arizona Cooperative Extension.

Diagnosing Plant Problems

1. Identify the Plant

    A. Determine what the plant should look like at this time of year, i.e., what is "normal."
    B. Know the environmental and cultural needs of the plant.
    C. Know what pathogens the plant is susceptible to.

2. Define the Problems

    A. Examine the physical evidence
        1) Examine the entire plant (roots, stems, and leaves). Based on what you learned in Step 1, describe the problem.
        2) Check any surrounding plants for similar symptoms.
        3) Identify symptoms or signs of animals, insects, or diseases.
    B. Collect all the pertinent information
        1) Onset of problem. When was it first noticed?
        2) Description of plant's environment (sun, shade, soil, lawn, crushed granite, container, animals).
        3) Plant's age.
        4) Any recent changes in cultural practices (planting, irrigating, fertilizing, pruning, applying pesticides).
        5) What plants grew here previously? Is there a history of disease?
        6) Weather (dust storms, lighting, rain, intense heat or cold, hail, strong winds).
        7) Any unusual occurrences (the house next door burned down, irrigation line broke, chemical spill, neighbor spraying).

3. Look for Patterns

    A. Pattern of symptoms on individual plant
        1) Location of damage on plant
            a) New growth vs. old growth. Is the plant growing out of the damage? Some nutrients can be moved (translocated) within the plant, thus the plant can "rob" the older leaves to feed the new. In such a case, the nutrient deficiency symptoms appear on the old growth. Other nutrients do not move within the plant, so those deficiency symptoms show up on the new growth.
           b) Which side of plant (west vs. east; interior vs. exterior)? Damage only on the west side may indicate sunburn; damage only on the external leaves may indicate chemical drift from nearby spraying.

2) Progression within plant and/or to other plants

    a) Progressive spread of damage on a plant, onto other plants, or over an area with time generally indicates the damage was caused by a living organism.

    b) If the damage occurs and does not spread to other plants or other parts of the affected plant, and if there is a clear line of demarcation between damaged and undamaged tissues, it is likely that the plant was damaged by non-living factors (weather, chemical, mechanical damage).

B. Pattern of symptoms on multiple plants

1) Types of plants affected

    a) Damage to only one particular type of plant indicates a living pathogen (insect or disease).

    b) Uniform damage to a large area and several different types of plants indicates a non-living pathogen (weather, mechanical, or chemical factors).

2) Any relationship between the location of damaged plants and the watering pattern?

4. Make a Tentative Diagnosis

A. Start with a good reference book for your climate. Most are indexed by plant. Some are also indexed by the pathogen or "causal agent."

B. Look up the plant in the index.

C. Review the potential pathogens listed for that plant.

D. Select and read about likely options.

E. Compare the information that you have gathered to the problem's description in the book.

F. Identify the causal agent. If you are unable to diagnose the problem, take a sample to your local nursery or Cooperative Extension office to get a professional opinion.

5. Develop a Plan for Managing the Problem

A. Based on your research, determine how to care for the plant to keep it healthy.

B. Use the three elements of the disease triangle to identify the best method of managing the problem. For example, modify the environment to have it better meet the needs of the plant or to make it inhospitable to the pathogen. Remove or directly manage the pathogen. It may be necessary to replace the plant with one better adapted to the environment and less vulnerable to the pathogen.❀

Rose Varieties for the Low Desert

Name of Rose[1]	Color[2]	ARS Rating[3]	Classification[4]	Fragrance	Bloom description	Foliage color, growth habit, and size (in feet)
Ain't She Sweet 1994 AARS	or	7.0	H	spice & rose	fully double, 30-35 petals	deep green, 4-5
America 1976 AARS	op	8.2	C	strong spicy	4-5" double, 40-45 petals	dark green, leathery, 10-12
Angel Face 1968 AARS	m	8.1	F	old fashion rose	4" double, 20-22 petals	dark leathery, compact, 2-4
Arizona 1975 AARS	ob	5.8	G	strong tea	4.5" double, 30-35 petals	bronze green, semi-glossy, 4-6
Arizona Sunset 1988 AARS	yb	8.0	M	none	hybrid tea type, 14-16 petals	medium green, 2-3
Artistry 1997 AARS	op	7.6	H	slight rose	large full, 30-35 petals	medium green, 4-5
Ballerina 1937	mp	9.0	O	slight apple	small flowers in clusters, 5-12 petals	medium green, 6-10
Baronne Prevost 1842	mp	8.5	O	rich rose	big flowers with button eye, 100 petals	medium green, bushy, 5-7
Beauty Secret	mr	8.4	M	none	hybrid tea type, 20-25 petals	dark green, 1-2
Belinda 1936	mp	8.6	O	slight apple	large hot pink clusters with a white eye	dark green shrub, 5-7
Belle Story	lp	8.5	S	strong anise	semi-double, cupped, scarlet-pink stamens	soft medium green shrub, 8-10
Betty Boop 1999 AARS	yb	*	F	mild tea	single yellow edged in orange, 6-12 petals	medium green shrub, 2-3
Black Jade	dr	8.3	M	none	velvety, hybrid tea type	dark glossy green, 1.5-2
Blue Girl	m	5.8	H	light fruity	large double, 30-35 petals	medium glossy green, bush, 4-6
Brandy	ab	7.0	H	mild tea	large double hybrid tea type, 25-30 petals	medium green, 4-7
Brass Band 1995 AARS	ab	7.8	F	moderately fruity	large full, 30-35 petals	bright glossy green, 4-6
Bride's Dream	lp	8.0	H	slight tea	large double hybrid tea type, 25-30 petals	dark shiny green, 4-7

Variety	Color	Rating	Class	Fragrance	Bloom	Foliage / Growth
Brigadoon	rb	7.9	H	mild tea	large double hybrid tea, 25-30 petals	dark glossy green, slightly spreading, 4-7
Candelabra 1999 AARS	ob	*	G	light sweet	large double, 25 petals	dark glossy green, 4-5
Caribbean 1994 AARS	ab	7.6	G	mild tea	medium double, 30-35 petals	bright green, 4-6
Cecile Brunner	lp	8.2	P	moderate tea	small clusters, 30 plus petals	dark green, low, bushy, 2-3
Cherish	op	8.4	F	slight tea	small clusters, 25-30 petals	medium green, 3-5
China Doll	mp	8.3	P	light tea	large clusters of fluffy doubles	medium green, dwarf bushy mound, 2-3
Chrysler Imperial 1953 AARS	dr	7.8	H	sweet, spicy	large velvety, very double	dark green, 4-7
Crimson Bouquet 2000 AARS	r	*	G	slight rose	4" blooms, 20-25 petals	deep green, 4.5-5
Crystalline	w	7.8	H	medium sweet tea	very large double, 35-40 petals	dark green, 4-7
Dainty Bess	lp	9.0	H	moderate tea	large single, 5 petals	dark green, leathery, 4-6
Don Juan	dr	8.2	C	strong rose	large full, 30-35 petals	dark glossy green, 10-14
Dortmund	mr	9.1	O	moderate apple	large single, 5-8 petals	deep shiny green, 10-12
Double Delight 1977 AARS	rb	8.9	H	strong spicy rose	very large hybrid tea, 30-35 petals	deep green, 4-7
Fairhope	ly	7.8	M	mild honeysuckle	large hybrid tea type, 15-20 petals	dark green, 2-3
Figurine	w	7.9	M	moderate rose	large double, 18-25 petals	medium green, 1.5-2
First Light 1998 AARS	lp	7.7	S	spice	2.5-3" blooms, 5-7 petals	medium green, 3-4
First Prize 1970 AARS	pb	8.9	H	mild tea	very large double, 25-30 petals	dark green, leathery, 4-7
Fourth of July 1999 AARS	rb	*	C	apple & rose	large sprays of semi-double, 10-15 petals	shiny green, 10-14
Francis Dubreuil 1894	dr	*	O	strong old rose	hybrid tea type	deep green, compact, 3-4
Gemini 2000 AARS	pb	*	H	spice	4.5" blooms, 25-30 petals	dark green, 4-6
Glowing Peace 2001 AARS	op	*	G	tea	3" blooms, 30-42 petals	deep glossy green, 4-5
Gold Medal	my	8.8	G	rich fruity	medium double, 30-35 petals	deep green, 5-8
Golden Celebration	dy	7.8	S	strong rose	large cupped, 50 plus petals	medium green, round compact bush, 5-6
Gourmet Popcorn	w	8.4	M	none	small flat blooms in clusters	dark green, compact bush, 2-3

Name	Color	Rating	Class	Fragrance	Bloom	Foliage / Habit
Graham Thomas	dy	7.9	S	slightly spicy	deep cupped, 50 plus petals	dark green, large upright bush, 6-8
Heritage	lp	8.7	S	sweet tea	large deep cupped, 50 plus petals	medium green, medium bush, 4
Hermosa 1837	mp	7.9	O	spicy rose	cupped, full blooms	olive green, 4
Honor	w	7.5	H	light honeysuckle	4-5" blooms, 20-22 petals	olive green, tall upright bush, 4-5
Hot Tamale	yb	8.1	M	none	hybrid tea in small clusters, 25-30 petals	dark green, 2
Hwy 290 Pink Buttons	lp	*	O	none	1" very double	bright green, small, 2-3
Iceberg	w	8.7	F	mild honey	medium blooms in clusters, 20-25 petals	very dark green, very bushy, 2-4
Incognito	m	7.7	M	mild rose	medium hybrid tea, 25 petals	medium green, 2-3
Ingrid Bergman	dr	7.1	H	slight rose	very large double, 35-40 petals	deep green, 4-6
Intrigue 1984 AARS	m	6.8	F	strong citrus/rose	medium-large double, 25-30 petals	medium green, 3-4
Irresistible	w	8.0	M	none	hybrid tea type, 45-50 petals	medium green, 2-3
Jean Kenneally	ab	9.7	M	none	hybrid tea type sprays, 25 petals	dark green, 2-3
Jingle Bells	dr	*	M	none	hybrid tea type, 25 petals	medium green, 1.5-2
Joseph's Coat	rb	7.5	C	light tea	large clusters of doubles, 23-28 petals	dark green, 10-12
June Laver	dy	7.9	M	none	hybrid tea type, 20-25 petals	medium green, 1.5-2
Just For You	dr	8.0	M	none	hybrid tea type, 25 petals	medium green, 2-2.5
Knock Out 2000 AARS	dr	*	S	tea rose	3-3.5" blooms, 5-7 petals	glossy green, 3-3.5
Kristin	rb	8.1	M	none	hybrid tea type, 25 petals	dark green 2-2.5
Lanvin	ly	7.1	H	none	large double, 25-30 petals	dark green, 4-6
Linville	w	7.8	M	none	hybrid tea type, 25 petals	medium green, 2-3
Love	rb	7.1	G	slight rose	medium double, 30-35 petals	dark green, upright bush, 3-4
Madame Hardy	w	9.0	O	strong rose	medium cupped, 100 petals	light green, upright bush, 5-6
Marmalade Skies 2001 AARS	ob	*	F	slight rose	2.5-3" double, 17-28 petals	olive green, 3
Martha Gonzales	mr	*	O	slight apple	single, 6-8 petals	dark green with red tinge, 3-4

Variety						
Margo Koster	ob	7.5	P	slight tea	small clusters, 25-30 petals	deep green, 2-3
Mary Rose	mp	8.7	S	strong rose	damask type, deep cupped, 50 plus petals	medium green, 4-5
Minnie Pearl	pb	9.4	M	none	hybrid tea type, 25-30 petals	dark glossy green, 2-3
Mister Lincoln 1965 AARS	dr	8.8	H	strong damask	pointed blooms, 30-35 petals	dark grey-green, 5-7
Monsier Tillier	op	9.0	O	spicy herbal tea	medium, 50 plus petals	medium green, upright, 4-6
Moonstone	w	*	H	mild tea & rose	large fully double, 30-35 petals	large dark green, 5-7
Mothers Love	pb	7.8	M	none	hybrid tea type, 25-30 petals	dark green, 2.5-3
Mutabilis (Butterfly Rose)	yb	8.7	O	slight tea	single silky, 5 petals	deep dark green, 5-8
My Sunshine	my	8.7	M	none	single, 5 petals	dark green, 2.5-3
New Zealand	lp	7.5	H	honeysuckle	large pointed blooms, 30-35 petals	deep dark green, 4-6
Nicole	rb	9.1	H	slight rose	clusters, 20-25 petals	medium green, 3-4
Old Blush	mp	8.8	O	slight rose	medium semi-double, 25-30 petals	medium green, 4-6
Opening Night 1998 AARS	dr	7.9	H	slight tea	4.5" blooms, 25-30 petals	dark green, semi-glossy, 5-6
Othello	mr	7.1	S	strong rose	large deep blooms, 50 plus petals	light green, 5-7
Olympiad 1984 AARS	r	9.1	H	light fruity	large double, 30-35 petals	grey-green, 4-6
Peace 1946 AARS	yb	6.8	H	mild fruity	large full, 40-45 petals	medium glossy green, 4-7
Perle d'Or 1884	ab	8.3	P	spicy rose	small clusters of full blooms	dark green, mounding, 3-4
Pierrine	op	9.4	M	none	hybrid tea type, 20-25 petals	dark green, 1.5-2.5
Playboy	rb	8.1	F	medium apple	large double, 7-10 petals	medium green, 3-5
Playgirl	mp	8.1	F	light fruity	medium single, 5-7 petals	medium green, 3-4
Popcorn	w	8.3	M	none	tiny blooms in clusters	dark green, 2.5-3
Pristine	w	9.2	H	mild rose	very large double, 25-30 petals	deep dark green, 4-6
Queen Elizabeth 1955 AARS	mp	9.0	G	moderate tea	large double, 35 petals	dark green, 4-8
Rainbow's End	yb	9.0	M	slight fruity	large full, 30-35 petals	dark green, 1.5-2

Name	Color	Rating	Class	Fragrance	Bloom	Foliage, Size
R.Rouletti	mp	6.7	M	mild fruity	small double, in clusters or single, 20-22	medium green, 2-3
Reine des Violettes	m	8.0	O	strong rose	deep cupped, 75 petals	medium green, 6-8
Rio Samba	yb	7.3	H	light tea	medium double, 25 petals	dark green, 3-5
Rise 'N' Shine	my	7.4	M	mild fruity	hybrid tea type, 30-35 petals	dark green, 1.5-2.5
Rose de Rescht	dp	8.6	O	mild damask	2" blooms, 50 plus petals	deep green, 3-4
Royal Highness 1963 AARS	lp	8.2	H	sweet tea	large full, 40-45 petals	bright green, 4-7
Sarabande 1960 AARS	or	8.0	F	light tea	large double, in clusters, 8-14 petals	medium green, 4-5
Sally Holmes	w	8.9	S	slight rose	large single, in clusters, 5-8 petals	dark green, 8-10
Santa Claus	dr	7.7	M	light rose	velvety hybrid tea type, 15-20 petals	medium shiny green, 1.5-2
Scentimental	rb	7.6	F	strong sweet	large double, 25-30 petals	dark green, 4-5
Secret	pb	7.6	H	sweet & spicy	large fully double, 30-35 petals	medium green, 4-6
Sexy Rexy	mp	9.0	F	slight fruity	medium double, 30-40 petals	deep green, 4-6
Sheer Elegance	w	7.8	H	light tea	large full, 30-35 petals	dark green, 4-6
Showbiz 1985 AARS	mr	8.6	F	light tea	medium, in clusters, 20-25 petals	dark glossy green, 3-4
Signature	dp	*	H	light fruity	large full, 30-35 petals	dark green, 4-6
Snow Bride	w	9.3	M	none	medium hybrid tea type, 20 petals	dark green, 1.5-2
Sombreuil	w	8.8	O	sweet tea	flat, quartered, 100 petals	dark green, 8-12
Souvenir de la Malmaison	lp	8.7	O	strong spicy	very double quartered, 35-45 petals	medium glossy green, 3-4
St. Patrick 1996 AARS	dy	7.7	H	mild apple	large fully double, 30-35 petals	grey-green, 4-6
Starina	or	9.0	M	slight tea	large full, 30-35 petals	dark glossy green, 2-2.5
Summer Fashion	yb	8.0	F	mild fruity	large full double, 35-40 petals	medium green, 3-5
Sunset Celebration 1998 AARS	ab	7.8	H	fruity	4.5" blooms, 25-30 petals	deep green, 4.5-5.5
Sun Sprinkles 2001 AARS	dy	*	M	musk	2" blooms, 25-30 petals	dark green, 1.5-2
Sunsprite	dy	8.7	F	sweet licorice	medium double, 25-30 petals	deep glossy green, 3-5

Variety	Color	Rating	Class	Fragrance	Bloom	Foliage/Habit
Sweet Chariot	m	7.7	M	strong rose	medium ruffled, in clusters, 45-50 petals	deep green, 1.5-2.5
Tamaro	ab	*	S	strong myrrh	medium deeply cupped, 40-50 petals	medium green, 3-4
The Fairy	lp	8.7	P	mild apple	small blooms in clusters, 20-25 petals	glossy green, 2-3
Timeless 1998 AARS	dp	7.7	H	mild rose	large double, 25-30 petals	deep green, 4-6
Touch of Class 1986 AARS	op	9.5	H	slight tea	large double, 30 petals	medium green, 4-7
Tournament of Roses 1989 AARS	mp	8.0	G	light spice	medium double, 25-30 petals	deep green, 4-6
Tropicana 1963 AARS	or	7.6	H	sweet fruity	large fully double, 30-35 petals	dark glossy green, 3-4
Veteran's Honor 1999	mr	*	H	tea	4.5" blooms, 30-35 petals	medium green, 4.5-5
Why Not	rb	7.9	M	light tea	medium single, 5 petals	deep green, 1-1.5
X-Rated	pb	7.7	M	light spice	medium hybrid tea type, 26-40 petals	dark green, 1.5-2
Zephirine Drouhin	mp	8.1	O	strong rose	medium cupped, 30-35 petals	medium green, thornless, 8-10

[1]AARS - All America Rose Selection winners. These are the roses judged to be the best of the year.

[2]Color Classification

ab	apricot & apricot blend	m	mauve & mauve blend
dr	dark red	mp	medium pink
dp	deep pink	mr	medium red
dy	deep yellow	my	medium yellow
lp	light pink	ob	orange & orange blend
ly	light yellow	op	orange pink & orange pink blend
or	orange red & orange red blend		
pb	pink blend		
rb	red blend		
r	russet		
w	white, near white & white blend		
yb	yellow blend		

[3]American Rose Society rating. Roses are rated as to their adaptability and growth habits. The roses are rated one through ten, with ten being the best. These ratings are for the low desert.

9.0 - 10.0 Best	8.8 - 9.2 Outstanding	8.3 - 8.7 Excellent	7.8 - 8.2 Very good	7.3 - 7.7 Good	6.8 - 7.2 Average
6.1-6.7 Below Average	6.0 Not recommended				

[4]Rose classification

H Hybrid Tea   G Grandiflora   S Shrub   F Floribunda   P Polyantha   M Miniature   O Old Garden Rose   C Climber

Resources

Chapter 1: The Magic of Desert Plants

The Desert Smells Like Rain: A Naturalist in Papago Indian Country. Gary Paul Nabhan, 1987. North Point Press, Berkeley, CA. 0-8654705-0-2.

Elements of the Nature and Property of Soils. Nyle C. Brady and Ray R. Weil, 1999. Prentice Hall, NY. 01301449-7-5.

Gardening Success with Difficult Soils: Limestone, Alkaline Clay, and Caliche. Scott Ogden, 1992. Taylor Publishing Company, Dallas. 0-8783374-1-5.

The Landscape Below Ground: Proceedings of an International Workshop on Tree Root Development in Urban Soils. Gary W. Watson and Dan Neely, 1994. International Society of Arboriculture, Savoy. 1-8819560-6-7.

Plants of Arizona. Lewis E. Epple and Anne Orth Epple, 1995. Falcon Press, Helena, MT. 1-56044-563-7.

Shrubs and Trees of the Southwest Desert. Janice Emily Bower and Brian Wignall, 1993. Southwest Parks and Monuments Association, Tucson.

Western Fertilizer Handbook. California Fertilizer Association, 1990. Interstate Publishers, Inc., Danville. 08134285-8-0.

Wild Food of the Sonoran Desert. Kevin Dahl, 1995. Arizona-Sonoran Desert Museum Press, Tucson. 1-886679-03-7.

Chapter 2: Selecting and Transplanting

Desert Accent Plants, 1992. Arizona Native Plant Society, PO Box 41206, Sun Station, Tucson, AZ 85717, http://aznps.org.

Desert Gardening for Beginners: How to Grow Vegetables, Flowers and Herbs in an Arid Climate. Cathy Cromell, Linda A. Guy and Lucy K. Bradley, 1999. Arizona Master Gardener Press, Phoenix, 0-9651987-2-3.

Desert Grasses, 1993. Arizona Native Plant Society, PO Box 41206, Sun Station, Tucson, AZ 85717, http://aznps.org.

Desert Groundcovers and Vines, 1991. Arizona Native Plant Society, PO Box 41206, Sun Station, Tucson, AZ 85717, http://aznps.org.

Desert Landscaping: How to Start and Maintain a Healthy Landscape in the Southwest. George Brookbank, 1991. University of Arizona Press, Tucson. 0-8165-1201-9.

Desert Shrubs, 1990. Arizona Native Plant Society, PO Box 41206, Sun Station, Tucson, AZ 85717, http://aznps.org.

Desert Trees, 1990. Arizona Native Plant Society, PO Box 41206, Sun Station, Tucson, AZ 85717, http://aznps.org.

Landscape Plants for Dry Regions. Warren Jones and Charles Sacamano, 2000. Fisher Books, Tucson. 1-55561190-7.

Low Water Use Plants for California and the Southwest. Carol Schuler, 1993. Fisher Books, Tucson. 1-55561271-7.

Native Plants for Southwestern Landscapes. Judy Mielke, 1993. University of Texas Press, Austin. 0-292-75147-8.

Natural by Design: Beauty and Balance in Southwest Gardens. Judith Phillips, 1995. Museum of New Mexico Press, Santa Fe. 0-89013-227-1.

Plant Handling Techniques for the Home Gardener. Allen D. Boettcher, 1990. University of Arizona Cooperative Extension, Tucson. Publication MC49.

Plant Selection and Selecting Your Plants. Elizabeth Davison, John Begeman, Jimmy L. Tipton, 2000. University of Arizona Cooperative Extension, Tucson. Publication AZ 1153.

Planting Guidelines: Container Trees and Shrubs. Jimmy L. Tipton, 1998. University of Arizona Cooperative Extension, Tucson. Publication AZ1022.

Plants for Dry Climates: How to Select, Grow and Enjoy. Mary Rose Duffield and Warren D. Jones, 2000. Fisher Books, Tucson. 1-55561-270-9.

College of Agriculture and Life Sciences, University of Arizona. Wide variety of arid southwest gardening information. http://www.ag.arizona.edu/gardening/.

Chapter 3: Watering Desert Landscapes

Arboriculture: Integrated Management of Landscape Trees, Shrubs, and Vines. Richard Harris, James Clark and Nelda Matheny, 1999, 3rd edition. Prentice Hall, Upper Saddle River, NJ. 0-13-386665-3.

Drip Irrigation for Every Landscape and All Climates. Robert Kourik, 1992. Metamorphic Press, Santa Rosa, CA. 0-9615848-2-3.

Garden Watering Systems. Susan Lang, 1999. Sunset Books, Menlo Park, CA. 0-3760383-9-X.

Guidelines for Landscape Drip Irrigation Systems. Arizona Landscape Irrigation Guidelines Committee, November 1999. Arizona Municipal Water Users Association, Phoenix, AZ. Call your city Water Conservation Office for a copy.

Ortho's All About Sprinklers and Drip Systems. Managing Editor, Sally W. Smith, 1998. Meredith Books, Des Moines, IA. 0-8972141-3-7.

Pruning, Planting & Care. Eric A. Johnson, 1997. Ironwood Press, Tucson. 0-9628236-5-1.

Xeriscape: Landscaping with Style in the Arizona Desert.
Arizona Department of Water Resources, 2000. Call your city
Water Conservation Office for a copy.

Arizona Municipal Water Users Association,
http:www.water.az.gov.

Chapter 4: Pruning

*Arboriculture: Integrated Management of Landscape Trees,
Shrubs, and Vines.* Richard Harris, James Clark and Nelda
Matheny, 1999, 3rd edition. Prentice Hall, Upper Saddle River,
NJ. 0-13-386665-3.

Pruning & Training. Christopher Brickell, David Joyce, 1996.
Dorling Kindersley Publishing, New York. 156458-331-7.

Pruning Handbook. Editors of Sunset Books and Sunset
Magazines, 1983. Sunset Publishing, Menlo Park, CA.

American Society of Consulting Arborists. Membership is for
practicing arborists who specialize in advising, diagnosing,
recommending treatments, making appraisals, and offering legal
testimony in court. Membership signifies a high degree of
professionalism in arboriculture with academic requirements,
extensive work experience, professional affiliations, and
references. Website contains a list of members by state and
specialty. 15245 Shady Grove Road, Suite 130, Rockville, MD
20850, 301-947-0483, 301-990-9771 (fax), asca@mgmtsol.com,
www.ascaconsultants.org.

Arizona Community Tree Council, Inc. A non-profit organiza-
tion that promotes communication and the exchange of information about trees, and the essential role they play in the well being
of all Arizona communities. Encourages and facilitates the
planting and care of trees throughout the state. Website contains
links to many tree-related sites. 1616 W. Adams, Phoenix, AZ
85007, 602-542-6191, http://aztrees.org/.

International Society of Arboriculture (ISA). ISA offers two
levels of certification: Certified Arborist and Certified Tree
Worker. Certification requires a broad knowledge of tree
biology, species identification and selection, soils and tree
nutrition, planting, pruning, cabling, bracing, and problem
diagnosis and management. It also requires 18 months of
experience in Arboriculture and 30 hours of continuing education
every three years. From the ISA web site, you may enter your
zip code or city and obtain a list of certified arborists in your
area. PO Box 3129, Champaign, IL 61826-3129, 217-355-9411,
217-355-9516 (fax), isa@isa-arbor.com, http://www.isa-
arbor.com/arborists/arborist.html.

National Arborist Association (NAA). Membership in NAA is
comprised of commercial tree care service firms. It has developed sets of standards for pruning, cabling, and other techniques
widely used in the industry. 3 Perimeter Road, Unit 1, Manches-
ter NH 03103, 800-733-2622, 603-314-5386 (fax),
naa@natlarb.com, www.natlarb.com.

Chapters 5 & 6: Plant Problems and Pests

Diseases of Trees and Shrubs. W.A. Sinclair, H.H. Lyon, and
W.T. Johnson, 1987. Cornell University Press, Ithaca, NY.
0-8014-1517-9.

In a Desert Garden: Love and Death among the Insects. John
Alcock, 1997. University of Arizona Press, Tucson. 0-8165-
1970-6.

Insects of the Southwest. Floyd Werner and Carl Olson, 1995.
Fisher Books, Tucson. 1-55561-060-9.

Insects that Feed on Trees and Shrubs. W.T. Johnson and H.H.
Lyon, 1991. Cornell University Press, Ithaca, NY.
0-8014-2602-2.

Master Gardener Entomology Manual. Dave T. Langston and
Roberta Gibson, 1995. The University of Arizona College of
Agriculture, Tucson. Order from
http://pubs.agforbes.arizona.edu/search/srch.cfm.

Maricopa County Cooperative Extension (Phoenix) gardening
website. Click on Timely Tips. Choose the appropriate month.
Scroll to find information on typical problems and Frequently
Asked Questions. http://www.ag.arizona.edu/maricopa/garden/.

Chapter 7: Frost Protection

*Arboriculture: Integrated Management of Landscape Trees,
Shrubs, and Vines.* Richard Harris, James Clark and Nelda
Matheny, 1999, 3rd edition. Prentice Hall, Upper Saddle River,
NJ. 0-13-386665-3.

"Basics of Frost and Freeze Protection for Horticultural Crops."
Katherine B. Perry. *HortTechnology*, January 1998, 8(1).

Chapter 8: Cacti & Succulents

Agaves of Continental North America. Howard Scott Gentry,
1982. University of Arizona Press, Tucson. 0-81650775-9.

Agaves, Yuccas, and Related Plants: A Gardener's Guide. Mary
and Gary Irish, 2000. Timber Press, Portland. 088192-442-3.

Cacti and Succulents for Modern Living. Laura Williams Rice,
1976. Merchants Publishing Company, Kalamazoo, MI. 0-
89484-003-7.

Desert Accent Plants, 1992. Arizona Native Plant Society, PO
Box 41206, Sun Station, Tucson, AZ 85717, http://aznps.org.

*Dry Climate Gardening with Succulents (The American Garden
Guides).* The Huntington Botanical Gardens, 1995. Pantheon
Books, New York. 0-679-75829-1.

Guide to the Aloes of South Africa. Ben-Erik Van Wyk and
Gideon Smith, 1996. Briza Publications, Pretoria, South Africa.
1-875093-04-4.

Landscape Plants for Dry Regions: More Than 600 Species from Around the World. Warren Jones and Charles Sacamano, 2000. Fisher Books, Tucson. 1-55561-190-7.

Native Plants for Southwestern Landscapes. Judy Mielke, 1993. University of Texas Press, Austin. 0-292-751478.

Simon and Schuster's Guide to Cacti and Succulents. Stanley Schuler (editor), 1985. Simon and Schuster, New York. 0-671-60231-4.

Cactus and Succulent Plant Mall. Contains information and links to cactus and succulent societies and suppliers of plants, seeds, and literature. www.cactus-mall.com.

Chapter 9: Growing Wildflowers
Desert Wildflowers, 1991. Arizona Native Plant Society, PO Box 41206, Sun Station, Tucson, AZ 85717, http://aznps.org.

Desert Wildflowers, A Guide for Identifying, Locating, and Enjoying Arizona Wildflowers and Cactus Blooms. Desert Botanical Garden Staff, 1997 fourth printing. Arizona Highways Book Division, Phoenix. 0-916179-68-0.

A Field Guide to Southwestern and Texas Wildflowers. Theodore F. Niehaus, 1984. Houghton Mifflin, Boston.

Flowers of the Southwest Deserts. Natt N. Dodge, 1985. Southwest Parks and Monuments Association, Tucson.

Grand Canyon Wildflowers. Arthur M. Phillips, 1990 revised. Grand Canyon Natural History Association. 0938216-01-5.

How to Grow the Wildflowers. Eric A. Johnson and Scott Millard, 1993. Ironwood Press, Tucson. 0-9628236-27.

The Low-Water Flower Gardener. Eric A. Johnson and Scott Millard, 1993. Ironwood Press, Tucson. 0-96282361-9.

Lady Bird Johnson Wildflower Center, 4801 La Crosse Avenue, Austin, TX, 78739-1702, 512-292-4200, 512-2924637 (fax), http://www.wildflower.org/index.html.

Wild Seed, Inc., P.O. Box 27751, Tempe, AZ 85285, 602-276-3536. Request a free catalog for native seed material.

Chapter 10: Landscaping for Wildlife
Coexisting with Urban Wildlife, A guide to the Central Arizona Uplands. Robert L. Hoffa, 1996. Sharlot Hall Museum Press, Prescott, AZ. 0-927579-07-3.

Desert Bird Gardening, 1997. Arizona Native Plant Society, PO Box 41206, Sun Station, Tucson, AZ 85717, http://aznps.org.

Desert Butterfly Gardening, 1996. Arizona Native Plant Society, PO Box 41206, Sun Station, Tucson, AZ 85717, http://aznps.org.

Desert Gardening for Beginners: How to Grow Vegetables, Flowers and Herbs in an Arid Climate. Cathy Cromell, Linda A. Guy and Lucy K. Bradley, 1999. Arizona Master Gardener Press, Phoenix. 0-9651987-2-3.

Gardening for Pollinators (brochure). Mrill Ingram, Stephen Buchmann, and Gary Nabhan, 1998. Arizona Sonora Desert Museum Press, 2021 N. Kinney Road, Tucson, AZ 85743. 1-886679-10-X.

Insects of the Southwest. Floyd Werner and Carl Olson, 1995. Fisher Books, Tucson. 1-55561-060-9.

Landscaping for Energy Efficiency. Arizona Public Service Company, 1999. http://www.aps.com/images/pdf/landscaping.pdf.

Landscaping for Wildlife, 1999, 2nd Edition. Arizona Game & Fish Department, 2221 West Greenway Road, Phoenix, AZ 85023, 602-942-3000, http://www.gf.state.az.us.

Native Plants for Southwestern Deserts. Judy Mielke, 1993. University of Texas Press, Austin. 0-292-75147-8.

A Sand County Almanac. Aldo Leopold, 1989 (special edition). Oxford University Press, New York. 0-19505305-2.

Xeriscape for School Gardens. Arizona Municipal Water Users Association, 1994. 4041 N. Central Avenue, Suite 900, Phoenix, AZ 85012.

Arizona Herpetological Association, PO Box 64531, Phoenix, AZ 85082-4531, 480-894-1625, http://www.azreptiles.com. Contains photos of snakes and lizards commonly found in Arizona. Volunteers will remove snakes from homes and yards.

California Department of Fish and Game, 1807 13th Street, Suite 202, Sacramento, CA 95814, 916-653-7664, http://www.dfg.ca.gov/dfghome.html.

New Mexico Department of Game & Fish, P. O. Box 25112, Santa Fe, NM 87504, 800-862-9310, ispa@state.nm.us, http://www.gmfsh.state.nm.us/.

Southwestern Herpetologists Society, P.O. Box 7469, Van Nuys, CA 91409-7469, 818-503-2052, http://www.swhs.org.

Texas Parks & Wildlife, 4200 Smith School Road, Austin, TX 78744, (800) 792-1112, (512) 389-4800, http://www.tpwd.state.tx.us/.

The Backyard Wildlife Habitat Certification Program was started in 1973 by the National Wildlife Federation to acknowledge and encourage individuals who garden for wildlife. The program encourages everyone to plan landscapes for the needs of wildlife. Today, with over 34,000 sites certified in the program, NWF provides information and assistance not only to homeowners, but also to schools, businesses, and community groups interested in creating landscapes friendly for wildlife and the environment. NWF, Backyard Wildlife Habitat Program Office, 11100 Wildlife Center Drive, Reston, VA 20190-5362, 703-438-6434, bkydint1@nwf.org, http://www.nwf.org/habitats/.

Chapter 11: Citrus Trees

All About Citrus & Subtropical Fruits. Editor Rick Bond, 1985. Ortho Books, San Ramon, CA. 0-89721-065-4.

Citrus. Lance Walheim, 1996. Ironwood Press, Tucson. 0-9628236-4-3.

Annual Citrus Clinics. Offered by The University of Arizona and Maricopa County Cooperative Extension, usually in January. Experts discuss aspects of citrus care including varieties, fertilizing, irrigating, pruning, and pest management. For dates and locations, contact Maricopa County Master Gardeners, 4341 E. Broadway Road, Phoenix, AZ 85040-8807, 602-470-8086, or http://ag.arizona.edu/maricopa/garden/.

Chapter 12: Roses in the Landscape

Compendium of Rose Diseases. R. Kenneth Horst, 1983. American Phytopathological Society, St. Paul, MN. 089054-052-7.

Consulting Rosarian Manual. American Rose Society, 1995. American Rose Society, Shreveport, LA.

The Graham Stuart Thomas Rose Book. Graham Stuart Thomas, 1994. Timber Press, Portland, OR. 0-88192280-3.

In Search of Lost Roses. Thomas Christopher, 1989. Summit Books, Simon & Schuster, New York. 0-38071987-8.

Landscaping with Antique Roses. Liz Druitt and G. Michael Shoup, 1992. Taunton Press, Newton, CT. 0942391-64-0.

Old Roses and English Roses. David Austin, 1996. Antique Collectors' Club Ltd, Woodbridge, Suffolk, UK. 185149-150-3.

The Organic Rose Garden. Liz Druitt, 1996. Taylor Publishing, Dallas. 0-87833-906-X.

Ortho's All About Roses. Dr. Tommy Cairns, 1999. Monsanto Corporation, San Ramon, CA. 0-89721-428-5.

The Rose Book. Maggie Oster, 1994. Rodale Press, Emmaus, PA. 0-87596-607-1.

The Rose Expert. Dr. D. G. Hessayon, 1995. Sterling Publishing, New York. 0-903505-25-8.

Roses in a Desert Garden. Hallie Beck, 1996. Phoenix Home & Garden Magazine, Phoenix. 0-9625961-1-6.

Secrets of the Miniature Rose. Elizabeth Abler, 1990. Lake Forest, IL. 0-9627217-0-0.

The Ultimate Rose Book. Stirling Macoboy, 1993. Harry M. Abrams, New York. 0-8109-3920-7.

American Rose Society. Contact for rose societies and Consulting Rosarians in your area. PO Box 30,000, Shreveport, LA, 71130, 800-637-6534, ars@ars-hq.org, http:// www.ars.org/.

Pacific Southwest District Rose Society. Contact for rose societies and Consulting Rosarians in Arizona, New Mexico, southern California, southern Nevada, and west Texas. http://www.geocities.com/pswdistrict/.

Antique Rose Emporium, 9300 Lueckemeyer Road, Brenham, TX 77833-6453, 1-800-441-0002, info@heirloomroses.com, http://www.weareroses.com.

Heirloom Roses, 24062 Riverside Drive NE, St. Paul, OR 97137, 503-538-1576, http://www.heirloomroses.com.

Vintage Gardens Antique Roses, 2833 Gravenstein Highway South, Sebastapol, CA 95472, 707-829-2035, http://www.vintagegardens.com.

Chapter 13: Growing a Healthy Lawn

Arizona Master Gardener Manual, Turf Chapter. D.M. Kopec and R. Call, 1997. University of Arizona Cooperative Extension, Tucson.

Drip Irrigation for Every Landscape and All Climates. Robert Kourik, 1992. Metamorphic Press, Santa Rosa, CA. 0-9615848-2-3.

Garden Watering Systems. Susan Lang, 1999. Sunset Books, Menlo Park, CA. 0-3760383-9-X.

Guidelines for Landscape Drip Irrigation Systems. Arizona Landscape Irrigation Guidelines Committee, November 1999. Arizona Municipal Water Users Association, Phoenix, AZ. Call your city Water Conservation Office for a copy.

Journal of Environmental Turfgrass, Spring 1990. "Lawns Can Heal the Environmental Wounds" and "Science Shows Turf Can Save Water Resources," Dr. J.B. Beard.

Lawn and Sports Turf Benefits. Eliot C. Roberts and Beverly C. Roberts. The Lawn Institute, Pleasant Hill, TN (undated).

Ortho's All About Sprinklers and Drip Systems. Managing Editor, Sally W. Smith, 1998. Meredith Books, Des Moines, IA. 0-8972141-3-7.

Salt-Affected Turfgrass Sites Assessment & Management. R.N. Carrow, R.R. Duncan, 1998. Ann Arbor Press, Chelsea, MI.

Xeriscape: Landscaping with Style in the Arizona Desert. Arizona Department of Water Resources, 2000. Call your city Water Conservation Office for a copy.

County Cooperative Extension. Contact your county's Cooperative Extension office for information on varieties and for growing advice specific to your region or www.ag.arizona.edu/turf.

Testimony of Dr. Thomas L. Watschke concerning H.R. 3950, "The Food and Agriculture Resources Act of 1990," before the Committee on Agriculture of the United States House of Representatives, April 18, 1990.

Index